THE MOST HOLY PLACE

Devotional Prayers in the Book of Hebrews

By Jeremy D. Vogan

Preface

"Long ago, at many times and in many ways, God spoke to us by the prophets, but in these last days He has spoken to us by His Son."

With these words, the writer of Hebrews draws us into one of the most profound and astonishing books in all of Holy Scripture. Angels, devils, signs and wonders, solemn warnings, the bodies of the defiant fallen in the wilderness, a Sabbath-rest for the people of God, a new high priest arising after the order of Melchizedek, the two unchangeable things by which God swears His faithfulness to us, the fulfillment of the pattern shown to Moses on Mount Sinai, a new Covenant written on our hearts, a new and living Way that fulfills the shadow of the Law, the dazzling array of those who by faith have conquered, our slow but sure approach to Mount Zion and the City of the consuming fire of the Living God; and, lifted high above all of these, the person and work of Jesus Christ, Who is the same yesterday, today and forever.

The Most Holy Place is a daily prayer meditation and Biblical synthesis from the Old and New Testaments based on the book of Hebrews, verse by verse, Monday through Saturday for fifty-two weeks. It is intended to be an aid to consistent and continuing reflection on the finished work of Jesus applied by the Holy Spirit in your life. May the Lord through this book continue to equip you with everything good that you may do His will, working in us that which is pleasing in His sight, through Jesus Christ, to Whom be glory forever and ever. Amen.

Jeremy D. Vogan

Staunton, Virginia, 2023

MONDAY

Hebrews 1:1 "Long ago, at many times and in many ways, God spoke to our fathers by the prophets"

L ord, You know how desperately I need to hear from You. This world is no friend to grace

I catch a glimpse of Your glory at dawn, but by nightfall my vision has faded

I plant Your words deep in my heart, but somehow they get shaken loose every time

I try to live Your truth, but my heart falls far short of Your holiness

Is anyone worthy? Is anyone whole? My heart sinks within me, for surely there is none

But Your Word continues, through my despair, like a pure note through the sounding chaos

You are not a God who remains distant, condemning, not clearing the guilty

Visiting the iniquity of the fathers on the children and the children's children, to the third and the fourth generation

You cared for people enough to become one, taking on flesh, knowing our weakness

You cared for this world enough to speak it into inheritance with Your divine fiat, even as You once spoke it into existence, separating light from darkness forever

You cared for Your glory enough to ascend on high, leading captives in Your train, showing Yourself a God of compassion and mercy

And You speak to us by Your Gospel of grace, as long as it is called Today, teaching us to humbly repent, helping us to hold our original confidence firm to the end

Canceling the record of debt that stood against us with its legal demands. This You set aside, nailing it to the cross

For You did not send Your Son into the world to condemn the world, but in order that the world might be saved through Him

Is there anything to be compared with such a salvation? Seat my faith firmly in Your promises today, and help me speak Your name with reverence to others, and may I never doubt again. Amen

TUESDAY

Hebrews 1:2 "but in these last days he has spoken to us by his Son, whom he appointed the heir of all things, through whom also he created the world."

L ord, You are not silent

Though it often seems that You are

As though evil has the upper hand

As though good has stumbled, never to rise again

As though the darkness has overcome the light

As though the kingdom of this world is not to become the Kingdom of our God, and of His Christ

As though He will not reign for ever and ever

Is it unbelief that convinces us of all this, that weighs us down?

Yes, our unbelief, and more than that

It is our not hearing Your Word

That Word which brought being out of nothing

That Word which brought order out of chaos

That Word which became flesh, and made His dwelling among us

The Revelation of God Himself, breaking in on the idolatry and sin of our hearts

We have seen Your glory, glory of the one and only Son

Who came from the Father, full of grace and truth

And in Him we have the prophetic word made more certain

Lord, we are holding onto it, as to a lamp shining in a dark place

Until the day dawns and the morning star rises in our hearts

For in Him there is provided for us an entrance into the eternal kingdom

And all our hope is in You. Amen

WEDNESDAY

Hebrews 1:3a "He is the radiance of the glory of God and the exact imprint of his nature, and he upholds the universe by the word of his power."

How many times have I asked to see Your glory

I have lost count, and the way still stretches long before me, and I have not seen it

Yet I will keep asking

For if You truly are, it would be worth a lifetime of waiting, to see You face to face

You who hung the stars, who brooded over the chaos, who knelt down to fashion life in Your image, after Your likeness

You who formed us faultless and commanded our obedience, as the morning stars sang together and all the sons of God shouted for joy

You who grieved over our sin and set a flaming sword between us and eternal life without You

You who took eternal counsel to take on flesh and walk among us, to know our sorrows, to work against evil with every word and touch, to be our Brother and great High Priest, yet without sin

You who humbled Yourself and were obedient to the point of death, even death on a cross

You who rose triumphant, and led captives in Your train

You whose Spirit gently teaches my captive heart now, and reminds me of Your words of wisdom: That I have indeed seen You, and that whoever has seen You has seen the Father

Help me, Lord Jesus, to treasure Your Word, and to be one who has not seen the fullness of Your glory, and yet has believed

Help me to know that in You there is a power greater than anything in this world

That everything Your Spirit says is life, and wisdom, and peace, and hope

That every trial You bring me to must be for Your glory and my good

That You uphold all things by the Word of your power

And You will surely bring me safely into glory. Amen

THURSDAY

Hebrews 1:3a-4 *"After making purification for sins, he sat down at the right hand of the Majesty on high, having become as much superior to angels as the name he has inherited is more excellent than theirs."*

L ord, I do not understand

You were already higher than the angels; why was it required that You attain to that again?

But the eternal wisdom of God knew that was needful

Mercy had to triumph over judgment

A Name had to be above all names

Evil had to be conquered

The Law had to be kept

Your promises had to be upheld

The word of the prophets had to be fulfilled

An innocent Lamb had to be found

The enemy forces had to be defeated

A death had to be died to sin, once for all

Your chosen people had to be made holy by Your obedience

The head of the serpent had to be crushed

That salvation into which angels long to look had to be accomplished

Your obedience to the Cross had to be finished

Faith had to be proved by its reverence

Hope had to be demonstrated by its appearance

But the greatest of these, Lord, was Love

We will spend all of eternity praising You for Your works, Lord Jesus

Amen

FRIDAY

Hebrews 1:5 *"For to which of the angels did God ever say, 'You are my Son, today I have begotten you'? Or again, 'I will be to him a father, and he shall be to me a son'?"*

I t is not to angels that our worship is lifted, Lord

For even if we or an angel from heaven should preach a Gospel contrary to the one given

Let them be accursed

It is not power that we worship

It is not appearance

It is not position or regard

It is not wisdom

It is not brilliance

We will not lift up our souls to any idol on earth or even in heaven

But we will serve You only, Lord

I saw a mighty angel proclaiming with a loud voice:

"Who is worthy to open the scroll and break its seals?"

And I began to weep loudly because no one was found worthy

But one of the elders said to me:

"Weep no more; behold, the Lion of the tribe of Judah, the Root of David, has conquered, so that He can open the scroll and its seven seals"

And I saw a Lamb, standing as though it had been slain

And we fell down before Him and sang a new song:

"Worthy is the Lamb who was slain, to receive power and wealth and wisdom and might and honor and glory and blessing!"

You alone, Lord Jesus, are our hope in life and death

Amen

SATURDAY

Hebrews 1:6 *"And again, when he brings the firstborn into the world, he says, 'Let all God's angels worship him.'"*

L ord, we were made to worship

You created the world so that Your glory would be more present for all

When we fell away, we did not cease to worship; we only ceased to worship You

Christ Jesus, Your Firstborn from eternity, came into this world to the adoration of angels

The highest heavens lift up Your name

The darkest depths resound with the chorus of Your praise

The waves of the seas are stilled at Your voice

Even the stones on the ground cry out Your glories

The wicked tremble at the sound of Your justice

The righteous rejoice for the coming of Your salvation

The farthest reaches of the earth tremble with the sound of Your name

The curtain of the Holy of Holies is rent, and all flesh falls silent before you

The earth is shaken, and the rocks are split

The dead are raised, and those who sleep are awakened

And faith and awe we cry, *"Surely this was the Son of God"!*

Give us a vision, O Lord, of the glory of Your Son

In holy fear we will worship and adore Him

Let us serve the Lord with fear, and rejoice with trembling

Let us kiss the Son, Whose wrath is quickly kindled

Blessed are all who take refuge in Him

Amen

MONDAY

Hebrews 1:7 *"Of the angels he says, 'He makes his angels winds, and his ministers a flame of fire.'"*

L ord, all things bow down to worship You

This world is dark and twisted, and along with us it has fallen far from the pattern You first set it in

The gardens of paradise are closed to us now, and the pathways of the stars are forbidden

Our lot is cast among the thistles and the gullies, and the sons of God are set to hard labor

We heard Your voice, and knew Your love for us, yet we have forsaken you and eaten of the tree of which You commanded us not to eat

In the cool of the day You found us, and covered our shameful nakedness, and did not shield us from death; for that would have been a curse eternal

Instead You set us out on a long, desperate journey through this lonely world without Your presence overshadowing us; yet You did not leave us, even then

For You had purposed to become a man like us, for very God to take on flesh

The angels longed to look into these things, but only fleeting glimpses were ever given, and then only to faithful seers who suffered long for the privilege

So the brightest of the seraphim tremble, and listen for Your command to them

The winds of Your Spirit blow over all the earth to bring Your will to life

None knows where they came from or where they are going, yet they do Your will

The will of Your Spirit burns intensely, to fan our hearts into flame for You

The Spirit wars against the flesh, with its passions and desires

By faith we see Your kingdom coming, that all might know and worship You

Spiritual pillars of smoke and fire to lead us through the wilderness

And in Your holy Temple all cry, *"Glory!"*

Amen

TUESDAY

Hebrews 1:8 *"But of the Son he says, 'Your throne, O God, is forever and ever, the scepter of uprightness is the scepter of your kingdom.'"*

F or so long we have searched for a king

The young, the strong, and the beautiful catch our eye, and we would crown them

They lead us into battle, and our hearts are raised up; they give us hope when the enemy is at the gates

The warm sun shines on our armor and the dark forces melt away before us

But the days of victory fade away just as quickly

And the long, gray spans of servitude set in, and we begin to know that our rulers are just as human as we are

They set us to hard labor and we groan under it, for we build nothing but their name

They take our sons and daughters to be their slaves, and our flocks to be their possessions

Their commands begin to contradict Your Word and set us against Your Spirit

And we grieve, for we know what we have done

We have set up another king in our own image, and Yours has begun to fade away in our hearts

May God have mercy on us, for we have committed two evils:

We have forsaken You, the Fountain of living waters

And hewed out cisterns for ourselves, broken cisterns that can hold no water

Ask among the nations: Who has heard the like of this?

Does the snow of Lebanon leave Sirion's crags? Do the mountain waters run dry?

Yet Your people have forgotten You, and made offerings to false gods

By Your faithful Spirit, lead us back to Your throne to worship You, O Lord

And never let our hearts stray away from Your presence again. Amen

WEDNESDAY

Hebrews 1:9 *"You have loved righteousness and hated wickedness; therefore God, your God, has anointed you with the oil of gladness beyond your companions."*

L ord, there is none like You

We are all sinful, fallen men, and we fall short of true righteousness

We condemn our brothers for the same sins that grip our own hearts

We hide behind webs of truth and appearances

Truth is dense, and when we stand behind it people often cannot see our true selves

Appearances are deceptive and though we often cannot see past them, You can

Teach us, Lord, to see Jesus

To hear His voice and recognize it

To walk in His steps and never turn away from them

To perceive by faith what He is doing and lay hold of it

To willingly suffer in His cause, and lay down our lives as He did

To accept the rebuke of His Spirit and turn from our sin

To build up the Body of Christ and encourage one another

To sing and make melody to Him

To plead for His mercy on us, every day of our lives

To buy from Him gold refined by fire, so we might be rich

To love His coming more than anything else in all this world

For it is only then that we will see the righteousness of God in the flesh

Let us anoint Him with the oil of gladness

For He is God, our God, and we lift up our hearts and lives in worship

Amen

THURSDAY

Hebrews 1:10 *"And, 'You, Lord, laid the foundation of the earth in the beginning, and the heavens are the work of your hands.'"*

When the foundations are shaken, I will trust in You

When hope grows dim, I will trust in You

When salvation seems far away, I will trust in You

When the flaming darts come thick, I will trust in You

When the enemy rejoices over me, I will trust in You

When my heart is foolish and wayward, I will trust in You

When strong arms of friends fail, I will trust in You

When darkness covers my eyes and I cannot see, I will trust in You

When my soul is of little faith, I will trust in You

When I suffer grievous loss, I will trust in You

When plans come to nothing, I will trust in You

When I do not feel Your presence, I will trust in You

When bitter war arises around me, I will trust in You

When disappointment pierces my heart, I will trust in You

When I do not know which way to turn, I will trust in You

When Your promises have not yet come to fruition, I will trust in You

When evil prospers, I will trust in You

When righteousness falters, I will trust in You

When heaven and earth fade away, I will trust in You

In silence and patience I will trust in You, for I am the work of Your hands

And I know that You will receive me into glory

Amen

FRIDAY

Hebrews 1:11 *"...they will perish, but you remain;*
they will all wear out like a garment"

L
ord, the world is unraveling, spinning out like tangled thread from a
broken loom

The span of life we see every day is fading before our eyes

The things we watch that make us feel safe:

Money

Food

Work

Activity

We thought in our foolishness that they would last forever

But in a single day they are fading into the ground they came from

And we know why it is that we are so afraid

For we came from the same place; we are dust, and to dust we will return

Calm our hearts with Your Spirit, and teach us to find in You:

Gold refined by fire

Bread of life

Hope for the journey

Believing in Him who was sent

A Sabbath-rest for the people of God

And after we have suffered a little while

You Yourself will restore, confirm, strengthen, and establish us

For You, O Lord, remain

Amen

SATURDAY

Hebrews 1:12 *"...like a robe you will roll them up, like a garment they will be changed. But you are the same, and your years will have no end."*

H ow many times have You said it:

All things we know in this world will surely pass away

Yet our hearts do not believe

We cling to all the things we love:

   To our comforts

   To that which makes us look good

   To that which strokes our ego

   To that we think will save us

   To that which increases our worldly holdings

   To that which seems to give us power over our circumstances

But deep inside we know

We know that life is only to be found:

   In our crosses

   In that which makes us into the image of Christ

   In that which denies self, and follows Jesus

   In that which puts our faith in Your salvation alone

   In that which gains eternal treasure

   In that which clothes us with power from on high

Bring my heart steadily today to apprehend the glory of who You are, and to reflect that unending vision with all obedient joy and soberness

Amen

MONDAY

Hebrews 1:13 *"And to which of the angels has he ever said, 'Sit at my right hand until I make your enemies a footstool for your feet'?"*

A ll things live under the shroud of Your power

The wicked man knows, deep within his heart, that he will answer for his crimes one Day

The righteous man cannot lose sight of his mighty Hope in Your justice

Your heavenly servants go about Your bidding

The winds and the waves obey Your Word, and the skies proclaim Your faithfulness

All things bow, sooner or later, to Your awesome strength

But none of the angels have ever been seated at Your right hand

They have never seen Your enemies brought to subjugation under them

They still long to look into the deep things of God, the dark truths that will one day be made light

They have power that You give them, and they speak words which You allow them

But only Your Son has been raised to Your right hand:

Only Christ Jesus, Who in His humility made Himself like a servant

Only the true Messiah, Who redeemed His people by His perfect sacrifice

Only the second Adam, Who kept Your perfect Law and crushed the serpent's head

Only the great I Am, Who has taken His seat on high, and Who intercedes for us today

Only the true Israel, Who kept Your covenant in the wilderness, and Who has gone over into the Promised Land for us

Grant us to keep our eyes on Him, and never to be awed by the things of this world again

Amen

TUESDAY

Hebrews 1:14 *"Are they not all ministering spirits sent out to serve for the sake of those who are to inherit salvation?"*

L ord, what do we have that we have not been given?

Even the heavenly spirits set to watch over us testify to our need, and to Your grace

The way is long, and we grow weary in it

The vision You gave us grows dim

Our spirits are willing, but the flesh is weak

The enemy opposes us at every turn

Many there are who live as enemies of the cross of Christ

The dogs, the evildoers, those who mutilate the flesh

But we are the circumcision, who worship by the Spirit of God

Who glory in Christ Jesus

Who put no confidence in the flesh

Whatever gain we had, we count as loss for the sake of Christ

Indeed, we count everything as loss because of the surpassing worth of knowing Christ Jesus our Lord

For His sake we have suffered the loss of all things and count them as rubbish

In order that we may gain Christ and be found in Him

Not having a righteousness of our own that comes from the Law

But the righteousness from God that depends on faith

That we may know Him and the power of His resurrection, becoming like Him in His death

That by any means possible we may attain the resurrection from the dead

And being raised incorruptible, that we may enter into Your Kingdom, Lord. Amen

WEDNESDAY

Hebrews 2:1 *"Therefore we must pay much closer attention to what we have heard, lest we drift away from it."*

L ord, You have given us all we need

We have Your Word of truth, and we have Your Spirit to illumine it for us

There are still faithful churches that proclaim Your glories, and faithful ministers who labor long to show us Christ crucified

Is there any situation that shall arise in this world, that the Holy Scriptures do not address?

Shall tribulation

Or distress

Or persecution

Or famine

Or nakedness

Or danger

Or sword?

For Your sake we are being killed all the day long; we are regarded as sheep to be slaughtered

And for all this, we have not yet resisted to the point of shedding our blood

Teach us humility, and cause us to pay much closer attention to what we have heard

To this message:

That by this we know love, that He laid down His life for us, and we ought to lay down our lives for the brothers

Help me not to drift away from this today

Amen

THURSDAY

Hebrews 2:2 *"For since the message declared by angels proved to be reliable, and every transgression or disobedience received a just retribution"*

Your Word, O Lord, is faithful

It tells me the truth when every other word does not; my own heart included

It does not entice me to seek after the promises of this world

It does not gratify the desires of my flesh

It does not echo the false testimony of the prince of the power of the air

Instead, Your Word begins with Your glory, which was before the world began

Your steadfast love, which never fails

Your power over all things, to make and to unmake

Your knowledge from which nothing ever will escape

Your great wisdom, which searches out and sets all things in order

Your unchangeableness that is my deliverance

Your justice like the noonday sun

Your truth, when all men are liars

Your goodness that I cannot even fathom

Your patience with my slowness of heart

And perhaps for me the most wonderful of all:

Your mercy like a mighty river of grace

Are not my sins ever before You? Yet You have taken upon Yourself the punishment for all my transgressions

I will praise you all my life

Amen

FRIDAY

Hebrews 2:3 *"How shall we escape if we neglect such a great salvation? It was declared at first by the Lord, and it was attested to us by those who heard"*

M y heart is so easily distracted, Lord

The world seems so important, as though I will miss out if I do not hang on its every word

As though life were the greatest good

Happiness the greatest goal

Accumulation of things the greatest achievement

Cultivation of one's image the greatest success

When in fact the opposite is true

Your Word tells me the real truth about this world

That there is a great death that overshadows us all, invisible as sky

That we have cut ourselves off from You

That we have turned, every one of us, to our own way

That our only hope is the death of Christ for us

That our only good the life of Christ in us

That to freely give our lives, as He did, the greatest goal

That to lose our lives in order to find them the greatest achievement

That to be loved by You the greatest eternal success

I am one of those blessed few who have heard. How, I do not know

But let Your Spirit indwell me today, that I may speak Your glories to those around me

Declare Your Gospel over me and let me see Your glory

Amen

SATURDAY

Hebrews 2:4 *"while God also bore witness by signs and wonders and various miracles and by gifts of the Holy Spirit distributed according to His will"*

L ord Jesus, when You ascended on high, You led captives in Your train

So often I forget where I came from:

The kingdom of darkness

A death sentence over me

A debt I could never repay

Hopelessly ensnared in sin

Enemy of God and man

You knew all these things, yet You sought me out until You found me

You washed me and put a new robe on me

You put a ring on my finger, and lifted up my head

Am I a slave to righteousness now? Yes, and never was there a more thankful prisoner:

In the kingdom of light

Eternal life promised to me

No debt still outstanding, except that to love one another

Free to follow You in righteousness

Under the smile of God and the fellowship of the Church

I remember that my trials are light and momentary, and that my suffering serves to guide others

But I eagerly desire the greater gifts

Give me faith, hope, and love; and in the morning let me see Your face

Amen

MONDAY

Hebrews 2:5 *"For it was not to angels that God subjected the world to come, of which we are speaking."*

A ngels are terrible in aspect; we cannot stand in their presence

We fear at the thought of them, of supernatural beings who are not bound by time and place

But more than that, we ought to fear their Maker

The One not only unbound by time and place, but who binds all things to do His holy will

The One before whom angels bow in reverence and awe

The One who commands the evil one, and that fallen angel does as He says

The One who formed heaven and earth and still makes the winds His servant

The One who is alone worthy of blessing and honor and glory

The One who became like us, yet without sin

Who was despised and rejected by men, a man of sorrows and acquainted with grief

Who for the joy set before Him endured the cross, scorning its shame

And is seated at the right hand of the throne of God.

For You, Jesus, I will raise my song of newness of life

For You I will endure the light and momentary afflictions You call me through

For You I will wait, till all things have passed away, and only Your love is left

Amen

TUESDAY

Hebrews 2:6 *"It has been testified somewhere, 'What is man, that you are mindful of him, or the son of man, that you care for him?'"*

L ord, I have spent so much of my life in wondering and longing

Wondering at the way life is

Longing for it to be different

And I am ashamed

Not because I have wanted too much; but surely, because I have wanted too little

When I look at Your heavens, the work of Your fingers

The moon and stars, which You have set in place

How is it that You remember me?

By what miracle do You care for me?

I know how often I have forgotten Your goodness and taken Your mercy for granted

Shape my heart once again, just as You once formed the universe, when the morning stars sang together and all the sons of God shouted for joy

Teach me to know You

To truly fear You

To listen to Your Spirit

To look for Your coming

To wonder only at Your love for me

And to long only for the day when I shall know You fully, even as I am fully known

Amen

WEDNESDAY

Hebrews 2:7 *"You made him for a little while lower than the angels; you have crowned him with glory and honor'"*

L ord, You have made us in Your image, after Your likeness

You set us as Your stewards, to rule over this world in Your name and to multiply in it

You put all earthly things under our dominion

You gave us every good thing for us to enjoy that would give us life

You kept back only that which would have brought our death

When we began to wonder whether You truly loved us:

    Whether You really had our good in mind

    Whether we could ourselves judge good and evil

    Whether life might be better if we were gods ourselves

    And whether, in fact, we needed You

You waited silently for us to choose of our own free will

And when we chose death You set, grieving, the flaming sword of the Law between us and life

And You thought of the day when our offspring (and Yours) would one day reenter the Garden:

    To crush the head of evil once for all

    To bring Your children back into Your presence

    To forgive their sin, and remove it as far as the east is from the west

    To lay hold of eternal life, for all those made into His image

Worthy is the Lamb who was slain, to receive power and wealth and wisdom and might and honor and glory and blessing

Amen

THURSDAY

Hebrews 2:8a *"'...putting everything in subjection under his feet.' Now in putting everything in subjection to him, he left nothing outside his control."*

Y ou accepted weakness, Lord

You accepted lowliness and poverty

For we know the grace of our Lord Jesus Christ

That though You were rich, yet for our sake You became poor

So that we by Your poverty might become rich

You did it to redeem for Yourself a chosen race

A royal priesthood

A holy nation

A people for Your own possession

That we may proclaim the excellencies of Him who called us out of darkness into His marvelous light

Once we were not a people, but now we are God's people

Once we had not received mercy, but now we have received mercy

This was Your work, Your crowning achievement

The reason You left Your throne, and the glory and fellowship You had at the right hand of the Father

And the Temple You are building will endure forever

Made up of living stones, built up as a spiritual house

To be a holy priesthood, and to offer spiritual sacrifices acceptable to God through Jesus Christ

One day all of Creation will consist in this new life, this glorified existence in a new Heavens and a new Earth

And all things will finally be according to Your good and gracious will

Come quickly, Lord Jesus. Amen

FRIDAY

Hebrews 2:8b *"At present, we do not yet see everything in subjection to him."*

Lord, that must be the greatest understatement in Your Word:

"We do not yet see everything in subjection to Him"

The entire universe has rebelled against us, and rightly so

We threw off Your fetters and broke Your chains

We declared that we would be the ones to judge right and wrong

That our innocence would no longer define us

That we could taste of death, and laugh of it, and live forever

That we needed only to stretch out our hand, and eternity would be ours

That need was the only barrier left between us and happiness

And at the end of all things

That we did not need You.

Lord, if You were not merciful, we would have been destroyed

And just as You told us, we have surely died

All is death and destruction around us, and there is no hope left – save one thing only

That You became one of us, to die with us

That we could become one with You, to live with You

In this narrow sliver of hope, hard as it is to see, painful as it is to know

We live, and move, and have our being

We take Your easy yoke on us, and feel Your burden is light

We lift Your name on high, Jesus

Amen

SATURDAY

Hebrews 2:9 *"But we see Him who for a little while was made lower than the angels, namely Jesus, crowned with glory and honor because of the suffering of death, so that by the grace of God He might taste death for everyone."*

L ord, how many times have I asked you: *"Let me see Your glory"*

You have never fully answered, yet I have kept asking

May I never stop asking; but Your Word gives me pause here, as always

It does not say "We saw Him" or "We shall see Him." It says, *"We see Him"*

And with the apostle I rejoice in this blessed vision:

The Son of God, the true God and eternal life

The Root of Jesse, even He who arises to rule the Gentiles

The Alpha and the Omega, who is and who was and who is to come

The Author and Perfecter of our faith, who for love's sake laid down His life for us

The Man of Sorrows, despised and rejected by men

The Bread of Life who came down from Heaven and gave life to the world

The Light of the world, who leads us into life

The Mediator between God and men, the man Christ Jesus

The Resurrection and the Life, in whom if we believe we will never die

The Victorious One, who has the right to sit on the throne of God

The Peace who has made the two groups one, destroying the dividing wall of hostility

The Lamb of God, who takes away the sin of the world – my sin

The Lamb who was slain, and is worthy to receive power and wealth and wisdom and might and honor and glory and blessing

To Him be blessing and honor and glory and might forever and ever!

Amen.

MONDAY

Hebrews 2:10 *"For it was fitting that he, for whom and by whom all things exist, in bringing many sons to glory, should make the founder of their salvation perfect through suffering."*

L ord, how can this be

How can suffering be fitting for the sinless Son of God

How can He who knew no sin be made to be sin, so that in Him we might become the righteousness of God

How can the perfect Lamb be forsaken, and the skies darkened over His agony, and the curtain of Your holy Temple be torn in two

These things are too great for me, and I must go back to what I know

I know You made all things for Your glory

I know we sinned against You, suspecting Your intentions, turning to our own way, setting up a god of our own desires instead of Your Holiness

And I know You justly sentenced us to death

But even while pronouncing the sentence, I know You stepped between us and death, promising a Savior who would one day crush the head of evil

For the only way that suffering could be fitting for God Himself

Is if God Himself were a God of love, one who would never abandon His people

Who for the joy set before Him endured the cross, despising its shame, and is seated at the right hand of the throne of God

To walk in those steps, to imitate that faithfulness, I will bear up under my light and momentary trials today

For You alone are faithful, and Your Spirit will dwell in me and give me the hope of glory

Amen

TUESDAY

Hebrews 2:11 *"For he who sanctifies and those who are sanctified all have one source. That is why he is not ashamed to call them brothers"*

T his, Lord

For all my sin

For all my foolish desires

For all my disobedience, the bitterness and the gall

For all the shame that has come on me and those I love

For all the pain we had to go through, for sanctification to be worked in our lives

For all the hard consequences that linger long

For all the senseless separation, the shattering of friendships

For all the darkness that covered my eyes

For all the triumphs evil boasted over me

For all the toil to regain the path of righteousness

For all the tears, every one precious in Your sight, over love and loss

For all the times we forgot where we were going, and more importantly, who we are:

See what kind of love the Father has given to us, that we should be called children of God

And so we are

Amen

WEDNESDAY

Hebrews 2:12 *"saying, 'I will tell of your name to my brothers; in the midst of the congregation I will sing your praise.'"*

T he Lord Jesus told us of Your Name, Lord God

He said that if we have seen Him, we have seen the Father

He told us of:

Yahweh who keeps covenant with His people

The Comforter who restores our health

The Fear of Isaac who keeps His miracle promises

The Desire of Nations who comes

The Guide who has walked in sorrow for us

The Prince of Peace who will rule with justice

The Glory of God who covers us

The Morning Star who rises in our hearts

The Root of David who sets up a throne for all time

The Foundation upon whom all eternal things are built

Emmanuel who did not despise our flesh

The Great Shepherd of the sheep who gave Himself for us

King of Kings and Lord of Lords, ruler over all

The Refuge to whom we can cling in the storm

The Sun of Righteousness who rises over us with healing in His wings

The Way, the Truth, and the Life who is our all and in all

You are the Alpha and the Omega, the First and the Last, the Beginning and the End. Blessed be Your name forever

Amen

THURSDAY

Hebrews 2:13a *"And again, 'I will put my trust in him.'"*

L ord, You know how many things I have put my trust in:

Myself

This world

Money

Others' esteem

Success

Friends

Confidence

Doing everything right

Every single one of them has been a snare to me

And I have been left broken hearted, sinning against Heaven and against You

Teach me to put my trust in You alone:

Dying to my self

Looking forward to a city with foundations, whose architect and builder is God

Being poured out like a drink offering

Despised and persecuted for the sake of Jesus

Chosen as foolish in the world to shame the wise

Forsaken by all, except for You

Boasting only in the Cross of Christ

Forgetting what lies behind, and straining forward to what lies ahead

Amen

FRIDAY

Hebrews 2:13b *"And again, 'Behold, I and the children God has given me.'"*

From first to last You have ordained the family as the means of Your grace to us

You said it was not good for the man to be alone, and You gave him a helper fit for him

You made your covenant with Noah and his family, and only they were saved from the destruction of the waters

You called Abraham Your servant to a land You would show him, and saved him out of ignorance and sin. And You called him out to show him the stars, and You said: "So shall your offspring be"

In Your wrath against the sin of Your people You told Your friend Moses that You would make a great nation out of him instead. But for the sake of Your glory he sought Your true heart and interceded for those You had called to bear Your name

From the sheepfolds You called Your son David, the man after Your own heart, and You set Him on a throne. You forgave his sin and strengthened his arm. And You promised him that he would never fail to have a son who would sit on it

To the people walking in darkness You brought a great light; You broke the yoke of their burden, and burned the garment rolled in blood. To them a child was born, to them a son was given, and the government would be on His shoulder

You called Your bride, faithless Israel, to return, and to circumcise their hearts; to remove their detestable things from Your holy presence, and to swear "As the Lord lives" in truth, justice, and righteousness

You called Your people back from adultery and unfaithfulness to you, and upon those who had no mercy You had mercy, and those who were not Your people You called My People

Your Suffering Servant came to redeem Your family from the darkness and bondage we had fallen into. He was oppressed, and He was afflicted, yet He opened not His mouth. Like a Lamb that was led to the slaughter, He opened not His mouth

But out of the anguish of His soul He saw the light of life: He saw the holy offspring You had kept for Him; He gave us eternal life, and we shall never perish, and no one shall snatch us out of His hand

Blessed be Your name

Amen

SATURDAY

Hebrews 2:14 *"Since therefore the children share in flesh and blood, he himself likewise partook of the same things, that through death he might destroy the one who has the power of death, that is, the devil"*

L ord Jesus, You know us within and without

You know how tenuous our lives are, how foolishly we cling to created things

And You know our greatest fear

You know death, and where it came from

But You did not only know; You also came

You came to take on flesh and blood, becoming fully man and fully God

You laid aside Your power and glory

You were born into poverty and ill repute and danger

No more than a handful knew of Your coming, and those not the powerful or the popular

The angels longed to look into these things; they rejoiced at Your birth, yet it was shrouded in mystery

For thirty years You worked at Your trade, living a quiet life

And then You set out to do Your Father's will

With compassion and wisdom You moved among Your people

You saw that they were like sheep scattered on the hills without a shepherd

You drew them near to You to teach them, to heal them, to give them hope

And You came into direct conflict with the accuser, Your enemy the devil

With the white-hot Word of God You defeated and turned him back

And You reminded him of the ancient prophecy: That he might bruise Your heel; but that You would one day crush his head

And through death destroy death forever

Lord Jesus, we place our everlasting hope in You. Amen

MONDAY

Hebrews 2:15 *"and deliver all those who through fear of death were subject to lifelong slavery."*

L ord, You know our deepest fears

For You created us in Your image, made us to walk with You, made us holy

When the morning stars sang together and all the sons of God shouted for joy

You knew when the tempter crept in to Your beautiful creation and brought ruin and sadness

Not by hurting or killing, but simply by questioning this one thing:

Whether You truly meant what You said

And when we opened our minds to that thought, taking on ourselves the unbearable burden of staking out right and wrong

The ruin and sadness turned to sickness and death

And for the first time in our existence

Fear entered in.

You knew the reasons for that fear, better than we did. Yet it was not enough in Your eternal purposes for You to know it only

But You also took on flesh, and felt that fear, handled it, tasted it, wept over it

The Lord Jesus lived a sinless life on our behalf to make for us a place in Your holy Heaven

He offered Himself a perfect sacrifice on our behalf, that through His death He might destroy the one who has the power of death

And He rose again in the power of an indestructible life, that we also may be where He is

From our lifelong slavery to the evil desires of our own hearts He rescued us, to make us slaves to grace, ambassadors in chains imploring those we love to be reconciled to God

For such a great salvation how can I express the joy that has replaced the fear in my heart?

I will praise you all my days, for You alone are worthy. Amen

TUESDAY

Hebrews 2:16 *"For surely it is not angels that he helps, but he helps the offspring of Abraham."*

L ord over all

You look down on heaven and earth, and all things do Your will

Even the wicked walk out the paths You have laid for them

The creation obeys you dumbly, proclaiming Your glory with each sunrise and bird's nest

The stars wheel in their courses by Your command

And the angels go out as Your messengers and soldiers to watch over Your people

You appeared to Abraham in Haran, calling him away from his home, to find his home in You

You covenanted Yourself to him with signs and wonders

You made of him a great nation, and You blessed him and made his name great

You blessed those who blessed him, and those who dishonored him You cursed

You multiplied his offspring as the stars of heaven and gave to them the land of Canaan

It was too small a thing for you to restore the tribes of Jacob, and gather Israel to Yourself. So You also made Abraham's Son a light for the Gentiles

That Your salvation might reach to the ends of the earth

Your Covenant was no longer made with the blood of bulls and goats

But with the life of Your own perfect Son, given a holy sacrifice for us to pay for sin and ransom from death

You did not call us as Moses, honored as a friend and faithful as a servant

You called us as Jesus Christ, adopted as sons and daughters into Your royal family, to reign with Him after we have endured a little while

We glory in our sufferings and long to know You face to face, even as we are fully known

Blessed be Your name. Amen

WEDNESDAY

Hebrews 2:17 *"Therefore he had to be made like his brothers in every respect, so that he might become a merciful and faithful high priest in the service of God, to make propitiation for the sins of the people."*

L ord Jesus

You were high and lifted up

You were rich beyond all measure

You knew the smile and the presence of God for all time

You had perfect fellowship, with the Father and the Holy Spirit

You could have left us to judgment, and it would have been perfectly just

Yet in the eternal counsel of Your wisdom You chose to take on flesh and tabernacle with us

You became like the least among us, like those from whom men turn their faces

You knew poverty and had not a place to lay Your head

You called out to Your Father in Your suffering, and He hid His face from You

You were alone, as no man in history has ever been alone

You faced the righteous judgment of the Law for sins You did not commit

And through all this, You showed love to Your enemies and prayed for those who persecuted You

In Your humility You showed us what it is for God to live with men

And You did this so that, one day, men might live with God

You did it all for love

I owe You my very self, Lord

Teach me, then, to live as You did; and bring me to life eternal in Your glory

Amen

THURSDAY

Hebrews 2:18 *"For because he himself has suffered when tempted, he is able to help those who are being tempted."*

L ord Jesus

The One who was before all things existed

Who sits now at the right hand of God the Father, to intercede for us

Who is coming back to judge the world and rescue the saints

Who has all glory and power

Who had done no violence, neither was any deceit in Your mouth

Who was crushed and forsaken by God, for our sin

Yet was faithful to the end, for love's sake:

You know what it is for the world to tempt with wrong:

For bread to be offered in the wilderness

For power to be offered in time of weakness

For a crown to be offered in return for worship

But You turned away from all these things

A Man of Sorrows, and acquainted with grief

For the joy that was set before You, You endured the cross, scorning its shame.

Therefore, since we are surrounded by such a great cloud of witnesses

Help us to lay aside every weight today and the sin that clings so closely

And run with endurance the race that is set before us

And whatever else we may lose in the running, may we never lose sight of you

Amen

FRIDAY

Hebrews 3:1 *"Therefore, holy brothers, you who share in a heavenly calling, consider Jesus, the apostle and high priest of our confession"*

L ord

You are the one who has made us holy

The one who first called us "brother"

Who gave us a heavenly calling, lifting us from the clutches of the world

You are the apostle who first told the world of a better hope

A hope for reconciliation with God

For forgiveness from sins

For the gift of salvation, full and free

For a temple not made with human hands

For a worship in Spirit and in truth, no longer in guilt and obscurity

You are the great High Priest, who stood between God and man

Not as a mediator only, but actually as a perfect sacrifice

To take the weight of the holy Law on Your shoulders

To make our heavenly calling sure, in spite of all our failings

To rend the veil that separated us from the unutterable holiness of God

To lift our faces to behold His own

To lift our hands to touch His hands, His feet, His side

The Lamb of God, who takes away the sin of the world

You who were slain are worthy, to receive power and wealth and wisdom and might and honor and glory and blessing!

Amen

SATURDAY

Hebrews 3:2 *"...who was faithful to him who appointed him, just as Moses also was found faithful in all God's house."*

L ord, we need a Savior

We need one who has kept Your holy Law

Who has not been corrupted by the world

Who still has compassion on the poor and the needy

Who has courage to confront evil

Who will not shrink from His calling, for the sake of those He pursues

Who lives the truth, not just speaks it

Who does not go after unjust gain

Who does not cover up wrongdoing

Who loves righteousness

Who delights in truth in the inmost being

Who will not accept a bribe, or be swayed by threats

Who will gather His people as a hen gathers her chicks under her wings

Who would set His face to Jerusalem like a flint, to suffer and to die for love

Who would triumph over evil by the power of an indestructible life

Who has taken His seat at the right hand of God the Father

Who rules over heaven and earth by the strength of His Word

Who will come again one day, as surely as the sun and the moon rise and set

Blessed be Your name, Jesus

Amen

MONDAY

Hebrews 3:3 *"For Jesus has been counted worthy of more glory than Moses –
as much more glory as the builder of a house has more
honor than the house itself."*

M oses was Your friend, Lord

You spoke with him face to face

He was faithful as a servant in Your house

If people would not listen to Moses and the prophets, they would not listen even if someone rose from the dead

He was more humble than anyone else on the earth

You showed him Your glory when You hid him in the cleft of the rock, and passed by

You even allowed him and Elijah to see Your glory as the promised God-man, and talk with you

But for as faithful as he was

There is One even more faithful

There is One who taught us not just law, but grace also

Who interceded not only with reason for the lives of His people, but also with His own blood

Who met us not with punishment, but with mercy

Who was not only humble, but was a Man of Sorrows and acquainted with grief; as one from whom men hide their faces He was despised, and we esteemed Him not

Who had power not just to declare the Word of the Lord, but also to declare the Day of the Lord, when the lame should walk and the blind receive their sight

Who delivered the sinful from the just demands of the Law, but then sent them out in power, saying, "Go and sin no more"

Worthy is the Lamb who was slain, to receive power and wealth and wisdom and might and honor and glory and blessing!

Amen

TUESDAY

Hebrews 3:4 *"(For every house is built by someone, but the builder of all things is God.)"*

L ord, You know our sitting down and our rising up

You have given us every good thing

Yours is the warm sun on the earth

The green of the fields as they grow

The wind going where it will

The fire that keeps the chill out

The food that gives us strength for another day

Yet these are only tokens of Your love

They are not the greatest good

You have said that if a person loses all these but gains the Kingdom, they will live forever

Teach us to look for a city with foundations, whose architect and builder is God

To see beyond the ruin of this world as it fades around us

To gain eternal treasure, to be rich toward You

To take up our crosses as Jesus did and throw off every sin that hinders

To build a home with its foundation on a rock

The rock of Your living Word, which will never pass away

And to look always for Your coming, though all be darkness around us

And may the glory for it be only Yours

Alpha and Omega, source of all true good

Amen

WEDNESDAY

Hebrews 3:5 *"Now Moses was faithful in all God's house as a servant,
to testify to the things that were to be spoken later."*

L ife is hard, Lord

We try to be faithful to Your holy Law

To love each other

To forgive from the heart

To stay away from sin

To work against the wiles of the evil one

To worship You in Spirit and in truth

But we fall so very short

We have forgotten the works of God

We have not kept His commandments

We have gone astray after mute idols

We have not revered Your Name as we should

We are like our fathers, a stubborn and rebellious generation

A generation whose heart was not steadfast

Whose spirit was not faithful to God

Have mercy, Lord

Teach us not to look to the holy Law for salvation

But to the One who has done all things well

Turn our hearts to Jesus, and let us never look away from Him again

Amen

THURSDAY

Hebrews 3:6 *"But Christ is faithful over God's house as a son. And we are His house if indeed we hold fast our confidence and our boasting in our hope."*

 house is one of our most basic needs

You made us to need shelter, to be with family, to adorn our surroundings with beauty

But this verse lifts the truth to a higher level

Your Word says that we are Christ's house

It was not that You needed a place to live

Behold, the highest heavens could not contain You; much less this house that we have built

Yet we did not even build it

Christ did.

He Himself is the Cornerstone, chosen and precious

Rejected of men, yet now become the head stone

And those who trust in Him will never be put to shame

For no one can lay any foundation other than that which is laid, which is Jesus Christ

And on it we ourselves, like living stones, are built up in Him

Built on the rock of the Word of God

Where You have founded Your beloved Church, and the gates of Hell shall not prevail against it

Help us to hold fast our confidence, Lord, that You might build us up to stand by faith, anchored upon grace alone

Help us to boast only in the Cross today

Amen

FRIDAY

Hebrews 3:7 *"Therefore, as the Holy Spirit says, 'Today, if you hear His voice'"*

L ord, Your Word is life

It brings us to Your presence, fills us, sustains us, instructs us, rebukes us, gives us hope

And it also warns us gravely:

"If you hear His voice"

Lord, we have heard Your voice

How many never did

How many continued in their blindness, sin & rebellion until it was too late

How many became friends with this world and enemies of You, only to realize that their bodies were mortal and their souls were not

And that this world and its desires are passing away, but You remain forever

How many hardened their hearts, having put You to the test and seen the works You did

Demanding bread in the wilderness, they lost sight of Him who is the Bread of Life

And they had been privileged to hear Your voice too, just as we have been

Lord, give us humble hearts

Help us to accept what Your prophets and apostles said as what it really is

Not the word of men, but the Word of God, which is at work in us who believe

Change our hearts with it

Let us be quick to repent, to forgive, to speak against evil, to speak Your Gospel

Help us to see Your Kingdom as it grows under Your faithful hand

And let us enter Your rest, by the faithfulness of Christ on our behalf

Amen

SATURDAY

Hebrews 3:8 *"...do not harden your hearts as in the rebellion,
on the day of testing in the wilderness"*

L ord, You know the depth of evil in our hearts

Much better than we do:

You know how quick we are to excuse ourselves

How good at assuring ourselves that we are not like other men

How clever at constructing barriers to hide our wrongdoing

How resolute in resisting the words of Your Spirit

How steadfast in insisting that we are rich, and have prospered, and need nothing

That we do not even need You.

Lord, open our eyes:

Show us that we were born with foolish hearts of stone, that will not inherit the Kingdom

Of your great mercy, give us hearts of spiritual flesh, that beat after Your own

Help us to accept Your forgiveness, offered full and free

To hear the truth that in the final analysis we are but unprofitable servants

To live in the joy of the light of Your holy Law, which shows us Jesus

To move and speak at the impulse of Your love, loving others even as Christ did

To boast only in the Cross, and freely own our poverty of spirit

And to seek the only fitness He requireth:

To know my deep and abiding need of You.

In part I see it now, and dimly

Haste the day when it shall be as fully as I am known by You

Amen.

MONDAY

Hebrews 3:9 *"...where your fathers put me to the test and saw my works for forty years."*

L ord, You are in Heaven, and we are on earth; You have all wisdom, and we are born foolish

You made all things, and we were to be Your stewards

You are righteous, and we are wayward

You see all ends, and we are blind to anything You do not show us

You punish evil, and we excuse our own while condemning others'

You judge justly, and we are swayed by appearance and opinion

You love truly, and we are unreliable friends

You tell the truth, and we are every man a liar

You have compassion on the perishing, and we harden our hearts

But in Your mighty mercy, You have brought us into Your family:

You redeem a people for Your own, to be made into the image of the Christ

You teach us to number our days aright, to get a heart of wisdom

You raise us from servants to sons, with a new robe and a ring on our finger

You give us sober hearts that joy only in Your holiness

You open our eyes to see Your eternal truth

You teach us humility to confess sin and repent of it

You give us Your Law, as a faithful schoolmaster to lead us to Christ

You show us Your hands and feet and side, and true love begins to grow in our hearts

You give us Your Word of life to guide us into all truth

You soften our hearts to tell others of what Jesus did for us

And You welcome us into eternal dwellings with You. Amen

TUESDAY

Your Word says the fear of the Lord is the beginning of wisdom

You know our hearts, better than we ever will

We were created in Your image, to reflect Your glory

We were supposed to have joy in Your fellowship

To walk with You in the cool of the day in the garden You set us in

To have dominion over the earth and rule over it

To be fruitful and multiply

For all of life to be worship, to fall under the light of Your presence

For our hearts to be open to Your Spirit and follow hard after Yours

But we sinned, and were driven from Your presence

The image You set in us was marred

We were afraid, because we realized we were naked; and we hid from You

We took the leaves of the trees we were charged with keeping to cover ourselves

All the earth was turned against us, and cursed was the very ground because of us

Pain was multiplied for us in childbearing and our offspring were born into the same despair

Your face was hidden from us, for You may not look on sin

And we provoked You to wrath. Our hearts have gone astray from You and we have not known Your ways

Give us to fear You before anything else in this world, Lord, that we might have wisdom to accept Your grace and forgiveness in Christ Jesus

Amen

WEDNESDAY

Hebrews 3:11 *"As I swore in my wrath, 'They shall not enter my rest.'"*

L ord, we bow before You in fear and trembling

It is not just in awe, or adoration, or amazement

It is actually in true godly fear

Fear of a God so holy that we cannot stand in Your presence unless we are found in Christ

Fear of a wrath against sin so fierce that it destroyed everything that had breath in the world, save for eight souls who heeded Your Word

Fear of a holiness so pure that You were ready to put Your covenant people to death, save for Your faithful servant Moses who intervened

Fear of a righteousness so high and lifted up that You sent the nation of Israel into exile, until they should learn not to have any other gods before You

Fear of a justice so penetrating that You sent Your prophet to confront the king, the man after Your own heart, and humble him for his sin before You

Fear of a Law so far above anything we can think or know, that You had to send Your only Son a redeeming sacrifice for us

Fear of a depth of sin in our hearts that surpasses our ability to know it, and remembrance of the times when you have shown us how desperately wicked we can be

Fear of a judgment so terrible that it took Jesus Christ Himself to drain the cup of Your wrath to its dregs. God, have mercy

Fear of an eternal punishment that can never fade away, driving me to share with the lost how they must cast their souls upon Christ

And fear of an evil, unbelieving heart that leads us to fall away from the living God. As so many times You have rescued me from my own foolishness. May I never presume on Your grace again

Lord of mercy, remember that we are but flesh. Visit us anew with Your Spirit, give us hearts that follow hard after you, pardon our sin, fit us for life everlasting in Your presence

Amen

THURSDAY

Hebrews 3:12 *"Take care, brothers, lest there be in any of you an evil, unbelieving heart, leading you to fall away from the living God."*

Our hearts are deceitful above all things, Lord

We have seen so much of Your faithfulness

We have seen You seek us out when we were aliens and strangers in a foreign land

You spoke to us a language we had not known, relieving our shoulder from the burden, our hands from the basket

You performed signs and wonders before the nations, proving that You were the God of all Creation:

We saw the waters turn to blood

The land swarm with frogs

The air fill with gnats

The houses covered with flies

The beasts of the field perish

Boils break out on the skin of the people

The crops ruined with hail

The increase devoured by locusts

Darkness stretch over the land, a darkness that could be felt

And the firstborn of all Egypt draw their last breath and die

We saw the destroying angel pause in front of our door and see the blood of the innocent lamb over it, and move on

And with Your words still echoing in our memory, *"Let my people go,"* we set off through the wilderness in search of Your Promised Land.

Lord, give us hearts that seek first Your Kingdom and Your righteousness

Amen

FRIDAY

Hebrews 3:13 *"But exhort one another every day, as long as it is called 'today,'*
that none of you may be hardened by the deceitfulness of sin."

L ord, each day of life You give is a gift

It is a treasure beyond price

Life is another chance to hear Your Word

To repent of sin

To tell the truth

To call on You for mercy

To have our hearts softened once again

To clearly see what destruction comes when we disobey Your Word

To understand the lie, mixed with truth, that so cunningly draws our hearts

To see the dreadful pedestal of rebellion we would place ourselves on to challenge Your Lordship

To hear the gentle word of rebuke from a brother or sister who loves us enough to speak it

To move in godly sorrow back into communion with Your Spirit

To willingly accept bitter consequences, knowing that You paid the higher debt

To make a clean break with sin, and embrace what is right and good

To speak to others our testimony of how You so faithfully saved us

To keep our hearts soft by prayer and confession, encouraging each other in it

To lift high Your Name with our obedience to Your Gospel

To long for that Day when we will sin no more

And to seek to bring You glory above all things

Amen

SATURDAY

Hebrews 3:14 *"For we have come to share in Christ, if indeed we hold our original confidence firm to the end."*

I t is so dark, Lord

Nobody will speak what truly is

Acquiescence is the sacrifice that must be brought to the altar

Silence is the fork that is plunged into the pot

And whatever truth is pierced by it belongs to the priest

There is no one who understands, none who seek after God

All have turned away

And are scattered on the hills like sheep without a shepherd

The shadow of the throne of the beast stretches long over the land

Who will stand and speak against it? For only Your Word has power to do that

The faithful are not those who are mighty to conquer in Your name

But rather they are those who have a little strength, and have kept Your Word, and have not denied Your name

Who have truly repented of their sin

Who have forgiven deep wrong, and interceded for the souls of those gone astray

Who have looked for Your coming, more than watchmen for the morning

More than watchmen for the morning

Who have stayed awake, and kept their lamps lit, and kept their garments on, that they might not be found naked and exposed in that great Day

And who have suffered all to know, in their original confidence, that there is only One faithful

And have stood in the strength of Your Spirit firm to the end.

Amen

MONDAY

Hebrews 3:15 *"As it is said, 'Today, if you hear his voice, do not harden your hearts as in the rebellion.'"*

L ord, Your voice is truth

You speak truth, and what You say remains, when all else has fallen away

When You repeat Yourself, it is well for us to listen

For it is for our benefit that the word is given again, not Yours

We have hardened our hearts again, Lord

The rebellion has begun again

In our hearts we have nurtured a dark thought, one that never should have seen the light of day

That You do not have our best interests at heart

That we must take our destiny into our own hands

That it is in ascending to a higher plane of knowledge that our salvation is to be found

That if smooth things were prophesied to us, we would at last be happy

That we would flee upon horses to at last find what we want

But for love You caught hold of us:

Our pursuers were swift, and we were left like a flagstaff on a mountain

Hard truths were spoken that pierced our hearts to heal them

In quietness and trust our salvation was found

A form of One who bore the bitter Cross for us rose before our wondering eyes

And His Spirit took us by the hand and led us where we did not want to go

Out of the darkness, and into the glorious light of the freedom of the children of God

Father, let us turn back and listen to You; and never lose the sound of Your voice again. Amen

TUESDAY

Hebrews 3:16 *"For who were those who heard and yet rebelled? Was it not all those who left Egypt led by Moses?"*

I am just a man, Lord

"Take my life, for I am no better than my fathers," the prophet said

We have all sinned and fallen short of the glory of God

We have turned every one to our own way

We have heard the voice of Your Spirit; there is no excuse for us

Our sin has been called out and our rebellion exposed

Our hearts have desired the leeks and the garlick of Egypt, of the land where our shoulders groaned under the lash

We have not believed Your promises, nor have we remembered Your mighty works in the desert

We do not deserve to gain Your inheritance

For we have faltered at the threshold of the Promised Land

Lord, You know that the blood of bulls and goats will never take away sin

Faithful as Moses was in Your house, we need One greater

We need One as much greater than Moses as grace is greater than law

One who is faithful as a Son, not as a servant

We need our hearts of stone removed and need You to give us hearts of flesh

Change us into the image of Christ, Lord

Let us see through His eyes, walk with His feet, know by His mind, love by His heart

And bring us by Your great mercy into Your everlasting rest

Amen

WEDNESDAY

Hebrews 3:17 *"And with whom was he provoked for forty years? Was it not with those who sinned, whose bodies fell in the wilderness?"*

I have sinned

Not just my people, but me

I have provoked the Lord, who bought us out of slavery

Who took the yoke from our shoulders

Who called us by His name, and set His sign of faithfulness on us

Who delivered us from the enslaving power of evil

Whose Spirit went before us as a flame of fire and as a mighty covering

Who taught us His holy Law

Who shielded us from the sword of the oppressor

Who made a way for us through the deep waters

Who put a song of praise in our mouths, where there was only weeping

Who spread a table for us in the wilderness, and brought forth water from the barren rock

Who lifted up the serpent in the desert to take death from on our heads

Who brought us to a land flowing with milk and honey

Who called us to courage and strengthened our hearts to go forth in His power

Who defeated our enemies and struck down those who sought to destroy His people

Who quieted our hearts and settled us in houses already built, vineyards already planted

Who fulfilled all that was spoken of Him, and stands now to forgive and to restore

Lord, to Whom shall we go? You have the words of eternal life

Amen

THURSDAY

Hebrews 3:18 *"And to whom did He swear that they would not enter His rest, but to those who were disobedient?"*

L ord, it is more than we can bear

Our sins rise up against us to condemn us

We cannot even remember how many times You have rescued us

And each time we have fallen away from You again:

We have disobeyed Your holy Law

We have profaned Your temple

We have trespassed on Your sacred mountain

We have turned away Your faithful love for us

We have sought after other lovers in our hearts, illicit lovers who know no vows

We have dishonored You on top of every hill and under every spreading tree

We have sacrificed our firstborn to our evil desires, and their innocent blood cries out against us

We have neglected Your worship

We have not listened to Your Word

We have slain Your messengers and persecuted Your prophets

We have forgotten Your love and compassion for us

We have forced You to send us away, and the ruin of our downfall haunts us every day

Lord, our exiled souls have mourned our sin, and have longed for Your Sabbath-rest

Hear our cry, and from Heaven Your dwelling place, forgive

We have no other hope save in the atoning power of Your life and death

Amen

FRIDAY

Hebrews 3:19 *"So we see that they were unable to enter because of unbelief."*

T he work of God in us is this: To believe in the One He has sent

Lord, it is Your work first and last

You have called us out of darkness into Your amazing light

You have drawn us away from the empty way of life handed down to us by our forefathers

Out of Egypt You have called Your son

To leave behind slavery forever

To learn Your ways, and speak Your name in holy fear

To put the blood over the doorway and watch the destroying angel pass over

To watch the cloud lead by day, and the fire by night

To worship the God of ages as He tabernacles with us

To think on the blood of bulls and goats as it points to a greater Sacrifice

To willingly give of our treasures for the Glory that abides among us

To look up on the Mountain of the Law and see the flame and smoke

To hear the holiness of God laid down as a testament and a rule for His people

To see the horse and the rider thrown down by the power of the sea, which does but obey its Maker

And to look over Jordan and see the land that was promised to our fathers

A land rich with Canaan's fruit and ripe for the taking

But which is far more than just a place to call our own

A dwelling place for us forever, close to the heart of God

Lord, work Your Gospel of grace in our hearts and give us faith to follow You home

Amen

SATURDAY

Hebrews 4:1 *"Therefore, while the promise of entering His rest still stands, let us fear lest any of you should seem to have failed to reach it."*

L ord, so much of my life is spent in fear:

Fear of missing out on something exciting

Fear of losing a friend

Fear of not enjoying life to the fullest

Fear of being punished

Fear of looking foolish to others

Fear of not getting what I want

Fear of dying

Fear of failure

Fear of people

Why do I fear those who kill the body but cannot kill the soul?

Lord, teach me to fear You alone:

To see Your mighty works

To watch the sun and moon obey Your will every day

To try to count the stars, and know that so shall the descendants of faith be

To see You keep Your promises that were sworn to David

To know that You hear the righteous when they cry, and the deeds of the wicked do not escape Your sight

To be shaken by Your holiness in Your temple, and to fall down before you with all the saints to cry, "Glory!"

To long for Your coming, and to desire above all things to enter into Your rest

Amen

MONDAY

Hebrews 4:2 *"For good news came to us just as to them, but the message they heard did not benefit them, because they were not united by faith with those who listened."*

F ather, I give you great praise today for Your Gospel of grace

It is light in a dark place

It is pardon for crimes I have committed against Your holy Law

It is hope in desperate times

It is a word that speaks peace in the midst of a world that cries for war

It is Your very heart, gone out looking for Your lost sheep on the hills

It is tidings of victory from a distant place

It is comfort for Your people

It is water in a dry and thirsty land

It is a rock in the wilderness

It is a glimpse of eternal glory, kept in Heaven for us

It is news that You have conquered sin and death by the precious blood of Jesus

It is strength for the weary, joy for the burdened, new life for those who walk in the Valley of the Shadow of Death

It is a glimpse of the Tree whose leaves are for the healing of the nations

It is the sight of home, on a journey we have long toiled on

And I thank You that You have revealed all these things in Your Word

That Your message is one of truth, and forgiveness, and renewal

That it is truth, as we have never known it before

Humble our hearts and give us spirits to receive the implanted Word, which is able to save us

Amen

TUESDAY

Hebrews 4:3 *"For we who have believed enter that rest, as he has said, 'As I swore in my wrath, "They shall not enter my rest,"' although his works were finished from the foundation of the world."*

T hese words have appeared again

It is uncomfortable for us to hear

It does not assure us that we cannot lose our salvation

It does not say that we need not fear God

It does not say that there is nothing we can do to make God love us less

It does not say any of the foolish things American evangelicals love to assure ourselves with

It simply says the truth:

That You are holy

That You have ordained salvation, as You have all things, from the foundation of the world

That You, and You alone, write people's names in the Book of Life

That You are worthy of all worship, and that one day all will bow in holy fear of You

That You have prepared for us a Sabbath-rest that will dry all our tears, and heal all our wounds

That if we have stubborn hearts and will not take Your yoke on us, we will perish like the heathen, like those who never even heard Your law

That belief is a gift; a gift of grace, from first to last

That we are no better than those who died in the desert from unbelief, and that we should fear lest any of us seem to have failed to reach it

Lead us into Your Promised Land, and teach us heart-obedience to Your holy Law, by Your Spirit

Amen

WEDNESDAY

Hebrews 4:4 *"For he has somewhere spoken of the seventh day in this way: 'And God rested on the seventh day from all his works.'"*

Y ou are our Lord and our God

You have made us, and we are Yours

You showed us what faithfulness was to be, in a world untouched by sin:

Work, creativity, joy, dutifulness, imagination, investment, blessing

And then when You were done, You rested

It was a picture of perfect creative power at work to breathe spiritual life into the dust of the earth

Man was one of the works You made, and all You did was very good

We walked with You in the garden in the cool of the day

We obeyed Your commands from a simple heart of innocence

We looked out on a world bursting forth with life, and knew that we had been made to have dominion over it, to work it and protect it and build it and name it

And then to rest from our labors, even as You did

But a suggestion entered into our minds; not evil yet, nor disobedience, but simply the idea that You had not really meant what You said

That You did not have our best interests at heart

That to reach our full potential, we should take of the fruit of the tree of the knowledge of good and evil, and live forever

And turning away from You we did; and grieved with our unfaithfulness You set a flaming sword between us and the garden; and all our descendants were plunged into death and despair

There is a new rest that You call us to now. It is not the rest of Eden, and not a door we can walk through in our own strength

It is the Sabbath-rest of the people of God, and it is freely offered by Your Son's blood

Amen

THURSDAY

Hebrews 4:5 *"And again in this passage he said, 'They shall not enter my rest.'"*

L ord, You are holy above all things

We worship You not because it is meaningful, or because we need something to worship

We worship You because You alone are worthy

For all eternity You have existed, in light unapproachable, the One only glorious

You have revealed Yourself to us by Your Son, Jesus Christ

Through the clamor of the dying world around us

Through the decay we feel deep in our bones, creeping slowly into our hearts

Through the stealth of the darkness that covers our eyes

Through the bitter untruth of all that is seen, is felt, is heard, is known by our broken senses

Through the terror of the world, the flesh and the devil hurling their furious assault on the last bulwark of our spiritual resistance

Through the gnawing grief of the memory of those we once called friends, who have renounced Your name and turned their faces against the crumbling walls of Zion

Through the subtle betrayal of our own hearts, now accusing, now even excusing us before You who judge all things

Through the shadow of a mighty Cross, pulling us down its lonely path with a voice that may not be denied, over a dark River beyond which we cannot see

And above all these, clear when all else is obscured, true when all else is false, enduring when all else fails, lifted up like the snake in the wilderness, condemned for the sins of the world, triumphing in the death of Death for the life of Life:

My only Lord Jesus Christ, Messiah and King.

Where else will we go, Lord? For You have the words of life

Remember me when You come into Your Kingdom

Amen

FRIDAY

Hebrews 4:6 *"Since therefore it remains for some to enter it, and those who formerly received the good news failed to enter because of disobedience"*

Y ou gave us the good news, Lord; You preached it from every rooftop

It was proclaimed to us by faithful witnesses who spoke it at great cost to themselves

It was written in Your holy Word, there in all the stories, presented in all the sermons, hidden in all the parables

Even Your creation declared Your glory, and the sky proclaimed Your handiwork

Your prophets declared it at the risk of their lives

Your apostles preached it to rulers and to kings

From the earliest days, Your people heard the good news of Your salvation which was for all

Noah saw it from the ark, when You saved eight people from the floodwaters

Abraham saw it when the ram in the thicket took the place of his son on the altar

Isaac saw it when the son of the covenant received his blessing, not the oldest and strongest

Jacob saw it when he told his sons not to leave his bones in Egypt when they came back to the Promised Land

Moses saw it when he lifted up the serpent in the wilderness

David saw it when his sin was forgiven and You promised that one of his sons would always be on his throne

Isaiah saw it when the Son to be born was revealed to him

Jeremiah saw it when God showed him the Righteous Branch, who would be called "The Lord Our Righteousness"

We have their testimony, sure and certain and unchanging

Give us faith to believe it, Lord, and by the obedience of Christ welcome us into Your rest

Amen

SATURDAY

Hebrews 4:7 *"again he appoints a certain day, 'Today,' saying through David so long afterward, in the words already quoted, 'Today, if you hear his voice, do not harden your hearts.'"*

I t is so long afterward, Lord

So long since the voice in Mesopotamia

Since the Pharaoh was afflicted for Abram's sake, and God said "Touch not mine anointed"

Since the journey in the desert where so many of Your people fell because of disbelief

Since Joshua led them boldly over the Jordan into the good land

Since their hearts grew hard again from years of peace and plenty

Since they began to go astray with the gods of the nations around them, and let their eyes wander among their women

Since worship crept up onto the high places and beneath every spreading tree, and Your holy Temple sat profaned and neglected

Since their priests stopped their ears to Your Word and took bribes for their sacrifices

Since their prophets were persecuted and their blood was shed when they said, "This is what the Lord says"

Since their kings forsook wisdom and justice, and embraced foolishness and cruelty, and those they ruled cried out because of them

Since the wolf grew bold on their borders and the lion ventured into their town square

Since the fateful day came when Zion fell to her enemies, and her daughters were led out in disgrace into captivity, and her sons broken under the bitter yoke of the ungodly

That day was a Today, when in Your anger You said to them "Be ever seeing but not perceiving" and "Be ever hearing but not understanding"

A few of them heard Your voice, feared Your name, put their trust in You, and obeyed Your Word

Have mercy on us, Lord, and help us to serve You Today. Amen

MONDAY

Hebrews 4:8 *"For if Joshua had given them rest, God would not have spoken of another day later on."*

Y ou are the God who sees

In a world lit only by flame, we can no longer see Your face

The plants of the field, which were to have been a garden for You to enjoy in the cool of the day, now bear sword against us with thorn and thistle

The animals which move on the face of the earth, which were to display Your joy in life and variety, now fear their stewards and live by tooth and claw

The creatures of the great deep and the birds of the air blindly pursue their own ends, with no connection to the word You spoke when all things came into existence

Men and women spend our days in foolish bondage, using each other and the world around us to build crumbling temples to our own evil desires

When the desolation of our sin rose up before You like smoke over the hilltops, You sent Your floodwaters to destroy all life – almost all life

For You always preserve a Remnant

A small collection of those who fear Your name

Who see Your bow set in the clouds, and remember Your promise that You will never again destroy the world with water

But who know that one day the world will be destroyed with fire, and there will be no restoration

Who know that You will make all things new, heavens and earth, and those who would live with You must surely also be made new

Who look intently into Your holy Law, and begin to see not Death, but the form of One who kept it perfectly for us

A Man of Sorrows, and acquainted with grief; One from whom men hide their faces

Who bore our sins in His body on the tree, that we might again see Your face

That in Him we might at last truly have rest. Amen

TUESDAY

Hebrews 4:9 *"So then, there remains a Sabbath-rest for the people of God"*

What is it that remains, Lord? We are so weary

The road through the wilderness has been long

Many are those who have been master over us, and many of us have fallen on the way

We have not feared You as we ought

We have seen Your deliverance, and forgotten it

We have known Your power in the cloud and the pillar of fire, and resented it

We have been healed by Your messenger lifted up, yet not worshiped You with pure hearts

We have heard Your thunder and seen Your smoke on the mountain, and have cried for You to go away from us, to veil Your glory

We have felt the very salt spray on our cheeks as Your enemies were dashed beneath the waves in front of us, yet our hearts were slow to rejoice

We have watched the rock hewn in two and life-giving water spring from it, yet provoked Your servant to wrath with our unbelief

We have had the meat from Your table between our teeth when we called out to return to the yoke of bondage, to the long sleep of slavery

We have longed with our foolish hearts for the leeks and the onions of Egypt, despising the pure, clear air of freedom You gave us to breathe

We have no soundness in us, from the soles of our feet even to our head

We are sick with the affliction of this world and of its desires, and with it we are passing away

What is it that remains, Lord?

You alone remain.

Forgive our sin with the faithful wounds of Your suffering servant, Your only Son

And grant us to find our home at last in You. Amen

WEDNESDAY

Hebrews 4:10 *"For whoever has entered God's rest has also rested from his works as God did from his."*

L ord, on the sixth day of Creation You made man

And all the heavens and the earth were finished, and all the host of them

And on the seventh day You rested from all Your work that You had done

And You blessed the seventh day, and made it holy

Work was good, and from it came life of every kind, and beauty all around

But the end of the matter was better than the beginning, and to be finished than to undertake

For when work ceased, and You were no longer doing, You were still being

And in Your Word Your Spirit still teaches us of this rest:

Of a rest from trying to gain life by keeping Your Law

Of a rest from striving with evil that only You can overcome

Of a rest from trying to earn the favor we so deeply need from You

Of a rest from trying to become Your sons and daughters by our works, who we already are by grace alone

Of a rest from trying to secure a lasting place in this fading world

Of a rest from following the vainglory of our foolish hearts into error and sin

Of a rest from wanting to take hold of our eternal reward before its time

Of a rest from any doing, no matter how good, that hinders who we are to be in You

Whom have I in heaven besides You? And there is nothing on earth that I desire besides You

But I have calmed and quieted my soul, like a weaned child with its mother

Help me to remember that You are the strength of my heart, and my portion forever. Amen

THURSDAY

Hebrews 4:11 *"Let us therefore strive to enter that rest, so that no one may fall by the same sort of disobedience."*

L ord, You know all things; You know that I love you

I hear "strive" and think that I must try harder, that I have to achieve it

Have I not learned that there is nothing good which You did not create in six days?

And knowing that, that there will be nothing good in eternity not found by resting in Your work?

The disobedience of Your people was not one of not trying hard enough

The Israelites disobeyed by not believing what You said

They disobeyed by not doing what You commanded

They disobeyed by not following Your appointed servant

They disobeyed by not laying hold of Your promises

And finally they disobeyed by not wanting any part in You

They chose the world and its blind striving unto death, over trusting Your Word

Show me how to feed Your lambs

Show me how to tend Your sheep

Show me how to feed Your sheep, Lord, and remind me that I am one of them

By Your Spirit stretch out my hands, and dress me and carry me where I do not want to go when I am old

Remove the heart of stone from me, and give me a heart of flesh to strive

Striving above all else to enter into Your rest

Not because it is my heart's desire, even though it surely is

Because You are there.

Amen

FRIDAY

Hebrews 4:12 *"For the word of God is living and active, sharper than any two-edged sword, piercing to the division of soul and of spirit, of joints and of marrow, and discerning the thoughts and intentions of the heart."*

I n the beginning was the Word, and the Word was with God, and the Word was God

You hovered over the waters and brought forth life from the darkness

By the power of Your Word You hung the sun and moon and stars, and made all things that are

You called forth Your servant Abram and proclaimed Yourself his shield, his very great reward

From Egypt You called Moses, and taught Him in the wilderness to fear You, and led him back to set Your people free

You commanded Aaron and His sons to minister before You, looking forward to a day when You would have a people who would be to You a kingdom of priests, and a holy people

You descended to Mount Sinai in smoke, in thick smoke like a garment, and gave Your holy Law to set apart a people unto Yourself

They heard the sound of Your words, but saw no form; there was only a Voice

You raised up Your son David and put a song in his heart, that he might teach Your people to worship You; and You swore to him that he would always have a descendant on the throne

You did mighty works through Your servants the prophets, who through faith conquered kingdoms, enforced justice, obtained promises, stopped the mouths of lions, quenched the power of fire, escaped the edge of the sword, were made strong out of weakness, became mighty in war, put foreign armies to flight. The world was not worthy of them

And the Word became flesh and dwelt among us, and we have seen his glory, glory as of the only Son from the Father, full of grace and truth

Teach me to hear Your voice and to know Your truth, above all else

Amen

SATURDAY

Hebrews 4:13 *"And no creature is hidden from his sight, but all are naked and exposed to the eyes of him to whom we must give account."*

There is no one to whom we can go, Lord

Evil has risen like smoke on the water, until it seems like there is nothing else around. People smile and turn their eyes from it, and pretend not to see

They stop their ears to the cries of those around them, and pretend not to hear

They rinse the blood from their hands with the very milk of Your Word, and pretend not to feel

They darken the doors of their minds to the entering of the light, and pretend not to know

And in their blindness and satisfaction they speak Your Name over their foolishness

But You are the Beginning and the End, who made all things for Your glory

The Consolation of Israel, who kept Your promises of a Messiah who would save

The Bread of Life, that whoever comes to You should never hunger again

The Root of David, who has conquered so that He can open the scrolls

The Refuge, by whom the afflicted of His people can come into Zion

The Sun of Righteousness who rises with healing in His wings

The great High Priest who calls us to His throne of grace

The Son of Man who knows our deepest sorrows

The Son of God who has brought us into Your own family

The God who Sees, though all the world should turn their eyes away

The Lover of our Souls, who knows the dark places in our hearts and yet pursues us

Make us holy and blameless in Your sight, Lord, until we reflect the very image of Christ. Amen

MONDAY

Hebrews 4:14 *"Since then we have a great high priest who has passed through the heavens, Jesus, the Son of God, let us hold fast to our confession."*

S ave us, O God, for the waters are over our head

The world scoffs at our hope

The flesh is weak, and cannot but listen to them

The enemy assails us at every turn, and there seems no defense against his vicious barbs

Yet our confession is a bold one:

That You, O God, are holy

And that You, O God, are merciful

A holy God is alone worthy of our worship, though every idol in the world topple and fall, helpless to save

A holy God makes His home in the heavens, and the highest heavens cannot contain Him; how much less any temple built by our hands

A holy God has power even over the demons, and when they have done going to and fro in the earth, and going back and forth in it, they must appear in obedience before His will

And our confession is a gracious one:

A merciful God shows us that our Redeemer lives, and that at the last He will stand upon the earth

A merciful God condescends to tabernacle with us and to take on human flesh, yet without sin, so that the dwelling of God might be with men

A merciful God crushes the head of His foe and delivers His people from the hand of the oppressor, bringing us into a rich and plentiful Promised Land

Lord, show us that the waters that pass over our head first passed over Your Son's

Help us to see Jesus, and to hold fast our faith in Him, though Heaven and Earth pass away

Amen

TUESDAY

Hebrews 4:15 *"For we do not have a high priest who is unable to sympathize with our weaknesses, but one who in every respect has been tempted as we are, yet without sin."*

Y ou made us for community, Lord

You yourself existed as Father, Son and Spirit before the world began

In unapproachable light You were holy and together, without fault and lacking nothing

But in Your eternal wisdom You purposed to create, and not just to create being, but to create being in Your image

Male and female You created us, and set us to work the garden that was Your delight

But we listened to dark counsel, and we doubted Your Word of truth, supposing that You were holding out on us

As if You could have given us anything more than perfect innocence and Your approving Presence

In grief You cast us from Your sight, and set a flaming sword between us and eternal Life, that the only way we could find it would be to go through You

And then You sent us out into a world rigged to harm, where thorns and thistles would choke our work, and anguish attend our childbearing

When we began to stray from You, You shortened our days, and Your Spirit did not abide in man forever

When our sin rose to the heavens, and the earth itself cried out under our evildoing, You sent water to cover the earth and kill everything with breath in its nostrils; save eight people only

When we sought to build a tower to the heavens and make a name for ourselves, You confused our language, and scattered us on the face of the earth

And when we were scattered on the hills, like sheep without a shepherd, Your heart went out to us, and You sent Your Son

He tended Your sheep and gently led those that had young; he knew what it was to be tempted, to know fear, to know despair, to be alone. Yet He was not ashamed to be called our Brother

Amen

WEDNESDAY

Hebrews 4:16 *"Let us then with confidence draw near to the throne of grace, that we may receive mercy and find grace to help in time of need."*

T his whole world is built on power, Lord

If you know how the world works, you treat the right people well, and stay away from the others, and people give you what you want

And this whole world is built on things

They surround us: Things to do, things to eat, to look at, to touch, to listen to, to focus on, to work for, to hold onto, to pile around us, to glory in

And for what?

Power fades away, and those who guarded the gates begin to stoop and tremble, and those who courted them turn away to gate-keepers who are younger and stronger

Things succumb to moths and rust, and are stolen away, and even as we feast our eyes on them they fade away, leaving us with a pile of ashes

And if we are telling the truth, as we watch the world crumble around us, we must know that it was all built on sand

That the power and things we pursued all our lives was no more than fear and greed, thinly disguised as wellbeing, melting away before eternity as a mist before the rising sun

With hearts broken and hands empty we come back to You, and we dare not even look You in the eye

And the only thing we can cry out is, "Father, I have sinned against Heaven and against You. I am no longer worthy to be called Your son"

But You saw us coming when we were yet a long way off; and You ran to gather us in Your arms, and to call us Your beloved child

You called all Heaven and earth to celebrate with You, for we were dead and are now alive again; we were lost, and now are found

And You send us out again, no longer to give in to the foolish desires of the world, or to judge those who do; but to boldly proclaim the mercy and grace of Jesus, until You come again

Amen

THURSDAY

Hebrews 5:1 *"For every high priest chosen from among men is appointed to act on behalf of men in relation to God, to offer gifts and sacrifices for sins."*

E ven the best of men who are chosen to serve before You are broken, Lord
They have fears

They have false hopes

They are blind to things

They put their trust in worthless idols that cannot save

They hide their eyes from the unceasing plight of the helpless

They lend their support to the unrelenting weight of the overbearing

They silence Truth when it speaks

They obscure the people's vision of God, until it is blurred beyond recognition

They forget what it is to stand in the presence of the Almighty:

To remove your shoes because you are on holy ground

To see the hot blood spilled on the altar, and remember what sins it is paying for

To hear the angels shout in joyful assembly for pure worship

To feel the wrath of God pass over the Lamb's blood on the doorpost, and know the joy of grace

To dance before the presence of the Lord and praise His mighty Name

To bow down before Him in His holy temple, and hear the angels shout "Glory!"

To hear the prophets condemn sin, and speak of a Messiah who will one day come to save us

To see the Chosen One appear and lead captives in His train

To place their faith in Him, though all the world should stand against Him

And to look for Your salvation

Amen

FRIDAY

Hebrews 5:2 *"He can deal gently with the ignorant and wayward, since he himself is beset with weakness."*

L ord Jesus, You are Lord over all things

You are before all things and in You they hold together

Your Spirit hovered over the waters when the earth was dark and formless

You spoke, and there was light amid the darkness

You separated the light from the darkness, and You said that it was good

And You made the waters under the Heavens; and You made the dry land

And You brought forth plants on the earth

And You hung great lights in the expanse of the skies, to be for signs and seasons and to give light on the earth

And You made living creatures in the waters and to fly in the air

And then You made man in Your image, after Your likeness. You made us to have dominion over the earth and to rule it, and You gave us every plant for food

And You saw that it was all good

And when, in the midst of all this good, evil came into our hearts and into the world You had made, it was not a surprise to You

For You knew in the eternal counsel of Your wisdom that we would fall

And You laid a course for our salvation which would call us to Resurrection

But You did not leave us alone; You took on flesh, and sojourned with us

You knew pain, and hunger, and loneliness, and temptation, and weakness

You dealt gently with the ignorant and wayward, for their salvation

And You taught us that every last one of us is ignorant and wayward, and that we need only freely confess it and come to You for eternal life

Amen

SATURDAY

Hebrews 5:3 *"Because of this he is obligated to offer sacrifice for his own sins just as he does for those of the people."*

T o lead is to suffer, to bear in your body the wounds of the people you love

For the Christian leader there is a double burden

He not only must lead the people to God for the forgiveness of their sins, but he must come to God himself to be forgiven

The temptation when you lead is to give in to pride

To think that you yourself are the hope of those who follow you

To suppose that when there is sickness in the body, you are not part of the cause

To continue in blindness to sin, which is to deny grace

To begin to suppose that you are the Shepherd Himself instead of the under-shepherd

To punish wrongdoing by your people but to excuse your own

To consider what the truth is less than you consider what the probable outcome of your decisions will be

To at last try to put yourself in the place of God, forgiving and excusing sin without having made sufficient sacrifice for it; for there is only One who is able to forgive sin

Lord, make our hearts content with the double burden You ask us to bear

Help us to be quick to resort to Your throne of grace

More inclined to pray for people than to lecture them

More dependent on Your Spirit than on our abilities

More enamored with Christ's glory than with the world's regard

And ready to lay down our lives for those we love, as Christ did for the Church

Amen

MONDAY

Hebrews 5:4 *"And no one takes this honor for himself, but only when called by God, just as Aaron was."*

L ord, You called me to leadership in Your Church once

It was one of the deepest honors and privileges of my life

I tended Your flock like an under-shepherd

I gathered the lambs in my arms

I carried them in my bosom

I gently led those that were with young

But always I remembered that they were not mine

That I was not their Lord, and they needed me most to point them to Jesus

And when the day came when I saw my sin between me and the good of the Church

I told the truth and quietly stepped down, and left them in Your hands

You know it, for You were there with me

Your Spirit slowly taught me that their protection was better than my happiness

That Your glory was higher than my desires

That to love anyone in this broken world, you have to let them go

Because if they are truly loved

They are with You.

Teach me this truth again, Lord

The deep honor of leading my wife, and loving my family

Of speaking Your glories to a dying world around

To know You and the power of Your Resurrection and the fellowship of Your sufferings

Amen

TUESDAY

Hebrews 5:5 *"So also Christ did not exalt himself to be made a high priest, but was appointed by him who said to him, 'You are my Son, today I have begotten you';"*

L ord, You did not take honor for Yourself

Even though it was Yours for the taking

You humbled Yourself, and became a man

Knowing poverty, and scorn, and separation

You walked this world in grace and truth

When You were reviled, You did not revile in return

When You suffered, You did not threaten, but continued entrusting Yourself to One who judges justly

Though You had come from the presence of God, You entered into the brokenness of our world without shrinking back

You dealt tenderly with those who had given away their innocence

You moved into relationship with those who had been driven away

You were called "friend of sinners" and so You still are

You reached out Your hand to the sick, and caused the lame to walk

But You had harsh words for the God-talkers who knew the truth and hid it, and used the Word of God to harm those who followed them in blindness

You spent Your time outside the camp, and called all those there to follow You to eternal life

The reproach of God for our sin fell on You, and it broke Your heart

Yet in Your sorrow You did not live for Yourself, but You accepted the priesthood conferred on you by the Father

Lord Jesus, help me to keep my eyes on You today, and accept the calling You place on my life

Amen

WEDNESDAY

Hebrews 5:6 *"as he says also in another place, 'You are a priest forever, after the order of Melchizedek.'"*

L ord, these are troubled times

Danger and lies seem to lurk at every corner

People twist and manipulate the truth to get what they want and control others

Brother rises up against brother, and sister betrays sister to harm

Rulers choose madness over wisdom

Evil is taught instead of good

Blindness is valued instead of sight

Truth is cast aside, and people are given over to a strong delusion

There is none remaining who knows how long, and few who look to You for their hope

We need a vision of Your power and glory

We need to hear Your voice, which we have come to know out of all others

We need to hear again of the Kingdom that is coming

We need to hear "Thus says the Lord" and turn from our wicked ways to do as You say

We need to see Your enemies defeated, and those who would harm Zion

We need to enter Your holy temple, and together cry "Holy"

We need to come to Mount Zion, the city of the living God

The assembly of the firstborn, and to God, the judge of all

The spirits of the righteous made perfect, and to Jesus, the mediator of a new covenant

And to the sprinkled blood that speaks a better word than the blood of Abel

You are our Priest forever, Lord; and we come to You. Amen

THURSDAY

Hebrews 5:7 *"In the days of his flesh, Jesus offered up prayers and supplications, with loud cries and tears, to him who was able to save him from death, and he was heard because of his reverence."*

L ord, You are our great example

You existed before all things in light unapproachable

You had perfection, purpose, community, and glory

You lacked nothing

Yet Your Spirit was pleased to create, out of nothing, all things that are

You gave us Your image

Your blessing and calling

And Your holy Law

But we rebelled against You, and tried to make You in our image

Tried to bless ourselves in our sin, and call ourselves forth in our utter foolishness

And set up our word over Yours

But our word could not create

Neither could it sustain all things by its power

If our word did not echo Yours, all it could ever do is destroy

But into that destruction, into the well-deserved condemnation, a Saviour was born

He came to bear our griefs and carry our sorrows

To offer up prayers and supplications, and to be heard because of His reverence

Like a lamb that is led to the slaughter, He opened not His mouth

But with His sacrifice we are brought near to You again, like sheep to the shepherd

Jesus, let me see Your glory today, and never lose sight of You. Amen

FRIDAY

Hebrews 5:8 *"Although he was a son, he learned obedience through what he suffered."*

L ord Jesus, You were faithful as a Son in Your Father's house

How is it that God can learn?

Yet Your Word says that in the days of Your flesh, You learned obedience

You learned to obey

To obey is to do the will of another, even if (especially if) it is different from your own

It means to spend time meditating on that will, understanding it, making it the sole purpose of your existence

It means looking at every situation and asking the question "What would the Lord have me to do?"

And then putting into practice the answer the Spirit gives, no matter what

Even if people judge you for doing it

Even if it makes you look bad

Even if the evil one tries to twist your obedience into his own designs

Even if the cost of doing God's will is very high

Even if your flesh rebels and sets itself against the coming of the Kingdom

Even if it feels like death.

And when you have stepped faithfully into the breach, the Spirit of Your Father descends upon you

And He says, "This is my beloved Son, with whom I am well pleased."

And when you have reached the end and your body gives up its spirit, you say, "It is finished."

All this You did for us, Jesus

We worship You and we follow You. Amen

SATURDAY

Hebrews 5:9 *"And being made perfect, he became the source of eternal salvation to all who obey him"*

L ord Jesus, You are perfect, without sin or fault

You existed in light unapproachable long before Creation

You saw the innocent joy of our first parents when they woke to the world Your Word had created for them

You knew the blessing of communion with the stewards of the earth, as they placed the sign of Your Lordship on all the animals

Your Spirit knew when the evil one tempted them in the garden, and the idea arose in their minds that perhaps they did not have to obey Your Word after all

"Did not have to obey Your Word"

The power that had brought all things into existence

That hung the sun and the moon and the stars

That kept the breath in their very nostrils, and though they were living dust, sustained them

And You grieved when they chose life without You; that is to say, when they chose death

You cast them out of the garden, that they should not stretch forth their hand and live forever

And You put enmity between the serpent and the woman, that one day he should strike Your heel, and one day You should crush his head

You came and lived a sinless life

In every one of Your words, deeds, and thoughts You glorified the God who is above all

You kept the holy Law perfectly

And in Your righteous sacrifice You offered salvation to all who would obey You

To all who would follow You in sincere repentance and faith, trusting in Your righteousness alone for their eternal hope

In this hope lead me today, Lord Christ. Amen

MONDAY

L ord Jesus

You are high and lifted up

You have all glory and power, all wisdom and knowledge

You formed all things by Your living Word

Your Spirit made us after Your image; male and female You made us

Your holy Law closed the door between us and the Garden, after we had sinned against You, so that to find life, we would first have to find You again

You set a limit to our days, and made them to be a hundred and twenty years

You turned Your face from our detestable offerings, for the blood of bulls and goats could not atone for our sin against You

You gave Moses Your Law, and spoke with him face to face, as a man speaks to his friend

But the Law, for all the truth it gave us, could only ever bring death.

You ordained priests to stand before Your holy temple and intercede for Your people

But Levi, for all the power of his line, could never bring others into Your family.

You saw this, and it displeased You that there was no justice; You saw that there was no man

Then Your own arm brought salvation, and Your righteousness upheld You

A helmet of salvation You put on, garments of vengeance, to wrap Yourself in zeal

You stood fully God and fully man, perfect as Your Heavenly Father is perfect, able to sympathize with our weakness

You became the Mediator of a new covenant to forgive our sins and make us Your children

And a Redeemer came to Zion, to those in Jacob who turn from transgression

Teach us today to place our faith in Your power and mercy. Amen

TUESDAY

Hebrews 5:10 "after the order of Melchizedek."

L ord, we spend so much time seeking what the world has to offer:

Peering down the halls of power

Looking longingly into inner circles

Currying favor with the gatekeepers

Hiding our insecurities and vaunting our strengths, putting forward a false self to convince others that we are better than we really are

Wondering whether we are enough to be included by those in positions of influence; accumulating the things that are valued by the world:

Power

Image

Money

Lord, teach us to seek only what You have:

To behold Your power and glory in the sanctuary

To know that a day in Your courts is better than a thousand elsewhere

To know Your ways, and by grace to enter into Your rest

To freely confess our sin and lay hold of the forgiveness that will bring us new life in Christ

To see You running down the road to welcome us home, and to accept Your embrace

And to seek after the things of Your heart:

Your glory

The image of Christ

Treasures in Heaven

Help us to find our high priesthood in Jesus. Amen

WEDNESDAY

Hebrews 5:11 *"About this we have much to say, and it is hard to explain, since you have become dull of hearing."*

L ord, wake us up

We have become slow of speech and slow of hearing

Sin has entangled us, its cords have held us fast

The world has entranced us with its pomp and show

Our flesh is gripped by the Law, now accusing, now even excusing us

The enemy wars against us with flaming darts that can only be extinguished by the shield of faith

Our feet had almost slipped, for we had seen the prosperity and the arrogance of the wicked

They say, *"How can God know? Is there knowledge in the Most High?"*

All in vain have we kept our hearts clean, and washed our hands in innocence

For all the day long we have been stricken, and rebuked every morning

If I had said, *"I will speak thus,"* I would have betrayed the generation of Your children

But when I went into the sanctuary of God – then I discerned their end

Truly You set them in slippery places and make them fall to ruin

How they are destroyed in a moment, swept utterly away by terrors!

I was brutish and ignorant, like a beast toward You

Nevertheless, I am continually with You; You hold my right hand

You guide me with Your counsel and will receive me into glory

Whom have I in Heaven but You? And there is nothing on earth that I desire besides you

My flesh and my heart may fail, but God is the strength of my heart and my portion forever. Amen

THURSDAY

Hebrews 5:12 *"For though by this time you ought to be teachers, you need someone to teach you again the basic principles of the oracles of God. You need milk, not solid food"*

L ord, to whom shall we go? You have the words of eternal life

You created all things by the power of Your Word

You looked, and saw that they were very good

You made man in Your image; male and female You made them

You put the breath of life in their nostrils

You put the sign of life on their heads, the names by which You called them

They walked with You in the cool of the day

But when they sinned against You, You confronted them

Your righteous Law condemned them

The doorway to the Garden was shut, and flaming swords barred the way

But Your Word prophesied a Redeemer who lives, and would stand again on the earth

One who would crush the serpent's head

Who would keep Your Law perfectly, loving Your creation as purely as He spoke truth

Who like a lamb was led to the slaughter, bearing the punishment that was for us

Who endured the cross, scorning its shame

Who saw the light of life and was satisfied.

He came to accomplish our salvation

To lose none of all You had given Him before the foundation of the world

To glorify You, the obedient Son in whom You were well pleased

Lord Jesus Christ, teach me to know You and to walk with You, and never let me desire any higher joy. Amen

FRIDAY

Hebrews 5:13 *"For everyone who lives on milk is unskilled in the word of righteousness, since he is a child."*

T ruly, Lord, You said to us, whoever does not receive the Kingdom like a child shall never enter it

We are arrested from the foolishness of playing in the mud by the simple joy of a promise

We drop our toys and look around for You, and when we hear Your voice we know it

We take off running, not knowing just where we are going, or what all it is that awaits us; only that You will be there

There are disappointments and dead ends, and our joy wanes, but still echoing in our ears is what You said to us:

"I will never leave you nor forsake you."

The world tries to draw our attention away with all its shiny surfaces, the false promise that what it offers will never fade away

The flesh would betray us, ever seeking its own, ever denying the blood that bought us, ever doubting the reality of the resurrected Savior

The devil's attacks grow more and more subtle, pitting us against Your Spirit with every new manipulation, breaking our hearts more deeply as we choose Your glory over our gain

The prophecies on which we based our keenest vision pass cruelly away

The tongues that spoke Your highest glories slow, and are stilled by the grinding press of time

The knowledge by which we bulwarked ourselves against the swift erosion of this present age totters and leans under the angry skies

But when the Perfect comes, the imperfect will pass away

We lift up the treasure hid in jars of clay, and even as we offer it up, we at last see Your face

The face of love, a divine love that can exist only in truth

Teach us to follow You where You lead us, and to leave childish ways behind forever. Amen

SATURDAY

Hebrews 5:14 *"But solid food is for the mature, for those who have their powers of discernment trained by constant practice to distinguish good from evil."*

L ord, You are the living bread that has come down from Heaven

You are the image of the invisible God, the firstborn of all Creation

You are the fullness of the glory of God in three persons, without beginning or end, with the glory You had with the Father and the Spirit before the world existed

Anyone who has seen You has seen the Father, and we have seen and testify that the Father has sent His Son to be the Savior of the world

That which was from the beginning, which we have heard, which we have seen with our eyes, which we looked upon and have touched with our hands, concerning the Word of life

That life was made manifest, and we have proclaimed it, the eternal life that was with the Father. This life was breathed into us at Creation

We were barred from it by the cherubim and the flaming sword, when we had sinned against You in the garden

It sustained Noah, the preacher of righteousness, when all life was destroyed on the face of the earth, save the few who were preserved by Your covenant

It called Abram out of the land of his fathers into a country Your Spirit would show him, and made of him a great nation, a blessing to the nations

It lifted David from the hills as he tended the sheep, and set him as king over Your people

It touched Isaiah's lips and atoned for his sin, and foretold through him a great light for the people who walked in darkness, a child born to them and a son given

It comforted Jeremiah as he looked over the lonely city, the princess become a widow

We have not obtained all this, nor are we made perfect, yet this one thing we do:

Forgetting what is behind and straining toward what is ahead, we press on toward the goal to win the prize for which God has called us heavenward in Christ Jesus

Lord Jesus, come quickly. Amen

MONDAY

Hebrews 6:1 *"Therefore let us leave the elementary doctrine of Christ and go on to maturity, not laying again a foundation of repentance from dead works and of faith toward God"*

L ord, there was a time when I thought my words and deeds did not matter so much

The faithfulness of Christ on my behalf was all that did

That I was chosen in Him before the foundation of the world

That His Spirit indwelled me to walk in His ways

That I was forgiven of all my sins, past, present, and future

That sin indeed had no power over me any more, but that Christ was on the throne of my heart

That His Kingdom was ordained to move forward, and that converts would be won to faith if their names were among the elect

And Lord, all this was not untrue. But I was wrong

What I say and what I do matters immensely, because truth matters immensely, and people matter immensely – to You

Your faithfulness to me calls me to a higher plane of duty than Law ever could

You chose me eternally to bring glory to Your name, not to vaunt my own

It is your same Spirit who works in me, to will and to work for His good pleasure

My sins cost You, my blessed and only Savior, more than I will ever know or comprehend

The Power that rules my heart is that same which hung the stars, which rejoiced with Wisdom in the dawn of time, which is building an everlasting city out of living stones

And Your Word solemnly warns me lest after preaching to others, I myself should be disqualified

For by grace I have been saved, through faith, and this not of my own doing, but the gift of God and not a result of works, lest any should boast

Give me a heart to follow hard after You today, Lord, that You might receive all the glory for it. Amen

TUESDAY

Hebrews 6:2 *"and of instruction about washings, the laying on of hands, the resurrection of the dead, and eternal judgment."*

L ord, we are created beings:

We live and move and have our being on this earth

All we know is what we see with our eyes

What commends itself to our senses as truth

What feels like the best way to stay out of trouble

What others tell us is common sense

What makes us feel alive

What will gain the approval of those whose opinion seems to matter most.

But all this is nothing but worldliness, and will surely pass away

For we are also New Creation:

We live and move and have our being in You

All we truly know is what by faith You show us

What Your Word says is truth

What will most please the Spirit who indwells us

What attains to the mind of Christ, and not to fleshly wisdom

What prompts us to take up our crosses as we follow Jesus

And what will finally hear You say, *"Well done, good and faithful servant."*

For if we live, we live to the Lord; and whether we live or die, we are the Lord's

Who shall separate us from the love of Christ? Shall tribulation, or distress, or persecution, or famine, or nakedness, or danger, or sword? As it is written, *"For your sake we are being killed all the day long; we are regarded as sheep to be slaughtered."*

No, in all these things we are more than conquerors through Him who loved us. Amen

WEDNESDAY

Hebrews 6:3 *"And this we will do if God permits."*

T here is a quiet power in faith, Lord

It is not the wisdom of this world

It did not come with signs to satisfy the Jews

Nor with wisdom to please the Greeks

It did not come with persuasive words

It did not call many who were wise according to worldly standards

Nor many who were powerful

Nor many who were of noble birth

But it came to make in our midst a people who were humble and lowly

Who would seek refuge in the Name of the Lord, those who are left in Israel

They shall do no injustice, and speak no lies

Nor shall be found in their mouth a deceitful tongue

For they shall graze and lie down

And none shall make them afraid.

Sing aloud, O Daughter of Zion!

Shout, O Israel

For the Lord your God is in your midst, a Mighty One who will save

He will rejoice over you with gladness

He will quiet you by His love

And by His wounds you shall be healed.

Amen

THURSDAY

Hebrews 6:4-5 *"For it is impossible, in the case of those who have once been enlightened, who have tasted the heavenly gift, and have shared in the Holy Spirit, and have tasted the goodness of the word of God and the powers of the age to come"*

L ord, help us to heed Your Word

To remember that Christian life is not a game

That Your Spirit indwells us for a purpose

And that purpose will not be thwarted, nor will any gainsay

We know that You chose us before the foundation of the world

That our names were written in the book of life

That Your eyes saw our unformed substance, before any of our days came to be

That You were enthroned forever, and remembered throughout all generations

That You arose and had pity on Zion

You favored her, for it was the appointed time

Your servants held her stones dear and had pity on her dust

You regarded the prayer of the destitute and did not despise their plea

And it was recorded for a generation yet to come:

That the Lord looked down from His holy height

From Heaven He looked at the earth, to hear the groans of the prisoners

To set free those who were doomed to die

That they may declare in Zion the name of the Lord, and in Jerusalem His praise

When peoples gather together, and kingdoms, to worship the Lord.

Let us worship the Lord in the splendor of holiness; tremble before Him, all the earth!

For You alone are holy. Amen

FRIDAY

Hebrews 6:6 *"and then have fallen away, to restore them again to repentance, since they are crucifying once again the Son of God to their own harm and holding him up in contempt."*

W ho is like You, Lord?

Who dwells in unapproachable light

Attended by the hosts of angels

Worthy not only of our worship and our holy fear, but of the glory of all things that are

Eternally proceeding from the Father

Image of the invisible God, firstborn of all Creation

By You all things were created, and You are before them, and in You they hold together

You are the Head of the body, the Church

You are the beginning, the firstborn from the dead, that in all things You might be preeminent

For in You all the fullness of God was pleased to dwell

And through You all things are to be reconciled to God, whether on earth or in Heaven, making peace by the blood of Your cross

Lord Jesus, our very bodies are the temple of Your Holy Spirit within us

We are not our own, for we were bought with a price

We, who once were alienated and hostile in mind, doing evil deeds! But you have now reconciled us in Your body of flesh by Your death

In order to present us holy and blameless and above reproach before You

Of Your great mercy, call us then to continue thankful in the faith, stable and steadfast, not shifting from the hope of the Gospel that we heard

And through us make known to all those who are lost how great are the riches of this mystery:

Christ in us, the hope of glory. Amen

SATURDAY

Hebrews 6:7 *"For land that has drunk the rain that often falls on it, and produces a crop useful to those for whose sake it is cultivated, receives a blessing from God."*

L ord, what do we have that we did not receive?

You are the Sun of righteousness; we are the living soil

You are the Sower; we are the seed

You are the Landlord; we are the vineyard

You are our Father; we are Your children

You are the Word; we are the hearers

You are the Bridegroom; we are the Bride

You are the First and the Last; we are the mist that passes

Teach us to know the measure of our days

To drink in the rain, which is like Your Word

Which goes out from Your mouth, and shall not return to You empty, but shall accomplish the purpose for which You sent it

To be content with Your blessing, and not to strive after earthly treasures

To lift up our eyes and see the fields white for harvest

To be about your work while it is daytime, before the night comes

To wonder at Your grace to us, and declare Your praises to a sin-sick world

To look in the mirror dimly, longing for the day when we will see You face to face

To eagerly desire the greater gifts, and offer our bodies as living sacrifices, to spend and be spent for more to know Your glories

To see Your Kingdom come and hold all things here lightly

Amen

MONDAY

Hebrews 6:8 *"But if it bears thorns and thistles, it is worthless and near to being cursed, and its end is to be burned."*

L ord, there is a reason You command us to forgive

There is a reason You exhort us to show mercy

There is a reason You remind us to remember the poor and the outcast

There is a reason You teach us to be humble, though that is not our nature

There is a reason Your Word tells us to remember those who are in prison as though we were in prison with them

Lord, is it not because You desire mercy, and not sacrifice?

Because You forgave a debt we could never repay

You first showed us mercy, when judgment was all we deserved

You brought us from death to life, when we were aliens and strangers to You

You destroyed our pride for the salvation of our souls

You delivered us from bondage and loosed our chains

You adopted us into Your family

You put the sign of Your Lordship on us, the names by which we are called before You

You gave Your Spirit to reveal Your truth to us

And to empower us to walk as Christ did

You pruned our leaves, and dug around our branches, and planted us in streams of water

And You waited patiently for fruit

Lord, help us to yield our fruit in season, and let not our leaf wither

That You might be praised in our lives

Amen

TUESDAY

Hebrews 6:9 *"Though we speak in this way, yet in your case, beloved, we feel sure of better things – things that belong to salvation."*

T ruth comes before salvation

   Hard things come before pleasant reward

Law comes before grace

Israel comes before Zion

The wilderness comes before the Promised Land

Exile comes before deliverance

Humility comes before exaltation

Rebuke comes before praise

Confrontation comes before restoration

Doubt comes before belief

Foolishness comes before wisdom

Youth comes before maturity

Failure comes before faithfulness

Despair comes before hope

Repentance comes before redemption

Dying to self comes before eternal life

Steadfastness comes before glory

At work in our lives are the things that belong to salvation, Lord

For we belong, body and soul, to You

Blessed be Your name

Amen

WEDNESDAY

Hebrews 6:10 *"For God is not so unjust as to overlook your work and the love that you have shown for his name in serving the saints, as you still do."*

L ord, we know that we are not saved by our works

But we also know that they matter

You do not plant trees to be unfruitful

Neither do you redeem sons and daughters to be without likeness to You

You are a hard master, reaping where You did not sow, and gathering where You scattered no seed

But neither do You break a bruised reed, or quench a smoldering wick

To the shrewd You show Yourself shrewd, but to the merciful You show Yourself merciful

So You do not overlook our work, and the love we show for Your name

But neither do You forget that we are but dust, that the wind blows over and we are gone, and our place remembers us no more

But You also remember

You remember the price at which we were bought

You remember Your own Son taking on flesh, for us

You remember His affliction and His wandering, the bitterness and the gall

The sorrow He took on Himself that we might know the oil of gladness

The darkness He entered into, that we might come at last into the glorious light

The perfect example He made for us, that even in our weakness we would have power to follow Him

The Spirit who leads us to look up from our little crosses and fix our eyes on Jesus

Lord, when You come into Your kingdom, remember me.

Amen

THURSDAY

Hebrews 6:11 *"And we desire each one of you to show the same earnestness to have the full assurance of hope till the end"*

W e know, Lord, that Your Word is truth; that You will be true, though every man be found a liar

What then is meant by "earnestness"?

If the meaning of Your Word is hidden from us, are there not two things we do?

We seek first Your face, imploring Your Holy Spirit:

> To show us the depths of Your wisdom, bringing out old treasures as well as new

> To show us the perfect Law, reviving the soul

> To show us that wisdom which is worth more than anything in this world, which we should buy and not sell

> To show us that fear of the Lord which is the beginning of knowledge

> To show us Jesus, and never let us lose sight of Him

And then we go to the rest of Scripture, that Your Word might interpret Your Word for us:

> O God, You are my God; earnestly I seek You; my soul thirsts for You; my flesh faints for You, as in a dry and thirsty land, where there is no water

> My soul yearns for You in the night; my spirit within me earnestly seeks You. For when Your judgments are in the earth, the inhabitants of the world learn righteousness

> But earnestly desire the greater gifts. And now I will show you a still more excellent way

> And He said to them, "The harvest is plentiful, but the laborers are few. Therefore pray earnestly to the Lord of the harvest to send out laborers into His harvest"

> Above all, keep loving one another earnestly, since love covers a multitude of sins

Can this mean anything but that we turn away from the world, the flesh, and the devil, to love and serve and know You more fully? Lord Jesus, work Your sovereign will in us today. Amen

FRIDAY

Hebrews 6:12 *"so that you may not be sluggish, but imitators of those who through faith and patience inherit the promises."*

L
ord, You are good; Your steadfast love endures forever

You see all things, and You know all things, and You have ordained it for Your glory

You have adopted us into Your family by no virtue of our own, but by Your grace only

Could anyone bear to know all the heartbreak and grief and loss that goes on around the world in one instant? Yet You do

And You do not change Your plan for our salvation

It goes forward still

The one perfect sacrifice that stands for all time, calling all to saving faith in Christ Jesus

Your Word, which goes out like the rain and snow which fall from heaven

And do not return there but water the earth, making it bring forth and sprout

So is Your Word which goes out from Your mouth

Which shall not return to You empty, but shall accomplish that which You purpose

And shall succeed in the thing for which You sent it

Your very Spirit, Who indwells us

The Helper You sent to walk with us, when You went to prepare a place for us

The Third Person of the Trinity, worthy of our adoration, who warms our hearts to form us closer to Your image

Your holy Father, into Whose presence we are drawn by your Word and Presence

Are there any promises more dear to us than this, that we should come and worship?

Quicken my heart today to find Your presence, and never to let You go again

Amen

SATURDAY

Hebrews 6:13 *"For when God made a promise to Abraham, since he had no one greater by whom to swear, he swore by himself"*

I think there is no greater enemy in all this life than doubt

I can do all things through Christ who strengthens me

But what when I will not accept His help?

What when the world catches at my heart, and I long again for the pleasures I for so long pursued?

When the flesh fails and the spirit weakens, and instead of praying and striving for Your Kingdom, I fall asleep in the garden?

When the devil reminds me of my sin, and the memory of it pierces me through, and I would forget the beauty of Your forgiveness and slide back into paralyzing regret?

It is in these times that I must remember the strong arm of the Lord

How You have delivered us out of the hand of our captors

Broken the chains and lifted up our heads

Led us out of the land of slavery, laden with the plunder of fear

Taught us Your name and given us the revelation of the great I Am

Gone before us in the towering pillars of smoke and flame

Given us Your holy Law with its picture of holiness

Drawn our hearts up into the breathtaking hope of life with You

Shown us a Promised Land, rich with milk and honey, its homes already built and fields already planted

Strengthened our hands to stand against the adversary; and swore by Yourself that we would not only be Your people

But that we would one day be Your holy Bride

Lord, I believe; help my unbelief. Amen

MONDAY

Hebrews 6:14-15 *"saying, 'Surely I will bless you and multiply you.' And thus Abraham, having patiently waited, obtained the promise."*

It is easy to attack in pride

It is easy to lash out at others in fear

It is easy to follow my own inclinations, instead of waiting for You to move

It is easy to speak my own words, instead of pondering Yours

It is easy to pursue my own desires instead of trusting Your heart

To provide my own solution instead of relying on Your miracle; to forge my own alliances, instead of placing my trust in Your armies

To surround myself with the assurance of this world, instead of waiting for Your promise

But that is not what Christ did.

He did not cry aloud

He did not lift up His voice, or make it heard in the street

A bruised reed He did not break

And a faintly burning wick He did not quench

He did not grow faint or be discouraged, till He had established justice in the earth

He is the Lord; that is His name, and His glory He gives to no other

Sing to the Lord a new song! And His praise from the end of the earth

He will lead the blind in ways they do not know

He will turn the darkness before them into light, the rough places into level ground

These are the things He does, and He will not forsake them

Hear, you deaf, and look, you blind, that you may see!

Lord, help us to wait for Your promise. Amen

TUESDAY

Hebrews 6:16 *"For people swear by something greater than themselves, and in all their disputes an oath is final for confirmation."*

P eople are unreliable, Lord

One minute we say one thing, another minute the next

Now we are staunchly conservative, now we veer liberal

Now we are faithful unto the point of death, now we hold our lives more dear than Your truth

Now we are a friend of God, now a friend of this worthless world

The best of us change like shifting shadows; yet You do not

You are the great I Am who spans all space and time, and You were before all things, and after they are no more, You still will be

You speak, and the mountains come forth, and the seas are in their place

The heavens proclaim Your glory, and Your grace is writ large in the skies

The winds and the waves obey Your will, and You bid them *Peace, be still*

From eternity Your sovereign power has been made known

You have raised up kingdoms, and brought them down

You have brought out a people from the land of darkness and called them by Your Name

You have kept covenant with them, and made them fruitful, bringing them out into a wide land

When they were unfaithful, You sent them into exile, yet You still preserved a Remnant

You sent Your son to be a living sacrifice and to make known Your great salvation

You made Your Spirit to indwell them and to teach them Your Word of life

Who can know Your greatness? Yet in Christ You were pleased to reveal Your glory

Teach us to know You, Lord, and in this power to boldly serve You today. Amen

WEDNESDAY

Hebrews 6:17 *"So when God desired to show more convincingly to the heirs of the promise the unchangeable character of his purpose, he guaranteed it with an oath"*

L ord, we are the heirs of Your promise

You promised Abram that he would have a son in his old age

That his descendants would inherit a great land, from the river of Egypt to the great river, the Euphrates

That he would become a mighty nation, as many as the stars in the sky

And that they would become a blessing to all the nations

This was Your promise, and when Abram heard it, in faith he believed You; and it was counted to him as righteousness

What is Your purpose for us, Lord? For we dwell in a land that is rich from coast to coast

We have money, and fine dwellings, and many things of great beauty, and can travel at will

We have books untold and have collected all knowledge from all of history

Yet for all our supposed wisdom, we have forgotten what Christ said, when He looked at the rich young ruler as he was walking away, and loved him:

"It is hard for the rich to enter the kingdom."

Behold, the wages of those we have defrauded are rising up against us, and the cries of the harvesters have reached the ears of the Lord of hosts

What is Your purpose, if not for us to buy from You gold refined by fire, so we may be rich?

And white garments, so we may clothe ourselves?

And salve to anoint our eyes, so we may see?

Lord, we are Your people, the sheep of Your pasture. We need to repent, and to see You

Though the end should come and all things collapse around us, we long for no other vision. Amen

THURSDAY

Hebrews 6:18 *"so that by two unchangeable things, in which it is impossible for God to lie, we who have fled for refuge might have strong encouragement to hold fast to the hope set before us."*

L ord, You know how bitter the struggle is here

The world punishes brutally any who would remain true to You

We have suffered the loss of all things so that we might seek first Your kingdom and Your righteousness

Surely we have this treasure in jars of clay, to show that the surpassing power belongs to God and not to us:

We are afflicted in every way, but not crushed

Perplexed, but not driven to despair

Persecuted, but not forsaken

Struck down, but not destroyed

Always carrying in the body the death of Jesus, so that the life of Jesus may also be manifested in our bodies.

We are the aroma of Christ to God among those who are being saved and among those who are perishing

To the one the fragrance from death to death, to the other a fragrance from life to life

Who is sufficient for these things?

And so, when we flee to Your throne of grace for refuge, we need a strong encouragement:

We need Your Word, which was in the beginning with God, and which was God,

And we need Your precious and very great promises, to become partakers of the divine nature.

In these show us Jesus, who for the joy set before Him endured the cross, despising its shame

And let us hold fast to Him, though all things give way around us

Amen

FRIDAY

Hebrews 6:19 *"We have this as a sure and steadfast anchor of the soul, a hope that enters into the inner place behind the curtain"*

The ground moves beneath me, Lord; nothing is solid

This world has changed, and changed again since I last looked at it

Now it seems to be wise, and now foolish

Now bold as a lion, and now fleeing at a sound

And when I condemn the world for its affectation – am I really any different?

My heart deeply loves security

It wants to know things will always stay the same

It desires wealth

It wants to heap up many good things, and never know want again

It would be warm and well-fed, even at the expense of others

And in much of its wandering, to get at all of these things:

My heart would even give up You.

That is desperate wickedness; who can know it?

For You are my only foundation

Your immutability my only promise

Your smile my only riches

Your Presence my one true good

Your calling my soul's only fulfillment

Your welcome my only eternal home.

Spirit of God, to whom alone I have fled for refuge, be my sure and steadfast Anchor today

Amen

SATURDAY

Hebrews 6:20 *"where Jesus has gone as a forerunner on our behalf, having become a high priest forever after the order of Melchizedek."*

L ord, You were high and lifted up before all worlds were made

You had all power and glory

You existed in perfect community, Father, Son, and Holy Spirit

In the Beginning was Your Word, and the Word was with God, and the Word was God

In You was life, and the life was the light of men

That light shines in the darkness, and the darkness has not overcome it

You had need of nothing, and You did not act out of need

You acted from pure desire for Your glory, that it should be over all things

And You acted from pure love for all You had created

You, the Mighty One, God the Lord, spoke and summoned the earth from the rising of its sun to its setting

Out of Zion, the perfection of beauty, God shines forth

You come, You do not keep silence; before You is a devouring fire, around You a mighty tempest

You call to the heavens above, and to the earth, that you may judge Your people:

"Gather to Me My faithful ones, who made a covenant with Me by sacrifice!"

The Lord has sworn, and will not change His mind:

"You are a priest forever after the order of Melchizedek!"

The heavens declare His righteousness, for God Himself is judge

For our Maker is our husband; the Lord of Hosts is His name, and our Redeemer is the Holy One of Israel

Blessed be Your name. Amen

MONDAY

Hebrews 7:1 *"For this Melchizedek, king of Salem, priest of the Most High God, met Abraham returning from the slaughter of the kings and blessed him"*

L ord, You are God Most High over all Creation

Not just over this physical world, and those who move in it

But over time and space as well

We see reflections of Your face in the most unlikely of places

Here after a little tribal war, where a few kings had decided to rebel against Chedorlaomer

And in the resulting rout, when the enemy looted Sodom and Gomorrah, they also took captive Lot, the nephew of Abram, and his household

You had charged him to walk through the length and breadth of that land, for You had promised to give it to Him

And the patriarch had built an altar there under the oaks of Mamre to worship You

So when his kinsman was taken by those who feared You not, he followed them

And when the rescue was done, Melchizedek came out to meet him, with bread and wine

Abram did not receive the glory; but Abram from Him received the blessing

First Melchizedek was king of righteousness; second He was king of peace

Without father or mother, without beginning or end of days He stood between God and men

Resembling the Son of God He continues a priest forever

And Abram gave to Him the sacred tenth

Who is king of righteousness and peace, but Christ alone?

And who the Alpha and the Omega, if not You?

We know Your voice, Lord. You are the image of the invisible God, the Firstborn of all Creation

And when Sin and Death are defeated, You will welcome us at Your table. Amen

TUESDAY

Hebrews 7:2 *"and to him Abraham apportioned a tenth part of everything. He is first, by translation of his name, king of righteousness, and then he is also king of Salem, that is, king of peace."*

We all have our idea of what is right, Lord

Justice we latch onto when we are young, and quickly protest whenever it eludes us

Truth we care about when it seems to be on our side

Faith is notable when we see it in another, but we quickly get impatient walking in it ourselves

Hope feels like foolishness, especially when the world seems to promise so much

Love is weakness

And the only thing weaker than love is forgiveness.

But these only show how very far short we fall of Your Heavenly wisdom

For You are first, by translation of Your Name, King of Righteousness:

And You administer a justice that even Your enemies will confess is sound

The question of who is right, must that not be the question of what is truth? And let Your Word be truth, though every man a liar

Faith breathes the very air of righteousness; I will serve Him, though He slay me

And You are second King of Peace:

Hope ceases to be wishing, and becomes a powerful chorus of outflowing testament from the souls of Your own

Love is the most powerful force this world has ever seen, demolishing strongholds and taking captive every thought to make it obedient to Christ

And forgiveness the most beautiful work love ever did. *"Father, forgive them"* is still our anthem

Teach us who you are, Lord Jesus, and then teach us to walk with You where You are going

Amen

WEDNESDAY

Hebrews 7:3 *"He is without father or mother or genealogy, having neither beginning of days nor end of life, but resembling the Son of God he continues a priest forever."*

L ord Jesus, we are bound by time, but You are not

We are but dust, but before Abraham was, You were the great I Am

Our sins were passed down to us by our fathers, but Your Father sent the Spirit down as a dove to declare that He was well pleased in You

Our fathers disciplined us for a short while as they thought best, but it was the will of the Lord to crush You, and put You to grief

Out of the abundance of our hearts our mouths speak, but You are the very Logos, the Word which was with God before the beginning, and which was God

We have sinned and fallen short of the glory of God, but You were put forward as a propitiation by Your blood, to be received by faith

Our days are as the grass that the wind passes over, but You are like a tree planted by streams of water that yields its fruit in its season, and its leaves do not wither

We think, and speak, and reason like a child; but as the heavens are higher than the earth, so Your ways are higher than our ways, and Your thoughts than our thoughts

The end of all things is always near for us, but to You belong glory and dominion forever and ever. Amen

For we were at one time disobedient to You, but now have received mercy. For You have consigned all to disobedience that You might have mercy on all

Oh, the depth of Your riches and wisdom and knowledge! How unsearchable are Your judgments, and how inscrutable Your ways!

For who has known the mind of the Lord, or who has been Your counselor?

Or who has given a gift to You that he might be repaid?

For from You and through You and to You are all things. To You be glory forever.

Amen.

THURSDAY

Hebrews 7:4 *"See how great this man was to whom Abraham
the patriarch gave a tenth of the spoils!"*

Worthy are You, our Lord and God, to receive glory and honor and power, for You created all things, and by Your will they existed and were created

We run around and try to heap up the things that make us happy; even the best of us do

Idols to stand over us and receive our misguided worship

Riches that give us a false sense of security

People's regard, unsteady and changing as it is

The appearance of happiness and ease

Control, that persistent illusion

Lying visions about this world that tell us we have finally arrived

For we say, We are rich, we have prospered, and we need nothing

Not realizing that we are wretched, pitiable, poor, blind, and naked.

In mercy and wisdom You counsel us to buy from You gold refined by fire, that we may be rich

White garments so that we may clothe ourselves and the shame of our nakedness may not be seen, and salve to anoint our eyes, so that we may see

Those whom You love, You reprove and discipline; therefore let us be zealous, and repent

And when we do, we find in Your presence fullness of joy

For Your yoke is easy, and Your burden is light

We have come to You, Jesus, we who labor and are heavy laden, and found rest for our souls

You have hidden these things from the wise and understanding, and have revealed them to little children

Yes, Father, for such was Your gracious will; and we offer up to You all we have. Amen

FRIDAY

Hebrews 7:5 *"And those descendants of Levi who receive the priestly office have a commandment in the law to take tithes from the people, that is, from their brothers, though these also are descended from Abraham."*

W e were made to worship, Lord

Something in us will always seek that which is higher, holier

You have commanded that we worship You, and for no other reason than that You are worthy

But the high places and the spreading trees have for so long drawn our hearts

The lofty grandeur of the stars that lifts our eyes

The glory of the sun as it makes its way across the heavens

The mountain ranges that rise so stately above us

The beauty we see in other human beings, fleeting as it is

The freedom and security that seem to come with wealth

All these catch at our hearts, and draw us to wonder and to bow down

And bow down we do, every one of us

And as if all these were not enough, we continually build new idols inside us

All in search of a replacement for You.

When it is so simple to follow the good You have told us:

To do justice

To love kindness,

And to walk humbly with our God.

This is our reasonable service

Shall we not gladly give a portion of what You have entrusted us with, to show where our life truly is?

For our life is caught up with Christ in glory forever. Amen

SATURDAY

Hebrews 7:6 *"But this man who does not have his descent from them received tithes from Abraham and blessed him who had the promises."*

L ord, You named Abraham the father of us all

Out of the darkness he was called, to go to a land You would show him

You made Your covenant with him, when the smoking fire pot and the flaming torch passed through the pieces

In a vision You spoke to him: *Fear not, Abram, I am your shield; your reward shall be very great*

And a dreadful and great darkness fell on him

And You made Your mighty promises to him:

That he would have a son in his old age

That his descendants would have a land of their own

That he would become a great nation, more in number than the stars in the sky

That his people would be a blessing to all the world

And Abraham believed You; and it was counted to him as righteousness

Not as work, or as wages, but by the very gift of faith

From him would come Moses, the giver of the Law

And the Law brings wrath; but blessed is the man against whom the Lord will not count his sin

And from him would come Levi, the first of the holy priesthood

But You rejected the tents of Joseph, and chose the tribe of Judah; Mount Zion, which You love

And from him would come a ruler who would shepherd Your people Israel

And they shall dwell secure, for He shall be great to the ends of the earth

And He shall be their peace, whose day Abraham rejoiced to see. Amen

MONDAY

Hebrews 7:7 *"It is beyond dispute that the inferior is blessed by the superior."*

G od, You are in Heaven, and we are on earth

Therefore let our words be few

You must increase, and I must decrease

Speak, Lord, for Your servants are listening

Amen

TUESDAY

Hebrews 7:8 *"In the one case tithes are received by mortal men, but in the other case, by one of whom it is testified that he lives."*

L ord, You call us to faithfulness with the things of this world

We are to steward them wisely

We are to give a portion of what You have entrusted us with

We are to give generously to those in need

And first to the household of faith

We are to care for our own, even as You do

Yet there is a higher faithfulness than the things of this world

For it is testified of Christ that He lives

It is testified of our Lord Jesus Christ that He is risen

Risen! and the gates of Hell did not prevail against Him

It is testified that He ascended on high, and led a host of captives in His train

It is testified that He gave gifts to men:

The apostles and the prophets

The evangelists, the shepherds and the teachers

To equip the saints for the work of ministry

To build up the body of Christ, until we all attain to the unity of the faith and of the knowledge of the Son of God

So that we may no longer be children, tossed to and fro by the winds and the waves

But may grow up in every way into Him who is the head, that is, into Christ

It is testified, O Lord, that You live; and that you are the life of the world

Glory to Your Name! Amen

WEDNESDAY

Hebrews 7:9-10 *"One might even say that Levi himself, who receives tithes, paid tithes through Abraham, for he was still in the loins of his ancestor when Melchizedek met him."*

Moreover it is required, Lord, of stewards that they be found faithful

A priest must follow Your instructions without deviating from them

They must lead the people in worship; they must receive confessions of sin

They must offer atonement for it, spilling the lifeblood of the perfect sacrifice as a substitute

They must present the grain and drink offerings as You prescribed

They may not offer strange fire, but must keep the censers burning, night and day

The smoke of the incense must go up before You without fail

But who among the sons of Levi has been found worthy of this?

Behold, You have sent Your messenger, and he has prepared the way before You

And the Lord whom we seek will suddenly come to His temple

But who can endure the day of His coming, and who can stand when He appeareth?

For He is like a refiner's fire.

He will purify the sons of Levi, and refine them like gold and silver

"Return to me," You have said, yet we cry, every one of us: "How shall we return to You?"

And the Lord heard those who feared Him, and a book of remembrance was written

"They shall be Mine," says the Lord, "in the day when I make up My treasured possession"

Then the offering of Judah and Jerusalem will be pleasing to the Lord, as in the days of old

Who is to condemn? Christ Jesus is the one who died — more than that, who was raised — who is at the right hand of God, who indeed is interceding for us. Amen

THURSDAY

Hebrews 7:11 *"Now if perfection had been attainable through the Levitical priesthood (for under it people received the law), what further need would there have been for another priest to arise after the order of Melchizedek, rather than one named after the order of Aaron?"*

Return, faithless Israel

We have sinned against Heaven and against our father, and are no longer worthy to be called His children

On every high hill and under every spreading tree we have played the whore

With stone and tree we have been unfaithful to our husband, our Maker, our God

We have bowed down to lifeless idols

We have committed two great evils:

We have forsaken You, the fountain of living waters

And we have hewn for ourselves broken cisterns that can hold no water

Be appalled, O heavens, at this

Be shocked and utterly desolate

Israel was faithless and forsook her first love

But Judah was treacherous, not returning with her whole heart, but in pretense

Those of us who have not sinned openly have denied You in our hearts

And we stand before You without hope, with no hope save in the pardoning power of the Cross

We would hear Your voice:

Return, faithless children, declares the Lord

For I am your Master

I will take you, one from a city and two from a family

And I will bring you to Zion.

Amen

FRIDAY

Hebrews 7:12 *"For when there is a change in the priesthood, there is necessarily a change in the law as well."*

L ord, the priesthood has failed

Aaron's shoulders were not able to bear the yoke of the salvation of Your people

And his sons were like him, frail and faithless

Only a few were steadfast

The sons of Levi obeyed Moses' command and slew their brethren, and stayed the anger of the Lord for the idolatry of their people

Phinehas son of Eleazar saw the brazen immorality of the Israelite man with the Midianite woman and slew them both in their chamber, and stopped the plague

Zadok the priest defied Adonijah and his deceitful bid for the throne, and anointed Solomon king over Israel, and caused the trumpet to be blown

Ahimelech, though he trembled, gave David the showbread, as a picture that Someone greater than the temple was coming

Joshua was clothed in pure vestments, and had a clean turban put on his head; and then a crown. For at last there would be a priest on the throne

But the Son of Man was lifted up as the snake in the wilderness, for our salvation

The blood of Jesus spoke a better word than the blood of Abel

Turning aside the cries of the people to crown him king, Christ accepted a crown of thorns

He offered His body and blood for the eternal life of all who partake in His sacrifice

And clothed in the garments of salvation, He welcomes all who will open the door to Him into the marriage-feast of the Lamb

The truth of the Law will stand until all things are brought into His Kingdom

But Jesus has fulfilled its righteous demands forever, and we no longer stand condemned by it

Glory to His Name! Amen

SATURDAY

Hebrews 7:13 *"For the one of whom these things are spoken belonged to another tribe, from which no one has ever served at the altar."*

L ord, You promised David: "You will never fail to have a man to sit before Me on the throne of Israel"

But he was a man of blood, and could not build the Temple for Your Name

He broke Your holy Law, taking another man's wife and shedding innocent blood

For he was only flesh and blood

As a flower of the field he flourished, and the wind passed over him, and he was gone

And his place knew him no more

But You knew him.

For David was a man after Your own heart

He loved Your holy Law

He longed for Your refining presence

He hated sin, and all the ruin it brings to those we love

He saw that this world was passing away, and the appointed time had grown very short

He laid the foundation that Jesus Christ would build on, the Temple and the Nation, which would become the Church, the Bride of Christ

No one from his tribe had ever served at the altar, just as none from Levi had ever sat on the throne

But one was coming who would be worthy

Who would be Prophet, Priest, and King

A bruised reed He would not break, and a smoldering wick He would not snuff out

Behold Your Servant, whom You uphold; Your Chosen, in whom Your soul delights

Behold the Lamb of God, who taketh away the sin of the world. Amen

MONDAY

Hebrews 7:14 *"For it is evident that our Lord was descended from Judah, and in connection with that tribe Moses said nothing about priests."*

L ord, You have seen our glory, and our weakness

It is but a faint reflection of what You created us for

Judah was a lion's cub; his father's sons bowed down before him

He was more noble than they

When his brothers would have slain Joseph, he pleaded for his life, and said, "What profit is it if we kill our brother and conceal his blood?"

His sin discovered him, when Tamar his daughter-in-law showed herself more righteous than he was, under sentence of death for the unfaithfulness both of them had

He did not give her the rights of a widow, and he condemned her for her immorality

Yet when his own immorality was discovered, he repented

Thus You were pleased to show Jacob that the scepter would not depart from Judah, nor the ruler's staff from between his feet

From such sinful stock You were pleased to bring Your glory

The Lion of Judah, the Root of David, Who has conquered, that He might open the scroll and its seven seals

A king who would reign in righteousness, and a prince to rule in justice

Whose blood would speak a better word than the blood of Abel

Who would reconcile us to God while we were enemies, by His death on the Cross

Who pronounced the woman caught in adultery free from condemnation, and called her to go and sin no more

Who was pierced for our transgressions, and was crushed for our iniquities

Who is seated at the right hand of Power, and coming on the clouds of Heaven

The Lord Christ, who must reign as King and Priest for ever and ever. Amen

TUESDAY

Hebrews 7:15-16 *"This becomes even more evident when another priest arises in the likeness of Melchizedek, who has become a priest, not on the basis of a legal requirement concerning bodily descent, but by the power of an indestructible life."*

L ord, You have made Your covenant with us

You first made it with Adam, the covenant of works that required simple obedience

You made it with Noah, when You destroyed all life because the only inclination of our hearts was only evil all the time

You set Your bow in the clouds, that all life should never be destroyed by water again, until the end of all things and the Judgment

Out of a land of darkness You called Abraham, and promised to make his descendants more in number than the stars in the sky. You promised him a son, the land, a nation, and a blessing

But in this covenant, You were the one who passed through the fire-pots, not him

You gave Your holy Law through Moses, and charged the people of Israel not to swerve from it, so they might live long in the land of their fathers

You set up the sacrifices and the Levitical priesthood, that Your people should never forget that death was the cost of sin

From the sheepfolds You took Your servant David, and gave him the kingship over Your people, to replace the unbelief and pride of Saul

A song You put in his heart, to mourn over his sin and to look for the coming of One who would sit on his throne forever, in justice and in mercy

On Your last night among Your disciples on earth, You took bread and wine, and offered up Your body and blood a living sacrifice for our sins. And a new covenant began, that would never fail

One that would not need the blood of bulls and goats, but that would call us to partake in the death and resurrection of the sinless, perfect Lamb of God

One that would send us out as priests and prophets together of a better covenant, proclaiming the day of the favor of the Lord, by the power of an indestructible life

Lord Jesus, You are our great and only Hope. Amen

WEDNESDAY

Hebrews 7:17 *"For it is witnessed of him, 'You are a priest forever, after the order of Melchizedek.'"*

L ord, You have not given us a faith that is without surety

The Spirit hovered over the waters when the earth was formless and void and saw You form life

When the only inclination of people's hearts was only evil all the time, and You purposed to destroy all life under the heavens, the Spirit was there

When You called Your servant Abraham out of darkness and unbelief to go to a land that You would show him, the Spirit was there

When You showed Moses the depths of his sin and led him into the wilderness for forty years to prepare him to lead Your people, Your Spirit was there

When You gave Your holy Law, knowing that Your chosen ones could not uphold it but pointing to one holy Lamb who one day would, Your Spirit was there

When You set Your servant David up to rule justly and truly before You and he prepared for the building of Your holy Temple, Your Spirit was there

When Your people sinned against you and went out to the nations to serve other gods, and You sent the prophets to open Your heart of restoration to them, Your Spirit was there

When the years grew long and the Messiah had not come, and the godly among Israel searched the Scriptures to inquire of His sufferings and glories, Your Spirit was there

When a voice appeared in the wilderness, crying, *"Prepare the way of the Lord!"* and the days of Your flesh drew near, Your Spirit was there

When You came to seek and to save the lost sheep of Israel, not breaking the bruised reed or quenching the faintly burning wick, and You brought forth faithful justice, Your Spirit was there

When You presented Your body as a living sacrifice for the sins of the whole world, holy and acceptable to God as Your act of spiritual worship, Your Spirit was there

When the God of peace brought again from the dead the great Shepherd of the sheep, by the blood of the eternal covenant, to work that which was pleasing in His sight, the Spirit was there

For it is witnessed of You, by the Spirit of truth, that You are our great High Priest forever. Amen

THURSDAY

Hebrews 7:18-19 *"For on the one hand, a former commandment is set aside because of its weakness and uselessness (for the law made nothing perfect); but on the other hand, a better hope is introduced, through which we draw near to God."*

L ord Jesus, You existed before all time and place. And Wisdom was with You, the first of Your acts of old

Before the mountains were shaped, before the hills, she was brought forth

When You established the Heavens, she was there

When You drew a circle on the face of the deep, and made firm the skies above

When You assigned to the sea its limit, so that the waters might not transgress Your command

When as a master workman You marked out the foundations of the earth, Wisdom was there

Daily Your delight, rejoicing before You always, rejoicing in Your inhabited world and delighting in the children of man

And now, O sons, listen to her: Blessed are those who keep her ways

Hear instruction and be wise, and do not neglect it

Blessed is the one who listens to her, watching at her gates, waiting by her doors

For whoever finds Wisdom finds life and obtains favor from the Lord

But all who hate her love death.

In Wisdom You gave Your holy Law, well knowing that it could not be life for us

Yet as a faithful schoolmaster it chastened us under the rod, and told eternal truth

Faithful as a servant in Your house it led us out to behold the coming of Your Son

The One who would finally live a righteous life, and show us perfection and power

And in Wisdom You set the Law aside, perfectly and powerfully fulfilled, for a better hope

One that would draw us near to You. Our abiding and only hope, the true Gospel of our Lord Jesus Christ. Amen

FRIDAY

Hebrews 7:20 *"And it was not without an oath. For those who formerly became priests were made such without an oath"*

L ord, when the foundations are destroyed, what can the righteous do?

Behold, the Lord's hand is not shortened, that it cannot save

Or Your ear dull, that You cannot hear

But our iniquities have made a separation between us and our God

And our sins have hidden Your face from us that You do not hear

For our hands are defiled with blood and our fingers with iniquity

Our works are works of iniquity, and deeds of violence are in our hands

Our feet run to evil and are swift to shed innocent blood

The way of peace we do not know, and there is no justice in our paths

Therefore justice is far from us and righteousness does not overtake us

We hope for light, and behold, darkness

For brightness, but we walk in gloom

Justice is turned back and righteousness stands far away

For truth has stumbled in the public squares and uprightness cannot enter

Truth is lacking, and he who departs from evil makes himself a prey

The Lord saw it, and it displeased You that there was no justice

You saw that there was no man, and Your own arm brought salvation, and Your righteousness upheld You

You put on righteousness as a breastplate, and a helmet of salvation on Your head

According to their deeds, so shall You repay wrath to Your adversaries

So shall they fear Your name. For You are righteous, and You love righteous deeds; and the upright shall behold Your face. Amen

SATURDAY

Hebrews 7:21 *"But this one was made a priest with an oath by the one who said to him: 'The Lord has sworn and will not change his mind, "You are a priest forever."'"*

We need a mediator, Lord

We need one who stands between us and Your consuming holiness

One who remembers our frame, and knows that we are dust

Who forgives all our iniquity and heals all our diseases

Who redeems our life from the pit

Who crowns us with steadfast love and mercy

Who satisfies us with good, so that our youth is renewed like the eagle's

The Lord, the Lord, a God merciful and gracious, slow to anger and abounding in steadfast love and faithfulness

Maintaining love to thousands, and forgiving wickedness, rebellion, and sin

He does not leave the guilty unpunished, but punishes the children and their children for the sin of the parents to the third and fourth generation

Yet Jesus was pierced for our transgressions

And He was crushed for our iniquities

Upon Him was the chastisement that brought us peace, and with His wounds we are healed.

For God has consigned all to disobedience, that He may have mercy on all

Oh, the depth of the riches and wisdom and knowledge of God! How unsearchable are His judgments, and how inscrutable His ways!

For who has known the mind of the Lord? Or who has been His counselor

But the steadfast love of the Lord is from everlasting to everlasting on those who fear Him

For from Him and through Him and to Him are all things. To Him be glory forever

Amen

MONDAY

Hebrews 7:22 *"This makes Jesus the guarantor of a better covenant."*

E verything in this world falls apart, Lord

Ideas fade and are forgotten

Buildings crumble away

Friends move away from us

Family disappears and bloodlines grow thin

Hopes dim

Dreams are gathered up into the dark hallways of time, never to come to life

The path You gave us to walk is narrow, and the Way is hard that leads to life

And few are those who walk on it

Your Spirit compels us to choose between the truth and those we love

It is only the knowledge that all truth is Yours, that You are behind that dark veil, that leaves us any hope at all

If Your glory were not the end of this road, we would be of all men most to be pitied

And if our good were not guaranteed in it, our sin would condemn us before we took the very first step

We have all turned aside; together we have become corrupt; there is none who does good, not even one

Have they no knowledge, all the evildoers, who eat up Your people as they eat bread, and do not call upon the Lord?

Oh, that salvation for Israel would come out of Zion!

When the Lord restores the fortunes of His people, let Jacob rejoice, let Israel be glad

Though all men turn away from us, we will hope in the finished work of Jesus Christ

Amen

TUESDAY

Hebrews 7:23-24 *"The former priests were many in number, because they were prevented by death from continuing in office, but he holds his priesthood permanently, because he continues forever."*

T here have been many physicians, Lord, but little healing

Many kings but not much peace

Many friends but no true kinship

Many counselors, but truth is lacking

Many priests but sin still lingers

Shall we seek You forever in vain? Yet for all who would confirm me, I have not sought You with my whole heart

I have turned aside after those who would heal my wounds lightly

"Peace, peace," they say, but there is no peace

Falsely have I dealt with the Lover of my soul

I came forth from my mother's womb speaking lies

And before the altar I have remembered the foolishness of my youth, the bitterness and the gall

Yet this I call to mind, and therefore I have hope:

The steadfast love of the Lord never ceases; His mercies never come to an end

Your mercies are new every morning; great is Your faithfulness

"The Lord is my portion," says my soul, *"therefore I will hope in Him"*

The Lord is good to those who wait for Him, to the soul who seeks Him

It is good that I should wait quietly for Your salvation

For the Lord will not cast off forever

But though You cause grief, You will have compassion

Amen

WEDNESDAY

Hebrews 7:25 *"Consequently, he is able to save to the uttermost those who draw near to God through him, since he always lives to make intercession for them."*

L ord, we sometimes think we are rich, having prospered and needing nothing

But indeed we are wretched, pitiable, poor, blind, and naked

We ought to always come seeking You in worship for Your holiness

Lifting up Your worthiness for all the world to see

Praising Your name before all, that all might come to faith in You

But we have returned to You sick, sad, and weary

Wounded from the fray, and not just from enemy swords

Full of longing for Your promises to be fulfilled, looking far out into the dark horizon for Your coming

Tired of bitter war and sorrowing from all the loss that continually rises up around us

Weary of the world, our selves, and sin

Despairing of any hope in man, that splintered reed on which we once leaned

Not holding over ourselves the name of "Reformed," or "Evangelical," or "Orthodox"

But clinging for all dear life to the name of "Christian"

And hoping in Your Word, which ever proves true; You are a shield to those who take refuge in You

Lord Jesus, You always live to make intercession for us

You know our frame, and remember that we are dust. And still You stand at the door and knock

Enter our hearts, and save to the uttermost those who in true faith have drawn near to You

And let us never lose sight of You again, till Your Kingdom come

Yes, Lord, for this is Your good pleasure. Amen

THURSDAY

Hebrews 7:26 *"For it was indeed fitting that we should have such a high priest, holy, innocent, unstained, separated from sinners, and exalted above the heavens."*

I told the truth, Lord, and he did not

She did what was wrong and would not acknowledge me

They would not listen to me or do what I told them

We are all convinced of our rightness, secure against our failure, wandering in our blindness and pride

We have lost sight of the splendor of Your holiness

We have forgotten the praise due to You in Zion, the vows we were to have performed

Once we were satisfied with the goodness of Your house, the holiness of Your temple

I was glad when they said to me, "Let us go to the house of the Lord!" Our feet were standing within your gates, O Jerusalem

Can a mother forget her nursing child? Even these may forget, yet You will not forget us

Behold, You have engraved us on the palms of Your hands

Our destroyers and those who laid us waste go out from us

Let us lift up our eyes and see; they all gather, they come to us

"As I live," declares the Lord, *"you shall put them all on as an ornament; you shall bind them on as a bride does"*

The children of our bereavement will then find the land too narrow for their inhabitants

Kings shall be their fathers, and queens their nursing mothers

The Lord will contend with those who contend with us, and save our children

Then we will know that He is the Lord

And those who wait for Him shall not be put to shame. Amen

FRIDAY

Hebrews 7:27 *"He has no need, like those high priests, to offer sacrifices daily, first for his own sins and then for those of the people, since he did this once for all when he offered up himself."*

L ord, who is a God like You, pardoning iniquity and passing over transgression for the remnant of Your inheritance?

You do not retain Your anger forever, but delight in steadfast love

Our sins are ever before us, Lord

They separate us from Your holiness

Listen to our cry, for we are brought very low

We need Your salvation more than the air we breathe or the food we eat

Yet it is not for our sake that You have come in the flesh

It was not for us that You have kept the holy Law, not swerving from its righteous requirements

Not for us that You resisted the temptations of the evil one

Not for us that You set Your face to Jerusalem like a flint, and were not ashamed to do the will of the Father who is in Heaven

Not for us that You gave the bread to Your friend who would betray You, knowing that his kiss would be that of death for You

Not for us that You offered up Your prayers and supplications, with loud cries and tears, to Him who was able to save You from death, and were heard because of Your reverence

Not for us that You said, "Father, into Your hands I commit my spirit" and breathed Your last

No, it was for Him to whom You prayed, "Father, glorify Your name"

And the Lord God Almighty has glorified His holy Name, and will glorify it again

And You, Lord Jesus, when You were lifted up from the earth, drew all men to Yourself

Help us while we have the light to believe in the light, that we may become sons of light. Amen

SATURDAY

Hebrews 7:28 *"For the law appoints men in their weakness as high priests, but the word of the oath, which came later than the law, appoints a Son who has been made perfect forever."*

Have mercy upon us, O Lord

Have mercy upon us, for we have had more than enough of contempt

Our soul has had more than enough of the scorn of those who are at ease, of the contempt of the proud

The best of us are weak and powerless to save; our justice is turned back, and our righteousness stands far away

The worst of us are blind guides, leading many away from the eternal truth to delight in the promise of this passing world

Where then is the worship that should be Yours? Where is the fear and the awe of Your Presence?

Where the praise due Your mighty deeds?

Where are the people who know the festal shout, who walk, O Lord, in the light of Your face?

Who exult in Your Name all the day, and in Your righteousness are exalted?

For You are the glory of our strength; by your favor our horn is exalted

You have found David, Your servant, and with Your holy oil You have anointed Him

The enemy shall not outwit Him and the wicked shall not humble Him

You will establish His offspring forever, and His throne as the days of the heavens

He shall cry to You, "You are My Father, My God, and the Rock of My Salvation"

Once for all You have sworn by Your holiness: His offspring shall endure forever, His throne as long as the sun before You

Like the moon it shall be established forever, a faithful witness in the skies. Selah

Blessed be the Lord forever!

Amen and Amen.

MONDAY

Hebrews 8:1 *"Now the point in what we are saying is this: we have such a high priest, one who is seated at the right hand of the throne of the Majesty in heaven"*

T he days swirl around us, Lord

The years ebb and flow, and their waves wash over us

When the Son of Man comes, will He find faith on the earth?

There are moments when we have hints of the glory that is to come

The praise of angels gathered around Your throne

The stern finality of the Day of Your justice as all hearts are opened before You

The prayers of the saints rising like incense from the altar

The joy of the redeemed who stand before You, who will never know sin or sorrow again

The last defeat of evil and of everything that resists Your eternal rule

The righteous pronouncement made over us, in that great Judgment, that the perfect obedience of Another was imputed to us once and for all

And the gathering up into Your Presence of all those who have longed for Your coming

And we know that You surely will find faith on the earth

For this was the will of Him who sent You, that You should lose none of those He has given You

But that they should be raised up at the Last Day

Who shall separate us from the love of Christ? Shall tribulation, or distress, or persecution, or famine, or nakedness, or danger, or sword?

As it is written, *"For your sake we are being killed all the day long; we are regarded as sheep to be slaughtered."*

No, in all these things we are more than conquerors through Him who loved us

Lord Jesus, You are our great High Priest

Amen

TUESDAY

Hebrews 8:2 *"a minister in the holy places, in the true tent that the Lord set up, not man."*

Our strength fails, Lord

The walls we build crumble

The words we speak fall to the ground

Our wisdom is not sufficient for the days

Our sight is not keen enough to pierce the smoke and cloud that surrounds us

Our sword is not strong enough to defend those we love

Our days are like an evening shadow

We wither away like grass.

But You, O Lord, are enthroned forever

You are remembered throughout all generations

You will arise and have pity on Zion; it is the time to favor her; the appointed time has come

For Your servants hold her stones dear, and have pity on her dust

Nations will fear the name of the Lord, and all the kings of the earth will fear Your glory

For the Lord builds up Zion; He appears in His glory

Let this be recorded for a generation to come, so that a people yet to be created may praise the Lord

That He looked down from His holy height to hear the groans of the prisoners, to set free those who were doomed to die

That they may declare in Zion the name of the Lord, and in Jerusalem His praise

Of old You laid the foundations of the earth, and the heavens are the work of Your hands

They will perish, Lord, but You will remain. Amen

WEDNESDAY

Hebrews 8:3 *"For every high priest is appointed to offer gifts and sacrifices; thus it is necessary for this priest also to have something to offer."*

L ord, You are high and lifted up

Glory in the highest Heaven is Yours, and also our worship

You alone have immortality, and dwell in unapproachable light, whom no one has ever seen or can see

Can a man stand before You? Yet You have sent Moses Your servant, and Aaron, whom You had chosen

They performed Your signs and miracles in the land of Ham

You brought Your people out with joy and Your chosen ones with singing

You gave them the lands of the nations, and they took possession of the people's toil

That they might keep Your statutes and observe Your laws. Praise the Lord

But they forgot You

Your people had a stubborn and rebellious heart; they turned aside and went away

They did not say in their hearts, *"Let us fear the Lord our God, who gives the rain in its season"*

Their iniquities turned them away, and their sins kept good from among them

Like a cage full of birds, their houses were full of deceit; therefore they have become great and rich, and have grown fat and sleek

An appalling and horrible thing has happened in the land: The prophets prophesy falsely, and the priests rule at their direction

My people love to have it so, but what will they do when the end comes?

For the End of all things is near. Lord Jesus, You stand to offer something new in the priesthood:

You offer us Your very Self.

Amen

THURSDAY

Hebrews 8:4 *"Now if he were on earth, he would not be a priest at all, since there are priests who offer gifts according to the law."*

I will seek You, Lord, while You may be found

I will call upon You while You are near

Let the wicked forsake his way, and the unrighteous man his thoughts

Let us return to the Lord, for He may have compassion on us

And to our God, for He will abundantly pardon

For My thoughts are not your thoughts

Neither are your ways My ways, declares the Lord

For as the heavens are higher than the earth, so are My ways higher than your ways

And My thoughts than your thoughts

For as the rain and snow come down from Heaven

And do not return there but water the earth, making it bring forth and sprout

So shall Your Word be that goes out from Your mouth

It shall not return to You empty, but it shall accomplish that which You purpose

And we shall go out in joy and be led forth in peace

The mountains and hills before us shall break forth into singing

Shout aloud, O daughter of Jerusalem! Behold, your King is coming to you

Righteous and having salvation is He; gentle, and mounted on a donkey

Serve the Lord with fear, and rejoice with trembling

Kiss the Son, lest He be angry and you perish in the way. For His wrath is quickly kindled

Blessed are all who take refuge in Him

Amen

FRIDAY

Hebrews 8:5 "They serve a copy and shadow of the heavenly things. For when Moses was about to erect the tent, he was instructed by God, saying, 'See that you make everything according to the pattern that was shown you on the mountain.'"

L ord Jesus, You are all and in all

By You all things were created, in heaven and on earth, visible and invisible

Whether thrones or dominions or rulers or authorities – all things were created through You and for You

You are before all things, and in You all things hold together

And You are the Head of the body, the Church

Who has known the mind of the Lord, that he should instruct You? But we have the mind of Christ

Teach us then by Your Spirit

Teach us to order our lives around Your glory

To come and worship before You in constant praise and prayer

To proclaim Your goodness to a world staggering beneath the load of evil

To confess our own sin and turn away from it, laying hold of Your righteousness

Teach us to work out our salvation with fear and trembling

To be blameless and innocent, children of God without blemish in a crooked and twisted generation

To hold fast to the Word of life, and know that by Your great mercy we shall not labor in vain

And after all is done, to fix our eyes on You, the Author and Finisher of our faith

Whom have I in Heaven but You, Lord? And there is nothing on earth I desire besides You

And in Your temple all cry *"Glory!"*

Amen

SATURDAY

Hebrews 8:6 *"But as it is, Christ has obtained a ministry that is as much more excellent than the old as the covenant he mediates is better, since it is enacted on better promises."*

R emember Your Word to Your servant, Lord, in which You have made me hope

This is my comfort in my affliction, that Your promise gives me life

At midnight I rise to praise You, because of Your righteous rules

You have dealt well with Your servant, O Lord, according to Your Word

It was good for me that I was afflicted, that I might learn Your statutes

I know, O Lord, that Your rules are righteous, and that in faithfulness You have afflicted me

May my heart be blameless in Your statutes, that I might not be put to shame!

My soul longs for Your salvation; I hope in Your Word

My eyes long for Your promise. I ask, "When will You comfort me?"

For I am like a wineskin in the smoke, yet I have not forgotten Your statutes

Forever, O Lord, Your Word is firmly fixed in the heavens

I am Yours. Save me, for I have sought Your precepts

Oh, how I love Your Law! It is my meditation all the day

Your Word is a lamp to my feet and a light to my path

You are my hiding place and my shield; I hope in Your Word

My eyes are awake before the watches of the night, that I may meditate on Your promise

Great peace have those who love Your Law, and nothing can make them stumble

Seven times a day I praise You for Your righteous rules

I long for Your salvation, O Lord, and Your Law is my delight

I have gone astray like a lost sheep; seek Your servant, for I do not forget Your commandments. Amen

MONDAY

Hebrews 8:7 *"For if that first covenant had been faultless, there would have been no occasion to look for a second."*

Y ou are the Lord, and there is no other. Besides You there is no God

You have made covenants with Your people

Out of the land of slavery You have brought us

In distress we called, and You delivered us

You answered us at the secret place of thunder

You tested us at the waters of Meribah

Selah

Hear, O My people, while I admonish you!

O Israel, if you would but listen to me

There shall be no strange god among you

You shall not bow down to a foreign god

I am the Lord your God, who brought you up out of the land of Egypt

Open your mouth wide, and I will fill it.

But my people did not listen to My voice; Israel would not submit to me

So I gave them over to their stubborn hearts, to follow their own counsels

Oh, that My people would listen to me, that Israel would walk in My ways!

I would soon subdue their enemies and turn My hand against their foes

And I would feed you with the finest of wheat

With honey from the rock I would satisfy you.

Lord Jesus, this cup is the new Covenant in Your blood. May we do this as often as we drink of it

Amen

TUESDAY

Hebrews 8:8 *"For he finds fault with them when he says: 'Behold, the days are coming, declares the Lord, when I will establish a new covenant with the house of Israel and with the house of Judah'"*

Y ou are the Lord; that is Your name

Your glory You give to no other, nor Your praise to carved idols

Behold, the former things have come to pass

And new things You now declare

Before they spring forth, You tell us of them

Thus says God, the Lord

Who created the heavens and stretched them out

Who spread out the earth and what comes from it

Who gives breath to the people on it

And spirit to those who walk in it

For all who are led by the Spirit of God are sons of God

For we did not receive the spirit of slavery to fall back into fear

But we have received the Spirit of adoption as sons, by whom we cry, *"Abba, Father!"*

The Spirit Himself bears witness with our spirit that we are children of God

And if children, then heirs – heirs of God and fellow heirs with Christ

Provided we suffer with Him, in order that we may also be glorified with Him

Where then is boasting? It is excluded. By the law of works? Nay, but by the law of faith

Righteousness is counted to us who believe in Him who raised from the dead Jesus our Lord

Who was delivered up for our trespasses and raised for our justification

Blessed be His Name. Amen

WEDNESDAY

Hebrews 8:9 *"Not like the covenant that I made with their fathers on the day when I took them by the hand to bring them out of the land of Egypt. For they did not continue in my covenant, and so I showed no concern for them, declares the Lord."*

L ord, we are born to trouble, as surely as the sparks fly upward

We have forgotten Your Law, and cast your words behind us

Your Spirit we have quenched, Who would have illuminated us with Your will

We have trembled at the smoke and fire on the mountain, but we have not listened to Your Word

You have given us water from the rock, yet we have quarreled against You

You fed us the bread of the angels, yet we tested You in the desert

Has a nation ever changed its gods? Though they are no gods

But Your people have changed their glory for that which does not profit

Be appalled, O heavens, at this. Be shocked and utterly desolate, declares the Lord

For My people have committed two evils:

They have forsaken Me, the fountain of living waters

And they have hewed out cisterns for themselves, broken cisterns that can hold no water

There is nothing left but punishment for us; nothing remains but ruin

Still You were not willing that we should perish, but You were patient with us, that all should reach repentance

Sacrifices and offerings You have not desired, but a body You have prepared for Him

Who can speak of His descendants? For Jesus Christ was cut off from the land of the living

But He will see His offspring and prolong His days

By His knowledge shall the Righteous One, Your servant, make many to be accounted righteous. Amen

THURSDAY

Hebrews 8:10 *"For this is the covenant that I will make with the house of Israel after those days, declares the Lord: I will put my laws into their minds, and write them on their hearts, and I will be their God, and they shall be my people."*

How long, O Lord

How long did Your people walk in darkness

How long did the thick smoke of incense rise in Your temple

And the hot blood of bulls and goats cover the ground

How long did priests in the frailty of their flesh stand to intercede

How long did the veil separate them from the Presence

Yet they knew it was impossible

They knew their transgressions and their sins were still before them

Against You, and You only, had they sinned, and done what was evil in Your sight

And they humbled themselves and called out to You:

Be merciful to us, O God, be merciful to us

For in You our soul takes refuge

In the shadow of Your wings we will take refuge, till the storms of destruction pass by

We cry out to God Most High, to God who fulfills His purpose for us

He will send from Heaven and save us. *Selah*

My heart is steadfast, O God

I will sing and make melody! Awake, my glory

I will awake the dawn

Be exalted, O God, above the heavens! Let Your glory be over all the earth

Amen

FRIDAY

Hebrews 8:11 *"And they shall not teach, each one his brother, saying, 'Know the Lord,' for they shall all know me, from the least of them to the greatest."*

W e want to see Jesus, Lord

The night is far gone and the day is at hand

We know the time, that the hour has come to wake from sleep

That salvation is nearer to us now than when we first believed

We have cast off the works of darkness, Lord, and have put on the armor of light

We make no provision for the flesh, to gratify its desires

Indeed, we count everything as loss because of the surpassing worth of knowing Christ Jesus our Lord

For we would gain Christ, and be found in Him

Not having a righteousness of our own that comes from the Law

But that which comes through faith in Christ, the righteousness of God that depends on faith

That we may know Him and the power of His resurrection

That we may share His sufferings, becoming like Him in His death

That by any means possible we may attain the resurrection from the dead.

The earthly forms we knew so well have faded away

The idols we bowed down to have all been toppled

Our hearts are open, the war rages all around, yet still we bring our solemn prayer before You:

We want to see Jesus.

Face to face, not in the mirror dimly, as for so long we have

Spirit, visit us with Your Presence and comfort, until our deepest longings are fulfilled

Amen

SATURDAY

Hebrews 8:12 *"For I will be merciful toward their iniquities, and I will remember their sins no more."*

Remember me, O Lord, when You show favor to Your people

Help me when You save them

That I may look on the prosperity of Your chosen ones

That I may rejoice in the gladness of Your nation

That I may glory with your inheritance

Both we and our fathers have sinned

We have committed iniquity

We have done wickedness

You rebuked the Red Sea, and it became dry

You led them through the deep as through a desert

Then they believed Your words, and sang Your praise

But they soon forgot Your works, and did not wait for Your counsel

The earth opened and swallowed them up

Fire broke out in their company also

But You looked on their distress when You heard their cry

For their sake You remembered Your covenant

And relented according to the abundance of Your steadfast love.

Save us, O Lord our God, and gather us from among the nations

That we may give thanks to Your holy name

And glory in Your praise

Amen

MONDAY

Hebrews 8:13 *"In speaking of a new covenant, he makes the first one obsolete. And what is becoming obsolete and growing old is ready to vanish away."*

L ord, we are bowed down to the earth in grief

Sin has come to dark fruition

Death has attended us in its wake

Innocent life has been brutally taken

The morning comes cold and answerless

We look to our leaders for hope, and there is none

None can explain the horrific callous sweep that sheds blood and delights in it

None can offer a way forward that will lead us out of this

There is only the spirit of destruction, which possessed the young man who committed the evil

It exults over the silent slain as they lie, beautiful golden stalks of young wheat, wrecked and trampled into the mud by the heedless thresher

Shall the Law not come to our aid? But what Law can change the heart

What Law can give back what has been taken

What Law can ever bring life out of death

For there is only One who has walked in that way

He was a Man of Sorrows, and acquainted with grief

He will tend His flock like a shepherd; He will gather the lambs in His arms

He will carry them in His bosom, and gently lead those that are with young

Comfort ye, comfort ye My people, saith your God

And the glory of the Lord shall be revealed, and all flesh shall see it together. For the mouth of the Lord has spoken it

Amen

TUESDAY

Hebrews 9:1 *"Now even the first covenant had regulations for worship and an earthly place of holiness."*

L ord, You are holy

Let Heaven and earth bow before You

Let the sun and stars and moon proclaim Your mighty deeds

Let the birds of the air show Your wisdom as they move through the skies

Let the beasts and creeping things lift their heads to the Hand that sustains them

Let the trees display their simple glory

The flowers of the field, which You have arrayed in beauty

They neither toil nor spin, yet each day they speak of Your faithfulness

How much more will God not provide for me? I, of little faith

But Your Spirit draws me to seek first Your Kingdom and Your righteousness

He softens my heart with conviction of sin

He strengthens me to tell the truth

To make the good confession that I am not the Christ

That I am unworthy even to be called Your son

But that I long to return to You with my whole heart

And You run to meet me. You bring quickly the best robe, and put a ring on my hand, and shoes on my feet

For Your son was dead, and is alive again; I was lost, but now am found

I will worship You and sing of Your mercy for all eternity, Lord

Who is a God like You, pardoning iniquity and passing over transgression for the remnant of Your inheritance? But You delight in steadfast love

Amen

WEDNESDAY

Hebrews 9:2 *"For a tent was prepared, the first section, in which were the lampstand and the table and the bread of the Presence. It is called the Holy Place."*

L ord, we come into Your presence with thanksgiving

We make a joyful noise to You with songs of praise

For the Lord is a great God, and a great King above all gods

In Your hand are the depths of the earth

The heights of the mountain are yours also

The sea is Yours, for You made it

And Your hands formed the dry land

How can we worship You in Spirit and in truth?

We are dust, and to dust we will return

We are no better than our fathers

We have hardened our hearts and gone astray, and we have not known Your ways

Sacrifice and offering You have not desired, but a body You have prepared for Him

For the One who came to do Your will, O Father God

Of whom it was written in the scroll of Your book

He is our God, and we are the people of His pasture, the sheep of His hand

He is the Head of the Body, the Church

He is the Beginning, the Firstborn from the dead, that in everything He might be preeminent

For in Christ all the fullness of God was pleased to dwell, and through Him to reconcile all things, whether on earth or in heaven, making peace by the blood of His Cross

Lord Jesus, You alone are worthy. Amen

THURSDAY

Hebrews 9:3 *"Behind the second curtain was a second section called the Most Holy Place"*

W e spend our lives searching, Lord

Searching for happiness

For purpose

For friendship

For redemption

For joy

For love

To find ourselves

But none of that is true. Even if we find it, it vanishes away from us like smoke on the water

Truth is a more costly thing

For it shows not only what we seek, but what we are

And in the light of eternity, there is only One who remains

And of Your great mercy You have named us for Yourself as a chosen race

A royal priesthood

A holy nation

A people for Your own possession

Called out of darkness into Your marvelous light, to proclaim the excellencies of Jesus Christ

Once we were not a people, but now we are Your people

Once we had not received mercy, but now we have received mercy

And we have sought You with all our heart; and here in the Most Holy Place, we have found You. Amen

FRIDAY

Hebrews 9:4 *"having the golden altar of incense and the ark of the covenant covered on all sides with gold, in which was a golden urn holding the manna, and Aaron's staff that budded, and the tablets of the covenant."*

T o the Law and to the testimony! If they speak not according to this word, there is no dawn for them

Lord, You alone see our hearts

Those of low estate are but a breath; those of high estate are a delusion

In the balances they go up, they are lighter than a breath

Who is it that stands before You? We have fallen, every one of us

We have leaned on that splintered reed that pierces every man's hand, this fading world

We have loved darkness more than the light

We have spoken evil of our brothers, and slandered our own mother's son

We have sinned against Your perfect Law

We have not obeyed Your Spirit when the wind of His breath has moved our souls

Heal me, O Lord, and I shall be healed

Save me and I shall be saved, for You are my praise

Behold, they say to me, *"Where is the Word of the Lord? Let it come!"*

I have not run away from being Your shepherd, nor have I desired the day of sickness

You know what came out of my lips, for it was before Your face

Be not a terror to me; You are my refuge in the day of disaster

O Lord, the hope of Israel, all who forsake You shall be put to shame

Those who turn away from You shall be written in the dust, for they have forsaken the Lord, the fountain of living water

Amen

SATURDAY

Hebrews 9:5 *"Above it were the cherubim of glory overshadowing the mercy seat. Of these things we cannot now speak in detail."*

S how me Your glory, Lord

Not because I am worthy, or because my people are worthy

But we give thanks because Your Name is near

And we recount Your wondrous deeds

Awake, awake, put on strength, O arm of the Lord

Awake, as in days of old, the generations of long ago

Was it not You who cut Rahab in pieces, who pierced the dragon?

Was it not You who dried up the sea, the waters of the great deep

Who made the depths of the sea a way for the redeemed to pass over?

And the ransomed of the Lord shall return, and come to Zion with singing

Everlasting joy shall be upon their heads, and they shall obtain gladness and joy, and sorrow and sighing shall flee away

I, I am He who comforts you

Who are you that you are afraid of man who dies, of the son of man who is made like grass

And have forgotten the Lord, your Maker, who stretched out the heavens and laid the foundation of the earth

I am the Lord your God, who stirs up the sea so that its waves roar

The Lord of Hosts is Your Name, and You have put Your Words in our mouth, and covered us with the shadow of Your hand

Establishing the heavens, laying the foundations of the earth, and saying to Zion, *"You are My people."*

Amen

MONDAY

Hebrews 9:6 *"These preparations having been made, the priests go regularly in the second section, performing their ritual duties"*

What is joy, Lord?

Is it what we try to cultivate within us

The knowing of accumulation

The subtle capture of a feeling, features, or form

The attenuation of thrill

The quick reflection of our own wishes glancing off the polished mirror of the world

They all vanish away so quickly. We have tried them, and they cannot fill the heart

They cannot feed the soul

Only in bringing our worship to You have we ever known satisfaction

Only in the good of singing praises to our God; for it is pleasant, and a song of praise is fitting

For the Lord builds up Jerusalem; He gathers the outcasts of Israel

He heals the brokenhearted and binds up their wounds

He determines the number of the stars, and calls them all by name

Great is our Lord, and abundant in power; His understanding is beyond measure

The Lord lifts up the humble; He casts the wicked to the ground

Sing to the Lord with thanksgiving, make melody to our God on the lyre!

The Lord takes pleasure in those who fear Him, in those who hope in His steadfast love

He declares His Word to Jacob, His statutes and rules to Israel

He has not dealt thus with any other nation; they do not know His rules

Praise the Lord! Amen

TUESDAY

Hebrews 9:7 *"But into the second only the high priest goes, and he but once a year, and not without taking blood, which he offers for himself and for the unintentional sins of the people."*

L ord, there is a place where Your holiness rests

Where we can come and enter into worship

Where nothing earthly or profane appears

Where our flesh can no longer stand between us and pure, spiritual worship

Where wickedness may not rebel against Your will

Where unbelief cannot make our hearts waver

Where Your Name is lifted high, for all to glorify You

Where Your mighty deeds and Your many mercies to Your people are recounted

How often we rebelled against You in the wilderness and grieved You in the desert! We tested You again and again, and provoked the Holy One of Israel

We did not remember Your power, or the day when You redeemed us from the foe

When You performed Your signs in Egypt and Your marvels in the field of Zoan

You turned their rivers to blood, so that they could not drink of their streams

You sent among them swarms of flies, and gave their crops to the destroying locust

You destroyed their vines with hail, and their sycamores with frost

You struck down every firstborn in Egypt

But You led out Your people like sheep, and guided them in the wilderness like a flock

You chose the tribe of Judah: Mount Zion, which You loved

You chose David, Your servant, and took him from the sheepfolds

With upright heart He shepherded them, and guided them with His skillful hand. Here, on David's Son, Your holiness has come to rest for us forever. Amen

WEDNESDAY

Hebrews 9:8-9a *"By this the Holy Spirit indicates that the way into the holy places is not yet opened as long as the first section is still standing (which is symbolic for the present age)."*

We live in an age of madness, Lord

When by their unrighteousness men have suppressed the truth

Without any excuse, for they knew the invisible attributes of God, but did not honor Him

Claiming to be wise, they became fools, and exchanged the glory of the immortal God for images resembling mortal man and birds and animals and creeping things

Therefore You gave them up in the lusts of their hearts to impurity, to the dishonoring of their bodies among themselves

Because they exchanged the truth about God for a lie and worshiped and served the creature rather than the Creator

Who is blessed forever! Amen

Shall we then in our worship continue to approach You with food and drink and washings, with rules destined to perish with use?

No, for we have been brought into a new and better covenant

One by which we are able to enter into Your presence in joyful worship

To know the eternal truth of Your holiness

To be known by You, and have our consciences washed clean by Your Spirit

To walk rightly before You, not from fear of Law, but from love worked in our hearts by grace

To in humility prefer each other and obey the authorities You have put over us

To build Your Kingdom one living stone at a time

To behold the glory of the One who is worthy, who has destroyed the old temple and in three days has raised up a new and glorious one

To become more like Jesus Christ as we offer our bodies as living sacrifices in His service. To Him be all the glory, forever and ever! Amen

THURSDAY

Hebrews 9:9 *"According to this arrangement, gifts and sacrifices are offered that cannot perfect the conscience of the worshiper"*

J esus, when You ascended on high, You led captives in Your train

Men and women from all walks of life

Not many of us were wise according to worldly standards

Not many were powerful

Not many were of noble birth

But You chose what is foolish in the world to shame the wise

You chose what is weak in the world to shame the strong

You chose what is low and despised in the world

Even the things that are not

To bring to nothing things that are

So that no human being might boast in the presence of God

And because of You we are found in Christ Jesus

Who became to us wisdom from God, righteousness and sanctification and redemption

So that, as it is written, *"Let him who boasts, boast in the Lord"*

When we were under the Law, we saw only faint shadows of the glory that was to come

We were without hope save in Your coming

But now, when we are under Grace, we have the prophetic word made more certain

This hope is not in gifts or sacrifices

It is in the greatest gift of all, that forms us into Your image:

The gift of Your very self, Lord Jesus. Amen

FRIDAY

Hebrews 9:10 *"but deal only with food and drink and various washings, regulations imposed for the body until the time of reformation."*

L ord, of old You spoke in a vision to Your godly one, and said:

"I have granted help to one who is mighty

I have exalted one chosen from the people

I have found David, My servant

With My holy oil I have anointed him

My arm also shall strengthen him

My faithfulness and My steadfast love shall be with him

He shall cry to Me, 'You are my Father

My God, and the rock of my salvation'

My steadfast love I will keep for him forever

And My covenant will stand firm for him"

As long as the sun You set his throne to endure. Like the moon it was established forever, a faithful witness in the skies. Selah

But now You have cast off and rejected; You are full of wrath against Your anointed. You have renounced the covenant with Your servant; You have defiled his crown in the dust

How long, O Lord? Will You hide Yourself forever? How long will Your wrath burn like fire?

Remember how short my time is! For what vanity You have created all the children of man!

Lord, where is Your steadfast love of old, which by Your faithfulness You swore to David?

Remember, O Lord, how Your servants are mocked, and how we bear in our hearts the insults of all the many nations with which Your enemies mock, O Lord, the footsteps of Your anointed

Blessed be the Lord forever! Amen and Amen

SATURDAY

Hebrews 9:11 *"But when Christ appeared as a high priest of the good things that have come, then through the greater and more perfect tent (not made with hands, that is, not of this creation)"*

L ord, we all stumble in many ways

We see Your glory, and then lose sight of it

We feel Your Spirit, and then fall out of step with Him

We hear Your Word, and then do not remember it

We know Your truth, and then turn away from it

We meditate on Your works, Your miracles of long ago, and then do not call on You to act

We pass under Your rod, the blood on the doorposts, and then do not make ready to leave Egypt with all of our own

We hear the threat of Your enemy, the chariots and horses that would bring us back into captivity, and our foolish hearts tremble at it

When the only fear we should know is that holy dread of You which first brought us to life

The only redemption we should look for is what You promised Your people

The only power we should follow is Your mighty arm

The only truth we should believe is what You have spoken

The only Word we should live by is Yours

The only Spirit who should move us is God's own

The only glory we should seek is from Your face

Are our bodies truly to be the temples for Your Presence? Then we need a great High Priest who has gone before us

May His Spirit indwell us today as we seek to follow You, even as we long for His appearing

For Jesus surely has appeared in us, and will come again to make all things new. Amen

MONDAY

Hebrews 9:12 *"he entered once for all into the holy places, not by means of the blood of goats and calves but by means of his own blood, thus securing an eternal redemption."*

L ord, we have had many saviors

They have promised us health, and purpose, and safety, and pleasure, and companionship, and meaning, and regard

Their promises seemed to be true, for the world always delivers what it offers

But once we held them in our hands, we knew them to be false

For there was no life in them, no eternal life

They slipped through our grasp like handfuls of sand, disappearing in the wind

And still Your Word was there

For You alone told us the truth:

You said that to serve You would be to offer ourselves up as living sacrifices

You said that our purpose in life is to bear witness to the Truth

You said that whoever would save his life would lose it, but whoever loses his life for Your sake would find it

You said that we would count it all joy when we meet with trials of various kinds

You said that anyone who has left houses or brothers or sisters or father or mother or children or lands for Your sake would receive again a hundredfold

You said the Father has hidden these things from the wise and learned and has revealed them to little children; yes, Father, for such was Your gracious will

And when the Spirit lighted on You and the light of Your Father was revealed from Heaven, and He said, *"This is My beloved Son, with whom I am well pleased"*

All that was for us, as we have been found in You, Jesus

And salvation is found in no one else, for there is no other Name under Heaven given to men by which we must be saved. Amen

TUESDAY

Hebrews 9:13 *"For if the blood of bulls and goats, and the sprinkling of defiled persons with the ashes of a heifer, sanctify for the purification of the flesh"*

L ord, who can pay for sin?

We do wrong every day

We take that which is not ours

We speak words which are not true

We speak against our brother and judge him

We speak against the holy Law, and judge it

We desire and do not have, so we murder

We covet and cannot obtain, so we fight and quarrel

We do not have, because we do not ask

We ask and do not receive, because we ask wrongly, to spend it on our passions

O adulterous people! For surely we do know that friendship with the world is enmity with God

It is not to no purpose that the Scriptures say, *"He yearns jealously over the spirit He has made to dwell within us"*

But You, O Lord, give more grace

You oppose the proud but give grace to the humble

Let us submit ourselves therefore to God

Resist the devil, and he will flee from us; draw near to God, and He will draw near to us

Cleanse our sinful hands, and purify our double-minded hearts

Be wretched and mourn and weep; humble ourselves before the Lord, and He will exalt us

For who can forgive sins except God alone? Only You, Lord Jesus. Amen

WEDNESDAY

Hebrews 9:14 *"how much more will the blood of Christ, who through the eternal Spirit offered himself without blemish to God, purify our conscience from dead works to serve the living God."*

L ife is not enough, Lord Jesus

Wisdom is not enough, for this world is too shrewd for us

Resolve is not enough, for it weakens

Perception is not enough, for it clouds over

Strength is not enough, for we falter

Words are not enough, for the pain goes deeper than words

Deeds are not enough, for they are soon past, and forgotten

What can we stand on? Where can we go

It is good to ask, as many times as we have, for the answer does not change

Only You are enough.

Only Your blood can purify us from sin

Only Your voice can tell us the truth

Only Your eternal Spirit can move us in the right way

Only Your work of faith in our hearts can be effectual

Only Your power can conquer our enemies, within and without

Only Your Word can reveal what we should do

And only Your finished work on the Cross can bring us out of dead works to serve the living God

Lord Jesus, have mercy on me, a sinner

Open the doors of my heart, strengthen my will, sharpen my mind, soften me to obey You

And never let me lose sight of You again. Amen

THURSDAY

Hebrews 9:15 *"Therefore he is the mediator of a new covenant, so that those who are called may receive the promised eternal inheritance, since a death has occurred that redeems them from the transgressions committed under the first covenant."*

H ear my prayer, O Lord; give ear to my pleas for mercy

In Your faithfulness answer me – in Your righteousness!

Enter not into judgment with Your servant, for no one living is righteous before You

For the enemy has pursued my soul; he has crushed my life to the ground

He has made me sit in darkness like those long dead

Therefore my spirit faints within me, my heart within me is appalled

But I remember the days of old

I meditate on all You have done

I ponder the work of Your hands

I stretch out my hands to You

My soul thirsts for You like a parched land. *Selah*

Answer me quickly, O Lord! My spirit fails

Hide not Your face from me, lest I be like those who go down to the pit

Let me hear in the morning of Your steadfast love, for in You I trust

Make me know the way I should go, for to You I lift up my soul

Deliver me from my enemies, O Lord! I have fled to You for refuge

Teach me to do Your will, for You are my God

Let Your good Spirit lead me on level ground; for Your name's sake, O Lord, preserve my life

And lead me in the Way everlasting

Amen

FRIDAY

Hebrews 9:16 *"For where a will is involved, the death of the one who made it must be established."*

L ord, who has believed our message?

Jesus Christ did not come to be served, or to condemn

He came to save and to give His life a ransom for many

He did not cry out, or raise His voice in the streets

He did not seek His own glory, but the glory of the One who sent Him

He was true, and there was no unrighteousness in Him

On the last day of the feast, the great day, Jesus stood up

And He cried out, *"If anyone thirsts, let him come to Me and drink"*

"Whoever believes in Me, as the Scripture has said, 'Out of his heart will flow rivers of living water'"

But He was despised and rejected by men

As one from whom men hide their faces, He was despised, and we esteemed Him not

And it was not until the curtain of the temple was torn in two, the earth shook, the rocks split, and the saints who had fallen asleep were raised

Then we looked up at his agony of faithfulness, and our hearts were stricken within us

And we cried, *"Surely this was the Son of God!"*

And we knew that we had turned – every one – to his own way, and the Lord had laid on Him the iniquity of us all

But after He had suffered, He saw the light of life, and was satisfied

Who can speak of His generation? For He poured out His life unto death, for the sin of many

So we have seen and testify, like rivers of living water, that the Father has sent His Son to be the Savior of the world. Amen

SATURDAY

Hebrews 9:17 *"For a will takes effect only at death, since it is not in force as long as the one who made it is alive."*

L ord, it is You who made us, and we are Yours. We are Your people, the sheep of Your pasture

You formed our inmost being and wove us in our mother's womb

When we took our first breath and opened our eyes to this unfeeling world, You were there; when we knew a mother's selfless love and comfort, You were there

When a father's strong hand led us in our first steps, faltering and daring, You were there

When we first began to explore with our play what we would do with our lives, You were there

When others began to appear in our consciousness and our sphere expanded, You were there

When we were first excluded from the graces of a friend, You were there

When an inner circle of favor appeared more lovely than anything else we knew, You were there

When adventure ended in injury and disappointment, You were there

When the soft glow of love appeared and someone else captured our heart, You were there

When we promised our life to another and became one with them, You were there

When sin crept in and darkened the light we had known in Your presence, You were there

When bitter consequences attended our unfaithfulness, and a long path of painful repentance lay ahead, You were there

When real loss confronted us and someone we loved went away, never to be known in this world again, You were there

When we came to know true beauty, not just appearances or feelings but lasting wonder at unfading delight, You were there

And when we take our last breath, gazing uncertainly across the dark path over Jordan, You gently take our hand. For You, Lord Jesus, have already walked it for us. Amen

MONDAY

Hebrews 9:18 *"Therefore not even the first covenant was inaugurated without blood."*

L ord, You are not a God who takes pleasure in evil

With You the wicked cannot dwell

You are the One who inhabits eternity, whose name is Holy

You dwell in the high and holy place

And also with him who is of a contrite and lowly spirit, to revive the spirit of the lowly, and revive the heart of the contrite

For You do not contend forever, nor will You always be angry

For then the spirit would grow faint before You

And the breath of life that You made.

But justice had turned back, and righteousness stood far away

For truth had stumbled in the public square

And he who departed from evil made himself a prey

You saw it, and it displeased You that there was no justice

You saw that there was no man, and wondered that there was no one to intercede

Then Your own arm brought salvation,

And Your righteousness upheld You

You put on righteousness as a breastplate, and a helmet of salvation

You put on garments of vengeance for clothing and wrapped Yourself in zeal as in a cloak

So shall they fear the Name of the Lord from the west, and His glory from the rising of the sun

"And a Redeemer will come to Zion, to those in Jacob who turn from transgression," says the Lord

Amen

TUESDAY

Hebrews 9:19 *"For when every commandment of the Law had been declared by Moses to all the people, he took the blood of calves and goats, with water and scarlet wool and hyssop, and sprinkled both the book itself and all the people"*

L ord, we are Your people

Not by blood, but by faith

The children You told Abraham would become a great nation, as many as the stars in the sky

The advantage of the covenant is much in every way

For we have Your great and precious promises

Your unchanging and powerful Word which spoke all things into existence

Your own Spirit, who indwells us to lead us in the Way everlasting

The sacrifice of Your Son, Jesus Christ, who bought us with His obedient life and faithful death

The adoption as sons and daughters into Your family

The mystery of Communion with You by His body broken and blood shed

The vision of faith, which looks on the bitter struggle of this world and sees Your hand at work

The bond of Christ in fellowship with others who confess Your name

The revelation of Your Gospel among the Gentiles, hidden for ages but now revealed to the saints, Christ in us, the hope of glory

A calling to walk in Him, rooted and built up and established in the faith, abounding in thanksgiving

To live as an aroma of life to life in them that are saved, and death to death in them that are perishing. Who is sufficient for these things?

But now a righteousness apart from the Law has been manifested, through faith in Jesus Christ for all who believe, whom God put forward as a propitiation by His blood, to be received by faith

Behold, death is swallowed up in victory! But thanks be to God, who gives us the victory through our Lord Jesus Christ. Amen

WEDNESDAY

Hebrews 9:20 *"saying, 'This is the blood of the covenant that God commanded for you.'"*

L ord Jesus Christ, You are my life

You are my joy

You are my shield and very great reward

You are the Word become flesh, that has dwelt among us

And I have seen Your glory, glory as of the only Son from the Father, full of grace and truth

You are my hope that does not disappoint

You are my great High Priest who intercedes for me

You are that You are, from eternity the only God

You are my King and conqueror, who has led me captive in Your train, and delivered me from bondage to sin and death

You are alone worthy

You are the Word, who was in the beginning, who was with God, and who was God

You are the Man of Sorrows who grieved at the grave of Your friend

You are the Teacher who brought out of the storehouse treasures old and new

You are the Alpha and the Omega, the Beginning and the End

You were before all things, and in You all things hold together

Ah, Lord God, it is You who have made the heavens and the earth by Your great power and by Your outstretched arm! Is anything too hard for You?

Your Spirit I will walk with, Your Word I will obey, Your will I will submit to, Your face I will seek

I will serve You with fear, Lord Jesus, and rejoice with trembling

Blessed are all who take refuge in You. Amen

THURSDAY

Hebrews 9:21 "And in the same way he sprinkled with the blood both the tent and all the vessels used in worship."

My soul clings to the dust

Give me life, Lord, according to Your Word

I have chased after the things of this world

My heart has desired to prosper

And to gain approval

And to be known

And to achieve success

And not to be harmed

And to be happy

But Your Spirit has lifted me up from all this

And instead of affirming my foolishness, You have made me realize that I am wretched, poor, pitiable, blind, and naked

You have counseled me to buy from you gold refined by fire, so that I may be rich

And white garments so that I may clothe myself and the shame of my nakedness may not be seen

And salve to anoint my eyes, so that I may see

And I know that those whom You love, You reprove and discipline

So by the power of Your Spirit, I will be zealous and repent

Whom have I in Heaven but You? And there is nothing on earth that I desire besides You

Cleanse me as a vessel for honorable use, set apart as holy, useful to the master of the house, ready for every good work

Amen

FRIDAY

Hebrews 9:22 *"Indeed, under the law almost everything is purified with blood, and without the shedding of blood there is no forgiveness of sins."*

Our betrayal of You runs deep, Lord; it began long ago in a garden when we first contemplated sin

Though You had given us every good thing, and made us a little lower than the angels

You gave us dominion over the works of Your hands; You put all things under our feet

All sheep and oxen, and also the beasts of the field

The birds of the heavens, and the fish of the sea, whatever passes along the paths of the seas

But we did not glorify Your Name or ascribe majesty to You

We questioned whether You really meant what You said, when You promised death with disobedience

And we saw that the forbidden tree was good for food, and that it was a delight to the eyes

And we saw that the tree was to be desired to make one wise. And we ate of it

We became like the Father, the Son, and the Holy Spirit in knowing good and evil; but a flaming sword was put between us and You, and we were cursed to toil and die here

And You were grieved with Your creation, and with man who had been made in Your image

But You really had meant what You said. And when You purposed in Your heart to save us, You knew there could be no life for man without the death of God

So You made Him for our sake to be sin who knew no sin, so that in Him we might become the righteousness of God

Therefore, if anyone is in Christ, he is a new creation. The old has passed away; behold, the new has come

In Christ God is reconciling the world to Himself, not counting their trespasses against them, and entrusting to us the message of reconciliation

May I be quick to speak of Your glories today. Amen

SATURDAY

Hebrews 9:23 *"Thus it was necessary for the copies of the heavenly things to be purified with these rites, but the heavenly things themselves with better sacrifices than these."*

This world is not our home, Lord

It is not just that the things around us are fading

But it is we ourselves

We have all become like one who is unclean, and all our righteous deeds are like a polluted garment

We all fade like a leaf, and our iniquities, like the wind, take us away

There is no one who calls upon Your name, who rouses himself to take hold of You

For You have hidden Your face from us, and have made us melt in the hand of our iniquities

But now, O Lord, You are our Father

We are the clay; You are the potter. We are the work of Your hand

Behold, please look, we are all Your people

Make known the riches of Your glory in vessels of mercy

Which You have prepared beforehand for glory

Even us whom You have called, not from the Jews only but from the Gentiles

The God who said *"Let light shine out of darkness"* has shone in our hearts to give the light of the knowledge of the glory of God in the face of Jesus Christ

And we have this treasure in jars of clay, to show that the surpassing power belongs to God and not to us

So we do not lose heart. Though our outer self is wasting away, our inner self is being renewed day by day, as we look not to the things that are seen but to the things that are unseen

To the Eternal God, who is our dwelling place; and underneath are the everlasting arms

Amen

MONDAY

Hebrews 9:24 *"For Christ has entered, not into holy places made with hands, which are copies of the true things, but into Heaven itself, now to appear in the presence of God on our behalf."*

A ll our lives are spent among shadows, Lord

What You created us to be, and what we are

The dreams we once cherished, and what remains of them

What the world seemed to be when we were young, and the bitter reality

Our own strengths and weaknesses, which are not what we thought

People like trees walking around, hard to make out, harder to know

The shadow of deadly sickness over our lives, that mows down the young and gathers in the old

The great dark gulf of separation that opens up between friend, spouse, co-laborer, brother, sister, parent, child, never to see each other again

The Valley of the Shadow of Death, that is near at hand all of our lives, waiting for that long last final journey over Jordan that each of us must make alone

But the people who walked in darkness have seen a great light

Those who dwelt in a land of deep darkness, on them a light has shone

For to us a child is born

To us a Son is given

The government shall be on His shoulder

And His Name shall be called Wonderful Counselor, Mighty God, Everlasting Father, Prince of Peace

And Jesus spoke to them, saying, "I am the Light of the World.

"Whoever follows Me will not walk in darkness, but will have the light of life."

Lord Jesus, draw us into the light of Your presence, and we will praise You with all of our hearts

Amen

TUESDAY

Hebrews 9:25 *"Nor was it to offer himself repeatedly, as the high priest enters the holy places every year with blood not his own"*

W ith one sin, Lord, we fell from our place as stewards of Creation before You

It began with doubt that You meant what You said

It was attended by the suggestion of the evil one that good could come of sin, and not destruction

It was borne up by pride, and the delusion that You did not have our best interests in mind

Our mother usurped authority, taking the fruit You had forbidden them to eat of

Our father abdicated his responsibility, failing to protect his wife and following in her error

And You cursed them, and their children, and the ground they walked on

Shame followed hard after them

Separation cut them to their hearts, a flaming sword that stood between them and communion with You

Condemnation rose up against them, and there was none to take their part

But great is the mystery of godliness

For You put enmity between the snake and the woman

And though His heel was bruised, her Offspring crushed the head of evil

He was manifested in the flesh

Vindicated by the Spirit

Seen by angels

Proclaimed among the nations

Believed on in the world

Taken up in glory

Lord Jesus, You are our perfect Sacrifice. Amen

WEDNESDAY

Hebrews 9:26 *"for then he would have had to suffer repeatedly since the foundation of the world."*

L ord Jesus, You are our living Hope

You are the Alpha and the Omega, the beginning and the end

You were before all things, and in You all things hold together

You were foreknown before the foundation of the world

But were made manifest in the last times, for the sake of us who through You are believers in God

Who raised You from the dead and gave You glory

So that our faith and hope are in God.

Is it nothing to you, all you who pass by?

Look and see if there is any sorrow like my sorrow, which was brought upon me

Which the Lord inflicted, on the day of His fierce anger

From on high He sent fire; into my bones He made it descend

My transgressions were bound into a yoke, by His hand they were fastened together

The Lord has trodden as in a winepress the virgin daughter of Judah

Zion stretches out her hands, but there is none to comfort her

The law is no more, and her prophets find no vision from the Lord.

But this I call to mind, and therefore I have hope:

The steadfast love of the Lord never ceases, and His mercies never come to an end

They are new every morning; great is Your faithfulness

For the Lord will not cast off forever, but will have compassion according to the abundance of His steadfast love

Amen

THURSDAY

Hebrews 9:27 *"And just as it is appointed for man to die once, and after that comes judgment"*

L ord God, who can know Your wisdom? How was it that You created us sinless, *posse peccare, posse non peccare*

That You gave us free will and left us naked and without shame, in a garden with one law

That You knew (for You had ordained it) that we would fall, yet You judged it still wise and good to create rather than not to create

That You asked after us when we were hiding from You, though You knew what we had done

That You spoke in righteous wrath to curse the ancient serpent who had led us astray

To curse Eve with pain in childbearing, and desire for what she could never have, since her sin was one of false longing

To curse Adam with futility in his work, and to labor with sweat on his face until he returned to the dust he came from, since his sin was one of abdication

And to set a flaming sword between us and communion with You, and sent us out into the earth not able not to sin, *non posse non peccare*

But even in Your judgment, Lord, You spoke of mercy

You spoke of the serpent's head being crushed by Eve's Offspring

You did not leave us in our death, but You spoke of a Savior, a second Adam

And as death reigned through that one man, much more will those who receive grace and righteousness reign in life through the one man Jesus Christ

For as in Adam all die, so also in Christ shall all be made alive

Delivered from the power of sin and walking in His Spirit, *posse non peccare*

For He must reign until He has put all His enemies under His feet. And the last enemy to be destroyed is Death

The saying is trustworthy, for if we have died with Him, we will also live with Him, raised imperishable with glory and honor, *non posse peccare*

Amen, Lord.

FRIDAY

Hebrews 9:28 *"so Christ, having been offered once to bear the sins of many, will appear a second time, not to deal with sin but to save those who are eagerly waiting for him."*

M*aranatha*

Hear my prayer, O Lord; let my cry come to You

Do not hide Your face from me, in the day of my distress

Incline Your ear to me; answer me speedily in the day when I call

For my days pass away like smoke

My heart is struck down like grass, and has withered

I eat ashes like bread, and mingle tears with my drink, because of Your indignation and anger

My days are like an evening shadow; I wither away like grass

But You, O Lord, are enthroned forever; You are remembered throughout all generations

You will arise and have pity on Zion. It is the time to favor her; the appointed time has come

For Your servants hold her stones dear, and have pity on her dust

Nations will fear the Name of the Lord, and all the kings of the earth will fear Your glory

For the Lord builds up Zion; He appears in His glory

He regards the prayer of the destitute and does not despise their prayer

Let this be recorded for a generation to come, so that a people yet to be created may praise the Lord: That He looked down from His holy height, from Heaven the Lord looked at the earth

To hear the groans of the prisoners, to set free those who were doomed to die

That they may declare in Zion the Name of the Lord, and in Jerusalem His praise, where peoples gather together to worship the Lord.

Lord Jesus, come quickly. Amen

SATURDAY

Hebrews 10:1 *"For since the law has but a shadow of the good things to come instead of the true form of these realities, it can never, by the same sacrifices that are continually offered every year, make perfect those who draw near."*

L ord, out of Egypt You called Your servant

He was a beautiful child, and they set him on the river for fear of the king

Pharaoh's daughter took him for her son and named him Moses, for she drew him out of the water

He raised his hand against the oppression of his people, and struck down the oppressor, and hid him in the sand

But when the thing became known, he had to flee to save his own life, and for many years he was a sojourner in a foreign land

But the cry of Your people came up before You, that they might be delivered from their slavery

In a flame that did not consume You met Moses at the burning bush, and called to him again

I AM WHO I AM was revealed, and this would be the sign: That when Moses had brought the people out of Egypt, they would serve God on that mountain

With signs of the covenant You bound him to Yourself, and he became a bridegroom of blood

You stretched out Your mighty hand and struck Egypt with signs and wonders, with blood, with unclean animals, with flying swarms, with death and festering boils, with hail flung down from the heavens

Locusts devoured their increase, and darkness settled over their land, yet Pharaoh would not let Your people go

Then the destroying angel walked through the land, and the firstborn of Egypt were struck down; but he passed over the houses where the blood was on the door

At Mount Sinai in the desert You gave them Your holy Law, and made a people for Yourself

But one day You would call Your Son, and He would deliver them from spiritual bondage

And everyone who called on the Name of the Lord would be saved. Amen

MONDAY

Hebrews 10:2 *"Otherwise, would they not have ceased to be offered, since the worshipers, having once been cleansed, would no longer have any consciousness of sins?"*

L ord, long did I wander in bondage to sin

Captive to every sinful passion of my heart

Dead in my rebellion against You

Repaying evil for good

Addicted to the gratification of my own desire

Blind to Your goodness, mercy, and love

Your grace hidden from my eyes, Your glory something strange to me

But was it sin that really held my heart?

No, it was simply self

The foolish desire to elevate my own wishes above any good that ever could have been

Which must always end alone, in destruction

Was it simple good, then, that would have rescued me?

No, it was You, for You *are* goodness

You are light

You are joy

You are meaning

You alone are worthy

Very God of very God, by whom all things were made

Holy, Holy, Holy is the Lord God Almighty, who was and is and is to come

I worship You and lift high Your Name before the world. Be glorified in me today, Lord. Amen

TUESDAY

Hebrews 10:3 *"But in these sacrifices there is a reminder of sin every year."*

L ord: Remember my affliction and my wanderings, the bitterness and the gall

I followed after my desires in the confidence of my heart

I acted in strength, sure in my convictions

Nothing slowed me or deterred me from the goal

I used people and discarded them

I sought after what the world had to offer, and foolishly held it up as a gift from You

I cherished my dreams over any other good, and pursued them at all cost. I even used You, and thought I had discarded You. Have mercy, Lord

But in truth, the only thing I was discarding was myself

Then Your Spirit halted me. You set before me Your holy Law, as a mirror, and when I looked into it, I was utterly lost

For I was a man of unclean lips, and I lived among a people of unclean lips, and my eyes had seen the King, the Lord of hosts

But when I confessed my sin, they gathered around me

My friends, my brothers, with whom I had enjoyed sweet fellowship in the house of God

They used me and discarded me, and laughed at my agony as they walked away

Yet this was not my greatest grief

I saw that I had wandered far from You, and my heart was broken forever

You have freely forgiven, O Lord, and washed me clean, and set Your seal of grace upon me

But I will not forget the height from which I have fallen

I too will freely forgive, and offer up a sacrifice of praise, the fruit of lips that confess Your name

Lord Jesus, You are everything to me. Amen

WEDNESDAY

Hebrews 10:4 *"For it is impossible for the blood of bulls and goats to take away sins."*

S in blinds us, Lord. It cripples and crushes

It divides

It ruins

It taints the truth with suggestion of evil

It draws our hearts from Your good way

It darkens our sight

And in the end, when we are given over to it, it destroys us

Who can bear up under it? Our most foolish moments are when we think we can manage it

Surely even Your Word in its wisdom tells us only to stand against the wiles of the devil

The sacrifices You gave Your people did not take away sins, for Creation could not do that either

But we know that Christ, being raised from the dead, will never die again

Death has no dominion over Him. For the death He died He died to sin, once for all

But the life He lives, He lives to God

So we also must consider ourselves dead to sin and alive to God in Christ Jesus

Let not sin therefore reign in our mortal bodies, to make us obey its passions

Nor present our members to sin as instruments for unrighteousness

But present ourselves to God, as those who have been brought from death to life

For sin will have no dominion over us, since we are not under law but under grace

For from Him and through Him and to Him are all things. To Him be glory forever! Amen

THURSDAY

Hebrews 10:5 *"Consequently, when Christ came into the world, He said, 'Sacrifices and offerings you have not desired, but a body you have prepared for me"*

Y ou are a Spirit, Lord, and they that worship You must worship in Spirit and in Truth

Yet the hour came, and indeed now has come, when neither at Mount Gerizim nor at Jerusalem has Your worship been commanded

"Destroy this temple," Jesus said, "and in three days I will raise it up"

But He was speaking of the temple of His body

"For life is more than food, and the body more than clothing," He said

And we knew that our immortal souls could never be fed on this world

He said, "Man shall not live by bread alone, but by every word that comes from the mouth of God"

And we apprehended Your eternal Word, and began to know it for Truth

"Do not fear those who kill the body but cannot kill the soul. Rather fear Him who can destroy both body and soul in Hell," He said

We were gripped by holy fear, for You alone are high and lifted up, who inhabits eternity, whose name is Holy

"The eye is the lamp of the body. So if your eye is healthy, your whole body will be full of light," Jesus said to us

And we saw that You were the Light of the world, and we followed You, and did not walk in darkness

Then He spread out His hands to us

"This is My Body, which is given for you. Do this in remembrance of Me," He said

And we took, and ate

And the life of Your Spirit falls fresh on us, and we lift up our heads to praise You, for at last we have tasted and seen that Your steadfast love is better than life

Amen

FRIDAY

Hebrews 10:6 *"in burnt offerings and sin offerings*
you have taken no pleasure."

O h give thanks to the Lord, for He is good, and His steadfast love endures forever

Blessed are they who observe justice

Who do righteousness at all times

Both we and our fathers have sinned

We have committed iniquity

We have done wickedness

Our fathers did not consider Your wondrous works, but rebelled at the sea, the Red Sea

Yet You saved them for Your Name's sake, that You might make known Your mighty power

You rebuked the Red Sea, and it became dry

You saved them from the hand of the foe, and redeemed them from the power of the enemy

Then they believed Your words, and sang Your praise

But they soon forgot Your works and did not wait for Your counsel. They had a wanton craving in the wilderness, and put God to the test

He gave them what they asked, but sent a wasting disease among them

Therefore He said He would destroy them, had not Moses, his chosen one, stood in the breach before them

Then they despised the pleasant land, having no faith in His promise

They yoked themselves to the Baal of Peor and ate sacrifices offered to the dead

They provoked the Lord to anger and poured out innocent blood

Nevertheless, He looked upon their distress when He heard their cry

For their sake He remembered His covenant, and relented according to His steadfast love. Amen

SATURDAY

Hebrews 10:7 *"Then I said, 'Behold, I have come to do your will, O God, as it is written of me in the scroll of the book.'"*

L ord, it is not because we were more in number than the nations that You chose us

Not because of anything in us, or anything we have done

But because of Your great love and mercy

See what kind of love the Father has given us, that we should be called children of God

And so we are

You once planted a vineyard, Lord

You put a fence around it and dug a winepress in it

You built a tower and leased it to tenants, and went to a far country

When the season for fruit drew near, You sent to Your tenants to get Your fruit

But they took Your servants and beat one, killed another, and stoned another

You sent other servants, more than the first. But they did the same to them

Finally You sent Your Son to them, saying, *"They will respect my Son"*

But when they saw Him, they said to themselves, *"This is the heir. Come, let us kill him and have the inheritance!"*

And they took Him and threw Him out of the vineyard and killed Him

And in a stark moment, heart laid bare by Your Word and Spirit:

I heard my voice among the scoffers.

The stone that the builders rejected has become the Cornerstone; this was the Lord's doing, and it is marvelous in our eyes

Lord Jesus, I can never repay what You have done for me

But as Your little child I can love not in word or talk, but in deed and truth

You who alone have done the perfect will of God, be glorified in me today. Amen

MONDAY

Hebrews 10:8 *"When he said above, 'You have neither desired nor taken pleasure in sacrifices and offerings and burnt offerings and sin offerings' (these are offered according to the law)"*

Your Law is holy, Lord

It is 613 commands that frame for us what it is to be set apart for Your purpose

Given to Moses the friend of God, when fire and smoke hid the Mountain

Passed down by Your people as the standard of faithfulness

After the threat of the devouring locusts had passed

And after the threat of judgment by fire had passed

Amos who was no prophet's son cried out, and You relented

So You stood beside a wall built with a plumb line, and You held up a plumb line beside it

And You said, *"Amos, what do you see?"*

And he said, "A plumb line"

And You said, *"Behold, I am setting a plumb line in the midst of My people Israel*

"I will never again pass by them; the high places of Isaac shall be made desolate

"And the sanctuaries of Israel shall be laid waste

"And I will rise against the house of Jeroboam with the sword"

And Your mercy stood forever as a testament to Your love

Your Son would one day follow that Law perfectly, keeping covenant with You

And guiltless, He would take its bitter punishment for us

(For cursed is everyone who is hanged upon a tree)

That through the Law we would die to the Law, and live to God

And the life we now live in the flesh we live by faith in the Son of God

Who loved us and gave Himself for us. Amen

TUESDAY

Hebrews 10:9 *"then he added, 'Behold, I have come to do Your will.' He does away with the first in order to establish the second."*

L ord, this world is tearing itself apart

For power, for money, for influence, for regard

But at the root of all the sin is one thing:

We will have our own way.

We will rule ourselves

We will be a law unto ourselves

We will make our own truth

We will make our own goodness

We will make our own eternity, without You

Should it be a surprise, then, that our Salvation came gentle and riding on a donkey

That He did not cry out or raise His voice in the streets

That a bruised reed He did not break, nor did He quench a faintly burning wick

That He was despised and rejected by men, a Man of Sorrows and acquainted with grief

That He set His face like a flint, to do the will of His Father in Heaven

And what was that will?

That everyone who looks on the Son and believes in Him shall have eternal life

And that He shall raise them up on the last Day

In this hope I will live

In this hope I will continue in faithfulness

In this hope I will take my last breath, still longing for His coming

All glory to You, Lord Jesus. Amen

WEDNESDAY

Hebrews 10:10 *"And by that will we have been sanctified through the offering of the body of Jesus Christ once for all."*

L ord, You are sovereign, high and lifted up. You inhabit eternity, and Your name is Holy

You speak, and the winds obey Your voice

You utter Your truth, and the skies are shaken

You look on the earth, and it trembles

You touch the mountains and they smoke

All things look to You to give them their food in due season

When You give it to them, they gather it up

When You open Your hand, they are filled with good things

When You hide Your face, they are dismayed

When You take away their breath, they die and return to their dust

When You send forth Your Spirit You create them, and renew the ground

What then was the will of God for the souls of men?

What could ever pay for our iniquity, or atone for our transgressions?

For we had no contrite or lowly spirit, that we should dwell with You

So it was the will of the Lord to crush the suffering Servant; He has put Him to grief

When His soul makes an offering for guilt, He shall see His offspring, and prolong His days

And the will of the Lord shall prosper in His hand

Out of the anguish of His soul He shall see and be satisfied; by His knowledge shall the righteous one, Your Servant, make many to be accounted righteous

Yes, Father, for such was Your gracious will. Amen

THURSDAY

Hebrews 10:11 *"And every priest stands daily at his service, offering repeatedly the same sacrifices, which can never take away sins."*

L ord, You know our weakness

You know that we cannot see

Our sin blinds us

Evil stuns us

Betrayal rocks us

The schemes of the devil confuse us

We grow weary in the fight, and our hope dwindles

But in the midst of our desperate worship, the Mighty One, God the Lord, speaks

You summon the earth from the rising of the sun to its setting

Out of Zion, the perfection of beauty, God shines forth

The heavens declare Your righteousness, for God Himself is judge! *Selah*

"Hear, O My people, and I will speak

O Israel, I will testify against you. I am God, your God

Not for your sacrifices do I rebuke you. For the cattle on a thousand hills are Mine

Offer to God a sacrifice of thanksgiving, and perform your vows to the Most High

The one who offers thanksgiving as his sacrifice glorifies Me;

To one who orders his way rightly, I will show the salvation of God!"

And we cast aside our fears, and listen to the Word of the Lord

For there is only One who has ever ordered His way rightly:

Lord Jesus, You are our only hope in life and death.

Amen

FRIDAY

Hebrews 10:12 *"But when Christ had offered for all time a single sacrifice for sins, he sat down at the right hand of God"*

A
ll of us, Lord

We have all sinned and fallen short of the glory of God

Is there any of us who does justice and seeks truth, that You may pardon us?

Though we say, *"As the Lord lives,"* yet we swear falsely

O Lord, do not Your eyes look for truth?

You have struck us down, but we feel no anguish

You have consumed us, but we refused to take correction

We have made our faces harder than rock; we refused to repent

And I said, *"These are only the poor; they have no sense*

For they do not know the way of the Lord, the justice of their God"

But we all alike had broken the yoke; we had burst our bonds

How can You pardon us? For our children have forsaken You, and have sworn by those who are no gods

"Shall I not punish them for these things?" declares the Lord, *"and shall I not avenge myself on a nation such as this?"*

The house of Israel and the house of Judah have been utterly treacherous to You

We have spoken falsely of the Lord, and have said, *"He will do nothing"*

Have You utterly rejected Judah? Does Your soul loathe Zion?

Why have You struck us down so that there is no healing for us?

We acknowledge our wickedness, O Lord, for we have sinned against You

Do not spurn us, for Your Name's sake; do not dishonor Your glorious throne

Are You not He, O Lord our God? For we set our hope on You. Amen

SATURDAY

Hebrews 10:13 *"waiting from that time until his enemies should be made a footstool for his feet."*

L ord, the waves rise and fall above me

Deep calls to deep, at the roar of Your waterfalls

Why are you cast down, O my soul? Hope in God, for I shall again praise Him

By day the Lord commands His steadfast love

At night His song is with me, a prayer to the God of my life

I say to God, my Rock: "Why have You forgotten me?

Why do I go about mourning, because of the oppression of the enemy?"

As with a deadly wound in my bones, my adversaries taunt me

While they say to me all the day long, "Where is your God?"

Why are you cast down, O my soul? Hope in God, for I shall again praise Him

For as in Adam all die, so also in Christ shall all be made alive

For in fact He has been raised from the dead, the firstfruits of those who have fallen asleep

And so it is with the resurrection from the dead

What is sown is perishable, what is raised is imperishable; what is sown in dishonor, is raised in glory; what is sown in weakness, is raised in power

Behold! I tell you a mystery

For we shall not all sleep, but we shall all be changed: In a moment, in the twinkling of an eye

And then shall come to pass that which is written: *O Death, where is thy sting? O Grave, where is thy victory?*

For the last enemy to be put under His feet is Death.

But thanks be to God, who gives us the victory through our Lord Jesus Christ

Amen

MONDAY

Hebrews 10:14 *"For by a single offering He has perfected for all time those who are being sanctified."*

G od is good

But as for me

My feet had slipped

For envy reigned

And evil prospered

They have no trouble

They are not stricken

They scoff and boast

They say, *"How can God know"*

Behold, their ease

My thoughts betrayed

Until I sought for You

And saw their end.

But You are here

You hold my hand

Whom have I

In Heaven, but You?

My heart may fail

But God is mine, forever

And I will tell Your works

Receive me into glory, Lord

Amen

TUESDAY

Hebrews 10:15 *"And the Holy Spirit also bears witness to us"*

L
ord, in the deeps of time

Before the world took shape

Before breath was drawn in our nostrils

Before the sun rose to rule the day

Or the moon rose to rule the night

Your Spirit hovered over the darkness

When Wisdom appeared

Beside You, like a master workman

The first of Your acts of old

When You established the heavens, she was there

When You drew a circle on the face of the deep

When You made firm the skies above

When You established the fountains of the deep

When You assigned to the sea its limit

So that the waters might not transgress Your command

There was observing all Your works a Witness

One who looked on, bore testimony, glorified, testified

That One is He who indwells us still

Who reminds us of Your Word

Who teaches us Your Wisdom

Who shows us Jesus, and bears witness to His image being formed in us

Give me ears to hear Your voice today, Lord. Amen

WEDNESDAY

Hebrews 10:16 *"for after saying, 'This is the covenant that I will make with them after those days, declares the Lord: I will put my laws on their hearts, and write them on their minds,'"*

L ord, the son of man prophesied to the mountains of Israel

He said, *O mountains of Israel, hear the Word of the Lord*

Because the enemy said of you, Aha! And, The ancient heights have become our possession

Thus says the Lord God to the mountains and the hills, the ravines and the valleys

The desolate wastes and the deserted cities

Which have become a prey and derision to the rest of the nations all around

Therefore thus says the Lord God: *I swear that the nations that are all around you shall themselves suffer reproach*

But you, O mountains of Israel, shall shoot forth your branches and yield your fruit to my people Israel. For they shall soon come home.

For behold, You are for us; and You will turn to us, and we shall again be tilled and sown

And You will multiply people on us, the whole house of Israel, all of it

You will vindicate the holiness of Your great Name, which has been profaned among the nations

And which we have profaned among them

And the nations will know that You are the Lord

You will take us from the nations and gather us from the countries, and bring us into our own land

You will sprinkle clean water on us, and from all our idols You will cleanse us

You will give us a new heart, and a new Spirit You will put within us

And You will remove the heart of stone from our flesh, and give us a heart of flesh

And we will soon come home. Amen, Lord Jesus

THURSDAY

Hebrews 10:17 *"then he adds, 'I will remember their sins and their lawless deeds no more.'"*

L ord, I struggle to forgive

I remember what they did to me, how calmly and cheerfully they did wrong

Evil spoke to them deep in their heart

There was no fear of God before their eyes

They said what was not true, and they were believed

They did what was not right, and were commended for it

They crushed Your people, O Lord, and afflicted Your heritage

They killed the widow and the sojourner, and murdered the fatherless

And they said, *"The Lord does not see; the God of Jacob does not perceive"*

But

Was it without Your knowledge that they sinned?

Is there not a God in Heaven who is just, who weighs our words and our deeds in the balance?

Will the Lord forsake His people, or abandon His heritage?

When I thought, *"My foot slips,"* has not Your steadfast love borne me up?

And, most powerful question of all, which Your Spirit reminds me when I falter:

Have they ever hurt me more deeply with their wrong, than I have hurt You?

If the Lord had not been my help, my soul would soon have lived in the land of silence

Forgive them, Father, for they know not what they do.

Teach us knowledge, You who know the thoughts of man, that we are but a breath

For justice will return to the righteous, and all the upright in heart will follow it

Amen

FRIDAY

Hebrews 10:18 *"Where there is forgiveness for these, there is no longer any offering for sin."*

L
ord, I am weary of the world, myself, and sin

Sin is impatient and unkind

It is envious

It vaunts itself, ever needing to be first

It is boastful

It is arrogant

It is rude

It always insists on its own way

It is irritable and resentful

It rejoices in wrongdoing

It does not love the truth

But because of the Cross – that is no longer who I am

I am dead to sin, and alive in Christ

I have been baptized into His death

I was raised to walk with Him in newness of life

My old self was crucified with Him, in order that the body of sin might be brought to nothing

So sin has no dominion over me, since I am not under law but under grace

Shall I then continue in sin, that grace may abound?

God forbid!

For the wages of sin is death, but the free gift of God is eternal life in Christ Jesus our Lord

Glorify Yourself in my faithful obedience today, Lord. Amen

SATURDAY

Hebrews 10:19 *"Therefore, brothers, since we have confidence to enter the holy places by the blood of Jesus"*

L ord, we have turned the corner here

Until now we have labored in our souls under solemn words

Hearing of those who would vie with the Lord Christ for supremacy

Being warned against neglecting our salvation

"Today, if you hear His voice, do not harden your hearts, as in the rebellion"

Your Spirit has cautioned us with this admonition, over and over, for a reason

The precious promise of the Sabbath-rest; the centrality of the Word of God; the awe of the throne of grace; the dreadful curse of falling away after tasting of Your heavenly gift

All these are good and necessary reminders for us

But now, Lord! Now

Now we catch a breath of the air from the very place where Your glory rests

Now is opened the door to the Most Holy Place, and by grace we are welcomed in

Now we can see the strong hand that has held us, the rock of Ebenezer that testifies to Your faithfulness

Now our faltering hearts rise up in faith, confident not in the flesh but in the finished work of Jesus Christ on our behalf. Confident in Him alone!

Now we are given strength to comprehend with all the saints what is the breadth and length and height and depth; to know the love of Christ that surpasses all knowledge

And to be filled with all the fullness of God

We behold an inheritance that is imperishable, undefiled, and unfading, kept in heaven for us

Who by God's power are being guarded through faith for a salvation ready to be revealed in the last time

Our hope is fully set, Lord, on the grace that will be brought to us at the Revelation of Jesus Christ. Amen

MONDAY

Hebrews 10:20 *"by the new and living way that he opened for us through the curtain, that is, through his flesh"*

L ord, we have spent all of our lives in the dark

We were born into generational patterns of sin

The empty ways of our forefathers

Selfishness, grumbling and disputing, a crooked and twisted generation

Not knowing the mind of Christ

Who, though He was in the form of God, did not count equality with God as a thing to be grasped

But emptied Himself, taking the form of a servant, being born in the likeness of men

And being found in human form, He humbled Himself by becoming obedient to the point of death

Even death on a cross.

Therefore God has highly exalted Him and has given Him the Name that is above every name

So that at the name of Jesus every knee should bow

In heaven and on earth and under the earth

And every tongue confess that Jesus Christ is Lord

To the glory of God the Father

So if there is any encouragement in Christ, any comfort from love, any participation in the Spirit, any affection and sympathy

Let us be of the same mind, having the same love, being in full accord and of one mind

Let what we heard from the beginning abide in us

For this is the promise that He made to us – Eternal life.

Amen

TUESDAY

Hebrews 10:21 *"and since we have a great priest over the house of God"*

L ord, we have been wandering for so long

We know this world is not our home

Our hearts have been broken here over, and over, and over again

Beauty beckons, and then fades away

Strength promises, but grows weak

Wisdom penetrates, but it fails

Hope shines out, but the darkness overcomes it

Friends turn away, enemies overthrow

We have given up houses and brothers and sisters and father and mother and children and lands

And for what? Surely all is loss, Lord

There is only one thing we have left

We stand before You, hands empty, hearts riven, nothing left but this one thing. And it is this:

We look like Jesus.

His beauty surrounds us

His strength upholds us

His mind instructs us

Our hope in Him will never disappoint

He has not called us Servants, but Friends

And at the end of all things, when what we live and know is gathered up into eternity

Jesus will call us home. Amen

WEDNESDAY

Hebrews 10:22 *"let us draw near with a true heart in full assurance of faith, with our hearts sprinkled clean from an evil conscience and our bodies washed with pure water."*

W hen Israel was a child, Lord, You loved him

And out of Egypt You called Your son

The more they were called, the more they went away

They kept sacrificing to the Baals, and burning offerings to idols

Yet it was You who taught Ephraim to walk

You took them up by their arms

But they did not know that You healed them

You led them with cords of kindness, with the bands of love

And You became to them as one who eases the yoke

You bent down to them and fed them

And Your heart recoiled within You

You would not execute Your burning anger

You would not again destroy Ephraim

For You are God and not a man, the Holy One in our midst

And You will not come in wrath

You will ransom us from the power of Sheol; You will redeem us from Death

O Death, where is your sting? O Grave, where is your victory?

For the sting of Death is sin, and the power of sin is the Law

So we come to You with a true heart now, not as Your captives, or prisoners

But as Your children.

Amen

THURSDAY

Hebrews 10:23 *"Let us hold fast the confession of our hope without wavering, for he who promised is faithful."*

People are not faithful, Lord

Even the best people cannot see all the way around things

They care, and they try, but their best efforts fall short

They do not have the power or the wisdom to protect the innocent, or punish the guilty

And the worst have no interest at all in what is just or right

They have made a covenant with Death

And with Sheol an agreement:

That when the overwhelming scourge passes through, it will not come to them

For they have made lies their refuge

And in falsehood they have taken shelter

Therefore thus says the Lord God:

"Behold, I am the one who has laid in Zion a stone, a tested stone

A precious cornerstone, a sure foundation

And I will make justice the line, and righteousness the plumb line

And hail will sweep away the refuge of lies, and water will overwhelm the shelter."

And it will be sheer terror to understand the message –

For the bed is too short to stretch oneself on, and the covering too narrow to wrap oneself in

And surely the Lord will rise up as at Perazim, and be roused as in the Valley of Gibeon, to do His work, His strange work

And all those who call on the Name of the Lord will be saved. For You alone are faithful. Amen

FRIDAY

Hebrews 10:24 *"And let us consider how to stir one another up to love and good works"*

L ord, our sin does not come from nowhere

We strive and war with each other

Our flesh vaunts itself; our pride is overweening

Yet our affliction does not come from the dust, nor trouble sprout from the ground

But man is born to trouble, as the sparks fly upward

The desires of the flesh are against the Spirit

And the works of the flesh are evident: Sexual immorality, impurity, sensuality, idolatry, sorcery

Enmity, strife, jealousy, fits of anger, rivalries, dissensions, divisions, envy, drunkenness, orgies

And the like. For those who do such things will not inherit the Kingdom

But the fruit of the Spirit is love, joy, peace, patience, kindness, goodness, faithfulness, gentleness, self-control

And against such things there is no law.

For those who belong to Christ Jesus have crucified the flesh with its passions and desires

Now if we have died with Him, we believe we will also live with Him

Let us then do nothing from selfish ambition or conceit

But in humility count others more significant than ourselves

That we may be blameless and innocent

Children of God without blemish in the midst of a crooked and twisted generation

Among whom we shine as lights in the world

Proclaiming the glories of our risen Lord, who came into the world as light, that whoever believes in Him may not remain in darkness. Amen

SATURDAY

Hebrews 10:25 *"not neglecting to meet together, as is the habit of some, but encouraging one another, and all the more as you see the Day drawing near."*

L ord Jesus, it is still Your Church. But she is beset with sin

She is dirty with the world

She is divided into warring factions

She is weary of well doing, even as the fields are white for the harvest

She has been sold for a trifle, and You have demanded no high price for her

She has been made like sheep for the slaughter, and is scattered among the nations

You have made her a byword for the nations, a laughingstock among the peoples

All this has come upon us, though we have not forgotten You or been false to Your covenant

If we had forgotten the name of our God, or spread out our hands to a foreign God, would not God discover this?

For You know the secrets of the heart

Yet for Your sake we are killed all the day long; we are regarded as sheep to be slaughtered

Awake! Why are you sleeping, O Lord

Rouse Yourself! Do not reject us forever

Why do You hide Your face? Rise up; come to our help

Redeem us for the sake of Your steadfast love

For Your Spirit has a godly jealousy over us, to present us a chaste virgin to Christ

So that He might present the Church to Himself in splendor, without spot or wrinkle, holy and without blemish

The Spirit and the Bride say, *"Come"*

Amen. Come, Lord Jesus

MONDAY

Hebrews 10:26 *"For if we go on sinning deliberately after receiving the knowledge of the truth, there no longer remains a sacrifice for sins"*

Holiness is a calling, Lord

It is not an accomplishment

It is not something within us that needs to be developed

It cannot be bought

We cannot get it from any other person

It cannot be gained with the wisdom of the world

And without it, we will surely not see You

It is a calling because there is only one way to lay hold of it

If any of us would come after Him, we must deny ourself and take up our cross and follow Him

For whoever would save his life will lose it, but whoever loses his life for Christ's sake will find it

For what will it profit a man, if he gains the whole world but forfeits his soul?

Or what shall a man give in return for his soul?

For the Son of Man is going to come with His angels in the glory of His Father

And then He will repay each person according to what he has done

Holiness, then, is not something of our own doing; it is how close we are to Jesus

How purely our beings reflect His love and compassion

How jealously the Spirit within us yearns to be set apart and sacred for His coming

How faithfully His truth rises on our lips, and His Gospel is borne out in our deeds

And in that calling most holy we make the good confession: *"Thou art the Christ, the Son of the living God."* Amen

TUESDAY

Hebrews 10:27 *"but a fearful expectation of judgment, and a fury of fire that will consume the adversaries"*

I saw all Israel scattered on the hills like sheep without a shepherd, Lord

Not a nation who did not know You

Nor a people who had not heard Your Word

But Your chosen race, Your covenant people

A people called by Your Name

And thus said the Lord God:

Ah, shepherds of Israel who have been feeding yourselves

Should not shepherds feed the sheep?

The weak you have not strengthened, the sick you have not healed

The injured you have not bound up, the strayed you have not brought back

The lost you have not sought

And with force and harshness you have ruled them

So My sheep were scattered, and wandered on every high hill, with none to search or seek for them

Behold, I am against the shepherds, and I will require My sheep at their hand

For thus says the Lord God:

Behold, I, I Myself will search for My sheep and will seek them out

As a shepherd seeks out his flock, so will I seek out My sheep

And I will rescue them from all places where they have been scattered, on a Day of clouds and thick darkness

For Your sheep hear Your voice, and we know You, and we follow You

Amen

WEDNESDAY

Hebrews 10:28 *"Anyone who has set aside the law of Moses dies without mercy on the evidence of two or three witnesses."*

The letter kills, Lord

For all its truth

For all its wisdom

For all the good and necessary reasons there are to have the Law

There is no life in it

The Law can reveal our hearts

The Law's six hundred thirteen commands show Your glory, as the only One who is good

The Law can punish sin

The Law can restrain wickedness

The Law can reflect truths to us, like a mirror

But if we look at ourselves, and then go away and forget what we look like

The Law has only death for us

But for the One who looks into the perfect Law, the Law of Liberty, and perseveres

Being no hearer who forgets but a doer who acts, He will be blessed in His doing

And in this vision – and this vision only – there is life for us

For the Law is a schoolmaster to bring us to Christ, to see His perfect obedience on our behalf

And Christ is the end of the Law for righteousness to everyone who believes

Let us then as we bow before Him, see that we owe no man anything, but to love each other

For the one who loves another has fulfilled the Law

And by Your Spirit we surely will. For the Spirit alone gives life. Amen

THURSDAY

Hebrews 10:29 *"How much worse punishment, do you think, will be deserved by the one who has trampled underfoot the Son of God, and has profaned the blood of the covenant by which he was sanctified, and has outraged the Spirit of grace?"*

There are some things, Lord, that should cause us to fear

They should cause us to turn toward You, and not toward the world

To revere You only

To listen to Your Word

To obey Your Spirit

To crucify the flesh with its passions and desires

To bless You, the God and Father of our Lord Jesus Christ

Who has blessed us in Christ with every spiritual blessing in the heavenly places

Even as You chose us in Him before the foundation of the world, that we should be holy and blameless before You

In love You predestined us for adoption to Yourself as sons through Jesus Christ, according to the purpose of Your will

To the praise of Your glorious grace, with which You have blessed us in the Beloved

In Him we have redemption through His blood, the forgiveness of our trespasses, according to the riches of His grace

Which He lavished on us, in all wisdom and insight making known to us the mystery of His will

According to Your purpose, which You set forth in Christ as a plan for the fullness of time

To unite all things in Him, things in Heaven and things on earth.

And by Your Spirit You said to us, *"Be holy, because I am holy."*

And so we live out our time here as exiles, in holy fear

For the grass withers, and the flower falls, but the Word of the Lord remains forever. Amen

FRIDAY

Hebrews 10:30a *"For we know him who said,
'Vengeance is mine; I will repay.'"*

L ord, Your power is a mystery

The forces of evil are arrayed against us

Their aspects are easily known, for anyone with eyes of faith

For we wrestle not against flesh and blood

But against the principalities

The powers

The rulers of darkness of this world

As we war against spiritual wickedness in high places

But You have entreated us, by the meekness and gentleness of Christ, not to walk according to the flesh

For the weapons of our warfare are not of the flesh

But have divine power to destroy strongholds

We destroy arguments, and every lofty opinion raised against the knowledge of God

We take every thought captive to obey Christ

And when we boast, we boast in the Lord

Let us put on, then, as Your chosen ones holy and beloved, compassionate hearts

Kindness, humility, meekness, patience

Bearing with one another and forgiving as You forgave us

And above all these putting on love, which binds everything together in perfect harmony

The peace of Christ will rule in our hearts

And the God of peace will soon crush Satan under our feet. Amen

SATURDAY

Hebrews 10:30b *"And again, 'The Lord will judge his people.'"*

L ord, sin has entered Your good creation

It came secretly, it was not spoken at Your command

It did not rail or threaten

Nor did it even seek to flatter

It merely asked a question: *"Did God really say, 'You shall not eat of any tree in the garden'?"*

A question that we turned over in our mind, and looked at fondly

And the longer we gazed at it, the deeper the idea sank into our minds and hearts:

"Does God really have our best interests in mind?"

Such foolish presumption led to our downfall, as we decided You had not really meant what You commanded us

And we took and ate of the forbidden fruit, and Death entered into our lives

It permeated everything we could see and know, until we could not even recognize Life anymore

And when the Lord of Life Himself came and walked among us, we turned our faces from Him

And even when Your Spirit came and raised us from the dead, it was a hard road we walked

A strait and narrow way, and few there are that go in it

Still warring against sin in our souls, and fighting to keep sight of Your glory, in a world that is set on its own destruction

In a strange and wondrous joy we persevere, always ready to give reason for the Hope in us

The spiritual man judges all things, but we do not even judge ourselves

Will not the Judge of all the earth do right? We are in Your hands, Lord

Arise, O God, judge the earth; for You shall inherit the nations. Amen

204

MONDAY

Hebrews 10:31 *"It is a fearful thing to fall into the hands of the living God."*

I saw the Lord sitting on a throne, high and lifted up, and the train of His robe filled the temple

And the seraphim called to one another and said, *"Holy, holy, holy is the Lord of hosts; the whole earth is full of His glory!"*

And the thresholds shook at the voice of Him who called, and the house was filled with smoke

And I said, *"Woe is me! I am lost. For I am a man of unclean lips, and I live among a people of unclean lips, and my eyes have seen the King, the Lord of hosts"*

So I have looked upon You in the sanctuary, Lord. I had heard of You by the hearing of the ear, but now my eye sees You

I have seen God face to face, yet my life has been preserved

Not that anyone has seen the Father except He who is from God; He has seen the Father

It is in and through Christ – and only in and through Him – that I have been drawn to You

For no one comes to the Father except through Him

Lord Jesus, I believe that You are in the Father and the Father is in You. From now on I do know You, and have seen You. Holy are Your judgments, Lord

And the seventh angel poured forth his bowl into the air, and there came a great voice out of the temple of Heaven, from the throne, saying, *"It is done."*

Alas, Babylon, O great city, you mighty city! For in a single hour your judgment has come

After this I heard the loud voice of a great multitude in heaven, crying out, *"Hallelujah! Salvation and glory and power belong to our God"*

And the twenty-four elders and the four living creatures fell down and worshiped God who was seated on the throne, saying, *"Amen. Hallelujah!"*

And from the throne came a voice saying, *"Praise our God, all you his servants, you who fear him, small and great"*

Amen, Lord! Hallelujah.

TUESDAY

Hebrews 10:32 *"But recall the former days when, after you were enlightened, you endured a hard struggle with sufferings"*

L ord, remember Your word to Your servant, in which You have made me hope

This is my comfort in my affliction

That Your promise gives me life

Who am I, Lord? You know my frame; You remember that I am dust

As a father shows compassion to his children

So the Lord shows compassion to those who fear Him

As for man, his days are like grass; he flourishes like a flower of the field

For the wind passes over it, and it is gone

And its place knows it no more

But the steadfast love of the Lord is from everlasting to everlasting on those who fear Him

And His righteousness to their children's children, to those who keep His covenant and remember to do His commandments

So we do not lose heart. Though our outer self is wasting away, our inner self is being renewed day by day

For this light momentary affliction is preparing for us an eternal weight of glory beyond all comparison

As we look not to the things that are seen but to the things that are unseen

For the things that are seen are temporal; but the things that are unseen are eternal

Let me see Your glory, Lord

Search me and know my heart, and see if there be any grievous way in me

And lead me in the Way everlasting

Amen

WEDNESDAY

Hebrews 10:33 *"sometimes being publicly exposed to reproach and affliction, and sometimes being partners with those so treated."*

L ord, we like to win

To have people cheer for us

To have the score say we came in first

To feel like we delivered when it counted most

To be thought well of by everyone

To hold joy tightly, and gaze long at it

But it is all an illusion, Lord

It is not true joy

Your Word says, *"Light is sown for the righteous, and joy for the upright in heart"*

And Your Spirit teaches us, with sorrows and loss, that there can be no joy without truth

And slowly we come to see down eternal corridors of meaning

That Your approval is worth more than any earthly praise

That many who are first shall be last, and the last first

That when we have done all we are commanded, we are unprofitable servants, who have only done our duty

That it is woe for us when all men speak well of us, as they did for the false prophets

That You make known to us the path of life; that in Your presence alone there is fullness of joy; and that at Your right hand are pleasures forevermore

That You are my Lord, and I have no good apart from You

I have set the Lord always before me; because You are at my right hand, I will not be shaken

And in Thy service, loss is gain. Amen

THURSDAY

Hebrews 10:34 *"For you had compassion on those in prison, and you joyfully accepted the plundering of your property, since you knew that you yourselves had a better possession and an abiding one."*

There is a prison, Lord

There is a place we cannot escape

A gaze we cannot avoid

Bars that are immovable

Walls of stone as hard as our hearts

A sentence that will not be commuted, but by Grace alone

And You have said that we shall be in the hands of those jailers, until we have paid back every cent of what we owe

So our Heavenly Father will do to every one of us, unless we forgive our brother from our heart

Should it not soften our hearts? To see someone held captive as we once were

Should we not accept it as the highest honor? To have our worldly goods seized for our faith

Will the Spirit not remind us of the word that You said to us? That a servant is not greater than his Master

For if they persecuted You, they will also persecute us

And that which is written in the Law must be fulfilled: *"They hated Me without a cause"*

But when the Helper comes, whom You sent to us from the Father, the Spirit of truth, who proceeds from the Father:

He will bear witness about You

And we also will bear witness, for we have been with You from the beginning

They can have all this world, but give me Jesus

My great and abiding treasure

Amen

FRIDAY

Hebrews 10:35 *"Therefore do not throw away your confidence, which has a great reward."*

L ord, You know our flesh

You know we are weak

We are affected by the world around us

By people and their words

By the very food we eat

The air we breathe

The hopes and despairs that have passed through our hearts

The fond dreams that have dissolved into nothing

The friends whose paths have taken a different turn, never to be seen again

Is there anything left for us to take confidence in?

But there is. There is a message from God, written on our hearts, to be known and read by all

Written not with ink but with the Spirit of the Living God

Not on tablets of stone but on tablets of human hearts

A ministry of righteousness, far exceeding in glory the ministry of death carved in stone letters

Since we have such a hope, we are very bold, not like Moses, who would put a veil over his face whenever the Law was read

For the Lord is the Spirit, and where the Spirit of the Lord is, there is freedom

And we with unveiled faces, beholding the glory of the Lord, are being transformed into the same image from one degree of glory to another

Such is the confidence that we have through Christ toward God

Who has made us sufficient to be ministers of a new Covenant

Blessed be His Name. Amen

SATURDAY

Hebrews 10:36 *"For you have need of endurance, so that when you have done the will of God you may receive what is promised."*

O Lord, God of my salvation

I cry out day and night before You

Let my prayer come before You; incline Your ear to my cry!

For my soul is full of trouble, and my life draws near to Sheol

Your wrath lies heavy on me, and You overwhelm me with all Your waves. *Selah*

Every day I call upon You, O Lord. I spread out my hands to You

Is Your steadfast love declared in the grave? Are Your wonders known in the darkness?

But I, O Lord, cry to You; in the morning my prayer comes to You

O Lord, why do you cast my soul away? Why do You hide Your face from me?

Your wrath has swept over me

You have caused my beloved and my friend to shun me

Darkness is my closest friend.

Yet even in this –

You too have known the darkness.

You have been shunned by those You loved

You have had the wrath of God sweep over You

Your soul has been cast away, the Father's face hidden from You

You cried to the Lord in the morning that His steadfast love would be declared in the grave

Your soul was full of trouble, and Your life drew near to Sheol

And after You had suffered, You saw the light of life, and were satisfied

O Lord, God of my salvation. Amen

MONDAY

Hebrews 10:37 *"For, 'Yet a little while, and the coming one will come and not delay,'"*

L ord, You have said that You are coming again

Days go by

Years stretch on

Time goes as it always has, and seems that it always will

We strive to enter Your rest, not to fall by disobedience

We abstain from the passions of the flesh, which wage war against our souls

Our conduct among the Gentiles is honorable, that they might glorify You on the day of visitation

They are surprised that we do not plunge into the same flood of dissipation

And we are maligned for our faith

It is hard – You, Jesus Christ, know exactly how hard it is – to remember that the fiery trials that test us are for our good

But somehow in them we rejoice; though now for a little while we have been grieved by them

So that the tested genuineness of our faith, more precious than gold though it perishes, be found to result in praise and honor and glory at the Revelation of Jesus Christ

But whose faithfulness is it? Shall we not lay our crowns before Your Throne in that Day?

Is it not Your finished work that justified us, Your blood that bought us, Your Word that feeds us, Your body broken for us, Your Spirit that burns within our hearts? Surely all is of grace

Then as the time grows short, we will speak of Your salvation to those who are perishing. A salvation by grace through faith, and not of ourselves, lest any man should boast

Multitudes, multitudes, in the Valley of Decision! For the Day of the Lord is near

But the Lord is a refuge to His people, a stronghold to the people of Israel. Amen.

TUESDAY

Hebrews 10:38a *"But my righteous one shall live by faith"*

L ord, Your Word says the race is not to the swift, nor the battle to the strong

Yet if there were any conclusion one would come to, here under the sun, that would not be it

If a person is strong enough, they can get what they want

If a person is smart enough, they can hide who they really are

If a person is a good enough liar, they can enjoy the support of others

If a person is unscrupulous, they let the weight of their sin fall on another

If a person is clever enough, perhaps, they can outwit God Himself

But Your Word also says that to the devious, You will show Yourself shrewd

For God is not mocked: Whatever a man sows, that he shall also reap

And the one who sows to his own flesh shall from the flesh reap corruption

But the one who sows to the Spirit will from the Spirit reap eternal life.

For Jesus Christ did not quarrel or cry aloud, nor was His voice heard in the streets

He bore all of our sins on His own body on the tree

He not only spoke truth, He was Truth, even as Pilate said, *"What is truth?"*

He had all wisdom and insight, yet the love of God was made manifest in Him

He could have called on His Father for twelve legions of angels; but how then would the Scriptures have been fulfilled, that it must be so?

And we see the Son of Man seated at the right hand of Power, and coming on the clouds of Heaven

Here is our vision; here our comfort; here our calling; here our joy; here, our blessed hope

The glorious riches of this mystery, which is Christ in us, the hope of glory

And in faith we long for Your appearing, Lord. Amen

WEDNESDAY

Hebrews 10:38b *"And if he shrinks back, my soul has no pleasure in him."*

L ord, things are not as they appear

Lot looked up at the Jordan Valley, and saw that the land of Sodom was well watered

The men of Israel saw the sons of Anak and were like grasshoppers in their eyes

The followers of Gideon were too many for the Lord to gain glory by their victory

Elisha's servant saw the Syrian army around the city, but could not see the chariots of fire

Saul heard the bleating of sheep and the lowing of cattle, and did not obey the Word of the Lord

Israel saw One from whom men turn their faces, and they crucified the Son of God

Where is the wise man? Where is the scribe? Where is the debater of this age? For God has made foolish the wisdom of this world

By faith Abraham obeyed God and set out, not knowing where he was going

By faith Joshua said *"Be strong and courageous!"* and led the people into Canaan

By faith Gideon led few against many, in the power and service of the one God

By faith Elisha said, *"Do not be afraid, for those who are with us are more than those with them"*

By faith Samuel rebuked Saul, and led the people to a king after God's own heart

By faith Simeon blessed the newborn Messiah in the temple, illumining Him with the fading light of his own life

The Kingdom of Heaven has suffered violence, and forceful ones lay hold of it

I thank You, Father, Lord of Heaven and earth, that You have hidden these things from the wise and understanding, and have revealed them to little children. Yes, Father, for such was Your gracious will

"Come to Me, all who are heavy laden, and I will give you rest." Yes, Lord Jesus. For Your yoke is easy and Your burden is light. Amen.

THURSDAY

Hebrews 10:39 *"But we are not of those who shrink back and are destroyed, but of those who have faith and preserve their souls."*

S o many voices, Lord:

Where is your God

The Lord does not see; the God of Jacob does not perceive

Let us close the doors of the temple, for by night they are coming to kill you

Curse God and die

Do not preach; one should not preach of such things; disgrace will not overtake us

Let us do evil, that good may come

Many are the afflictions of the righteous, but the Lord delivers him out of them all

So for every foolish and evil suggestion, Your Spirit has truth from Your Word for us:

I am the Lord, and there is no other

The eyes of the Lord are on the righteous, and His ears attend to their prayer

Fear not, for I am with you

Though He slay me, yet will I serve Him

I will tell of Your goodness; all day long I will speak of Your salvation

Be holy, as I am holy

And the Word became flesh and dwelt among us, and we have seen His glory

Glory as of the only Son from the Father, full of grace and truth

And to us who have received Him, who believe in His Name, He gave the right to become children of God: Born not of blood nor of the will of flesh or of the will of man, but of God

Jesus, we belong to You. Lead us in all boldness and humility to follow You today. Amen

FRIDAY

Hebrews 11:1 *"Now faith is the assurance of things hoped for, the conviction of things not seen."*

L ord, I have had this all wrong, most of my life

I have begun with my dreams

The things I hoped for

The things I wanted so badly

The things in this world that promised me life

The things that spoke to my heart so convincingly

The things that seemed like they would at last bring purpose and fulfillment

And beginning with what I most wanted

I went out and looked for those things

But that is not the way of the Christian

For us it all begins in the moment when You saw us lost in our blindness

And You turned aside to lay Your hands on us, and all of a sudden we could see

And it was not the brilliance of the blue sky, or the lush green of the grass, or the people all around us that captured our hearts

It was the sight of Your face; it was the very sight of Love

And in that new vision, You sent us out with a new mission for our lives:

To tell everyone about what the Lord has done for us

And what it is we hope for, because of what it is we have seen by faith

For from His fullness we have all received, grace upon grace

And we have seen and borne witness that this is the Son of God

Our hope is in You, Lord. Amen

SATURDAY

Hebrews 11:2 *"For by it the people of old received their commendation."*

I t is the great temptation, Lord

Shrewd leaders figure out two things about their followers:

1) What they really want, and

2) What they are most afraid of

With practiced skill they dangle the prize for blind obedience

And carefully hint at what perils will come about if they do not comply

"Do not preach" – thus they preach – *"one should not preach of such things.*

Disgrace will not overtake us"

And as long as people do what the leaders tell them to do, and say what they tell them to say

The leaders will surely commend them

But that is not the word of Your Spirit to us

He says, *"Arise and go, for this is no place to rest*

Because of uncleanness that destroys, with a grievous destruction

I will gather the remnant of Israel; I will set them together like sheep in a fold

Their King passes on before them, the Lord at their head."

Thus says the Lord concerning the prophets who lead my people astray, who cry *"Peace"* when they have something to eat, but declare war against him who puts nothing into their mouths

But as for me, I am filled with power, with the Spirit of the Lord, and with justice and might, to declare to Jacob his transgression, and Israel his sin

And there is only one commendation for which I wait, one blessing I long for:

To walk in the Name of the Lord our God forever and ever

Amen

MONDAY

Hebrews 11:3 *"By faith we understand that the universe was created by the Word of God, so that what is seen was not made out of things that are visible."*

L ord, the sun rose again today at Your command

The light of the stars was dimmed and gave way to the morning

The moon kept its faithful witness for another evening

The creatures of the earth went their way as You bid them

The winds blew as You directed

The fields of grain moved at their whisper

The trees held up their stately torches as Your Spirit passed

The mountaintops gave their silent salute

The dew fell on the mown grass, like Your Word, which does not return without accomplishing Your purpose

And men rose to another day of life as a gift from Your hand

A day with joy and hardship, truth and falsehood, good and evil, love and hatred, and at the end of all things, redemption

And together we lift up holy hands to give You Thanksgiving in it

Give the King your justice, O God, and Your righteousness to the royal Son!

May He have dominion from sea to sea, and from the River to the ends of the earth

May all kings fall down before Him, all nations serve Him

For He delivers the needy when he calls; He redeems their life, and precious is their blood in His sight

Blessed be the Lord, the God of Israel, who alone does wondrous things

Blessed be His glorious Name forever; may the whole earth be filled with His glory!

Amen and Amen

TUESDAY

Hebrews 11:4a *"By faith Abel offered to God a more acceptable sacrifice than Cain, through which he was commended as righteous, God commending him by accepting his gifts."*

W hat is worship, Lord

Is it a ceremony

Is it a show

Is it priestly ritual

Is it cultural expression

Is it a way to convince people that we enjoy Your favor

Or, is it something entirely different

Shall it come to pass in the latter days that the mountain of the house of the Lord

Shall be established as the highest of the mountains

And be lifted up above the hills

And shall all the nations flow to it

And many peoples come, and say,

"Come, let us go up to the mountain of the Lord

To the house of the God of Jacob

That He may teach us His ways, and that we may walk in His paths"

For out of Zion shall go forth the Law

And the Word of the Lord from Jerusalem

He shall judge between the nations, and they shall beat their swords into plowshares

Nation shall not lift up sword against nation; neither shall they learn war anymore

O house of Jacob, come, let us walk in the light of the Lord. Amen

WEDNESDAY

Hebrews 11:4b *"And through his faith, though he died, he still speaks."*

J ustice, Lord

We all call for it from our earliest days

Wrong is done

Loss is known

Beauty is wrecked

Life is lost

Trust is destroyed

Innocence vanishes away

Nothing is left, save the triumph of the victor and the despair of the victim

We appeal to the Law for redress:

"Punish the evildoer! bring about fairness! let there be a reckoning!"

But the Law, for all its truth, can only ever strike down. It can never restore

And we seek to levy its power against those who have wronged us, we end up speaking evil

And when we speak evil against our brother, we speak evil against the Law and judge it

Yet there is only one Lawgiver and Judge, the Lord Christ

In His great mercy and compassion, He has stepped between us and the Law

And the righteousness of God has been manifested apart from the Law

So that he might be just and the justifier of the one who has faith in Jesus

And boasting is excluded, not by the Law of works, but by the Law of faith

So by this we have power to forgive one another instead of to condemn

And mercy triumphs over judgment. Amen

THURSDAY

Hebrews 11:5 *"By faith Enoch was taken up so that he should not see death, and he was not found, because God had taken him. Now before he was taken he was commended as having pleased God."*

I have spent so much of my life trying to please people, Lord

Wondering what they noticed

Whether they saw me cut that corner

Whether they heard me say that word

Whether they judged me for failing

Whether they appreciated me for succeeding

Whether I looked good in their eyes

Whether they would favor me with attention

Whether I would gain preference with them

But it all vanishes like smoke, like trails of smoke on the wind

Because people change, and people pass away

But You the Lord do not change, and so the children of Jacob are not consumed

And those who feared the Lord spoke with one another, and the Lord paid attention and heard them

And a book of remembrance was written of those who feared the Lord and esteemed His Name

"They shall be Mine," says the Lord of Hosts, *"in the day when I make up My treasured possession*

"And I will spare them as a man spares his son who serves him"

Then once more we shall see the distinction between the righteous and wicked, between one who serves God and one who does not serve Him

And in Your perfect Son, You are well pleased. Blessed are all who take refuge in Him

Amen

FRIDAY

Hebrews 11:6 *"And without faith it is impossible to please him, for whoever would draw near to God must believe that he exists and that he rewards those who seek him."*

Y ou are holy, Lord

Your promises are true

They are yea and amen in Christ Jesus

Your testimonies are my heritage forever, for they are the joy of my heart

You are my Hiding Place and Shield

You are the Creator and the Giver of life

You are a consuming fire, a jealous God

The heavens proclaim Your righteousness, for God Himself is Judge. Selah

The Lord, the Lord, the compassionate and gracious God, slow to anger, abounding in love and faithfulness, maintaining love to thousands, and forgiving wickedness, rebellion and sin. Yet You do not leave the guilty unpunished; You punish the children and their children for the sin of the parents to the third and fourth generation

Have we not known? Have we not heard? The Lord is the everlasting God, the Creator of the ends of the earth. You do not faint or grow weary; Your understanding is unsearchable

Your way is perfect, and Your Word is flawless

And the Word became flesh and tabernacled among us. And we beheld Your glory, glory as of the only Son of the Father, full of grace and truth

You are the Christ, the Son of the living God

A bruised reed You will not break, and a smoldering wick you will not snuff out

For this You were born, and for this You came into the world, to testify to the truth. Everyone who is of the truth hears Your voice

And we have conquered by the blood of the Lamb and the word of Your testimony

To the King of the Ages, immortal, invisible, the only God, be honor and glory forever and ever! Amen

SATURDAY

Hebrews 11:7a *"By faith Noah, being warned by God concerning events as yet unseen, in reverent fear constructed an ark for the saving of his household."*

S o many speak of the fear of the Lord as if it were not really fear

"It means Awe," they say, smugly; *"or Wonder. It does not mean Fear"*

That is because they have surely never met You

And it is because first of all they live in the fear of man

Man, who has only the breath in his nostrils. Of what account is he?

Should we not rather fear Him who is able to destroy both body and soul in Hell?

Should we not fear Him who laid the foundation of the earth, when the morning stars sang together and all the sons of God shouted for joy?

Who bound the chains of the Pleiades and loosed the cords of Orion?

Who knows when the mountain goats give birth, by whose understanding the hawk soars?

Who made Behemoth, first of the works of God?

Who drew out Leviathan, king over all the sons of pride?

Who has first given to You, Lord, that You should repay him?

Shall we look on everyone who is proud, and tread down the wicked where they stand?

I know that You can do all things, and that no purpose of yours can be thwarted

I had heard of You by the hearing of the ear, but now my eye sees You

Therefore I despise myself, and repent in dust and ashes

But through the abundance of Your steadfast love, I will enter Your house; I will bow down toward Your holy temple in the fear of You

Let all who take refuge in You rejoice; let them ever sing for joy

Spread Your protection over them, that those who love Your name may exult in You. Amen

MONDAY

Hebrews 11:7b *"By this he condemned the world and became an heir of the righteousness that comes by faith."*

T his world is no friend to You, Lord

It seems to go on, through everything, as if it were all that endures

It rewards evil and punishes good

It promotes what is wrong and obscures what is right

It builds up lies and tears down the truth

It delights in harm; it scoffs at compassion

It promises the heart's desire, and gives assurance that none will ever know the subtle betrayal that was its cost

It destroys friendships, it wrecks marriages, it divides believers, it ruins families, it shatters relationships

And when it has done all this, it wipes its mouth and says, *"I've done nothing wrong"*

And turns to do it again

Is it truly the world, Lord? Or is all this from sin

Is all this surely contained in my own heart

The foolishness, the pride, the malice, the greed, the false witness, the lust, the wrath

For this reason You have called me to crucify the flesh

To let it not reign in my mortal body, making me obey its passions, but rather to die to sin and live to righteousness

Revealed in the Gospel, a righteousness by faith from first to last

For such a righteousness I will live and die in Your service

Let me hear in the morning of Your steadfast love; make me know the way I should go

For to You alone, Jesus, I lift up my soul. Amen

TUESDAY

Hebrews 11:8 *"By faith Abraham obeyed when he was called to go out to a place that he was to receive as an inheritance. And he went out, not knowing where he was going."*

Our life seems a fruitless journey, Lord

We wander through this forbidding world in search of our hearts' desires

Trackless wastes lie before us

Enemies threaten to overpower us

The heat oppresses during the day

The cold seeps in during the night

We find what we have sought and it withers in our hands; we throw it aside and go off after something else

In pain we bring forth children, and by the sweat of our brow we eat bread

Till we return to the ground, for we are dust, and to dust we shall return

The earth gives way and the mountains move into the heart of the sea

Its waters roar and foam, and the mountains tremble at its swelling. *Selah*

But there is a river whose streams make glad the city of God

The holy habitation of the Most High

God is in the midst of her; she shall not be moved

God will help her when morning dawns

Come, behold the works of the Lord, how He has brought desolations on the earth

He makes wars cease to the ends of the earth; He breaks the bow and shatters the spear

"Be still, and know that I am God."

By faith we will follow Your Spirit's leading, for we know that You will bring us home. Amen

WEDNESDAY

Hebrews 11:9 *"By faith he went to live in the land of promise, as in a foreign land, living in tents with Isaac and Jacob, heirs with him of the same promise."*

I am a stranger here, Lord

I hear a language I had not known

An alien people surround me

They offer up strange fire on their altars

Their gods are not like You

Moloch, the despicable fire-god, who demands innocent life to be sacrificed in his tophets, and devours their young as he did the children of Ammon

Ba-al, the loathsome storm-rider of the farmers' prayers, at the cost of their purity and devotion

Ashtoreth, the evil fertility goddess under the Babylonian moon, she-demon of Ur who was worshiped with swine's blood and orgies

Power, Money, and Regard are the idols they have set up before them

But surely their true names are Destruction, Corruption, and Death

"Come out from among them, and be ye separate," says the Lord. *"Touch no unclean thing, and I will receive you"*

But O Lord, the one true God of Abraham, Fear of Isaac, Fortress of Jacob

Too long have we tabernacled with those who pay regard to worthless idols

And our souls are unclean too, Lord, like the land on which we tread before You

Remind us from Your faithful Word that You alone made the heavens

Splendor and majesty are before You; strength and beauty are in Your sanctuary

Let us say among the nations, *"The Lord reigns! He will judge the peoples with equity"*

And since we have these promises, beloved, let us cleanse ourselves from every defilement, bringing holiness to completion in the fear of the Lord

For our confidence is in Your perfect righteousness, Lord Jesus. Amen

THURSDAY

Hebrews 11:10 *"For he was looking forward to the city that has foundations, whose designer and builder is God."*

There is a place, Lord

Far from the blood-soaked ziggurats in the land You called our father from

Far from the spreading trees and high places of Israel's idolatrous youth

Far from the pagan temples of the nations You exiled them to

There was a hint of it long ago, when Melchizedek blessed Abraham, and brought out bread and wine

When God stayed the hand of His obedient servant, and provided a sacrifice for the offering, that Isaac the child of promise might live

When the tent of the Tabernacle was raised, and the image of Your glory began faintly to appear

When David longed to build Your temple, yet You said, *"A man of blood shall not build a house for My Name"*

When Solomon stretched out his hands over the new place of worship and prayed, *"Hear from Heaven Your dwelling place, and when You hear, forgive"*

When the older people wept at the laying of the new foundation in the days of Ezra, because they remembered the beauty of the old temple

When Isaiah cried out at the unveiling of the glory of Your Throne, and the foundations of the thresholds shook, and the house was filled with smoke

When Jesus said, *"Destroy this temple, and I will raise it up again in three days"*

When Jesus in His resurrected body answered Thomas, *"Have you believed because you have seen Me? Blessed are those who have not seen, and yet have believed"*

And with John we see a vision of the Holy City, the New Jerusalem, coming down out of Heaven from God, prepared as a bride adorned for her Husband. Behold, the dwelling place of God is with man, and He will wipe every tear from their eyes

Blessed are those whose strength is with You, in whose hearts are the highways to Zion

Amen

FRIDAY

Hebrews 11:11 *"By faith Sarah herself received power to conceive, even when she was past the age, since she considered him faithful who had promised."*

People have sought power since You first made us, Lord

Leaders seek a following

The cruel seek someone they can wrong

Those cast off want someone to hear their grievance

The gifted seek to impose their will on the world around them

Those with a voice would have all men listen to them

Those with perception try to strip away the veils from reality

All of us want to be able to make things go our way

This is power, right? So we tell ourselves

And so we are told by the false prophets of the idols we once served

But that is not power

Power is life, and it has only ever come from Your hand

Power is what You spoke over the darkness, when all that is was not

"Let there be light," You said, and that which was nothing came into being

The world, the land, the sea, the creatures, the trees, the mountains, the lowest depths, the lights of highest heaven, our very selves – all existed at Your Word

This, then, is power: To step from death into life, from doubt into faith, from fear into boldness, to offer our bodies as a living sacrifice, holy and acceptable to God, which is our spiritual worship

And to see Your faithful Spirit do what You promised to do

And to know that You always have, and always will

In such power let us live and one day even die, in full assurance that Your Kingdom is coming

Amen

SATURDAY

Hebrews 11:12 *"Therefore from one man, and him as good as dead, were born descendants as many as the stars of heaven and as many as the innumerable grains of sand by the seashore."*

How long have we looked up to the stars, Lord

They are spread over the sky, farther than the keenest sight can tell

They are more in number than the mind can take in

Their beauty is compelling, as we look up to them night after night

Yet their message is inescapable:

He who made the Pleiades and the Orion, and turns deep darkness into the morning

And darkens the day into night

Who calls for the waters of the sea, and pours them out on the surface of the earth

The Lord is his name

Who makes destruction flash forth against the strong, so that destruction comes upon the fortress.

For You know how many are our transgressions and how great are our sins

Therefore he who is prudent will keep silent in such a time, for it is an evil time

For You alone, Your righteous Son, has sought good and not evil

You alone have hated evil and loved good

And established justice in the gate

You alone have been gracious to the remnant of Joseph

You have let justice roll down like waters, and righteousness like an ever-flowing stream

And it shall be as You promised Your servant Abraham: *"Look toward heaven, and number the stars, if you are able to number them. So shall your offspring be."*

Amen

MONDAY

Hebrews 11:13 *"These all died in faith, not having received the things promised, but having seen them and greeted them from afar, and having acknowledged that they were strangers and exiles on the earth."*

W ho am I, Lord?

The world we live in tells me that my identity is my most valuable possession

That I can be whoever I want to be

That who I am determines my destiny

That I can have whatever I want, be whoever I want, and do whatever I want with no consequences or ill effects

That anyone who warns me is just being hateful and ignorant, and the greatest tragedy imaginable is me not laying hold of everything the world offers

But even in the saying of it, it all rings hollow

People are born into this life, they spend their days grasping at the sand running down all around them, and they slip into eternity empty-handed and desperate

For it is the wrong question we have been asking all along.

Who are You, Lord?

By faith we see Your holiness, and it is more precious than gold

You are the blessed God and Father of our Lord Jesus Christ

Your salvation was foreknown before the foundation of the world

Your Word remains forever, though the grass withers and the flower falls

There is none who can say to You, *"What have you done?"*

It is by Your wounds that we have been healed

And You will surely bring all things to Your righteous judgment

With honor and holy fear we will bear the name of Elect Exile, for in You we lack no good thing

Teach us to live as people who are free, longing for Your Kingdom to come. Amen

TUESDAY

Hebrews 11:14 *"For people who speak thus make it clear that they are seeking a homeland."*

Something is wrong, Lord

We have known it since the beginning

Since we first knew what sin was

Since the desire to have things our way started growing in our hearts

Since the temptation to lie first pushed the truth aside

Since we discovered that you can try to hide after you have done wrong

Since we sought to receive honor from one another

Since desire was conceived and gave birth to sin

And since the desolation of sin settled in and all hope fled away

Your Spirit showed us Your perfect Law, and we turned around

And we became born again, of water and the Spirit

We sought the honor that comes from You only

We came into the light of grace and confessed our enduring need of You

We told the truth and discovered how costly it truly is

More than anything, we wanted Your Kingdom to come, Your will done

And we found out what holiness is

What You have known since the beginning

For You, Lord, are the only right there is

And when we began to understand that, our hearts began to know why Your Spirit yearns so jealously over us

Because, after a lifetime of wandering, You are slowly but surely calling us home.

Amen

WEDNESDAY

Hebrews 11:15 *"If they had been thinking of that land from which they had gone out, they would have had opportunity to return."*

T hose who have given up much for the Kingdom know that following You is costly, Lord. Houses, brothers, sisters, father, mother, wife, children, lands

Holding all things with an open hand

Destroying arguments and every lofty opinion raised against the knowledge of God

Taking every thought captive to obey Christ

For we have learned, and dear has it been in the learning, that friendship with the world is always enmity with God

You said, Yourself, that anyone who comes to You and does not hate his own father and mother and wife and children and brothers and sisters, cannot be Your disciple

Not that we are to bear anyone ill will, but that we are willing to lay on the altar anything – *anything* – that stands between us and You

Because You are able to raise it all up at the last day

And knowing this, we place it all in Your hands; we leave it all at the foot of Your Cross

For there is no hope in anything save the resurrection from the dead

The destruction of all that is false

The passing away of all that is visible

The rending of that last veil that enshrouds all nations, which is death

The restoration of all things to Yourself

And the revelation of Your glorious coming

As You do what You promised to do, and make all things new

We do not look back, Lord; there is nothing in this world which would keep hold on our hearts

It is for You alone that we wait. Amen

THURSDAY

G reed is a sin, Lord

Your holy Word says so

Avarice it was called in the ancient church, and many a soul fell victim to it

For it is not one of the more open or notorious sins; it tends to come after and not go before, as the sins of many

Greed takes unto itself with no thought of others

It is the sin of Demas and draws us off the path of heaven

It is the secret love of this present world

It breaks the second great commandment, for in it we love not our neighbor as ourself

We would covet our neighbor's goods, and have him to go without so we could have more

Yet it surely breaks the first great commandment also, for who can love their neighbor, without first and truly loving You?

We would exchange Your immortal glory for created things, and the Eternal for that which will pass away

Come now, you rich, weep and howl for the miseries that are coming upon you

Your gold and silver have corroded; you have laid up treasure in the last days

Behold, the wages of the laborers who have mowed your fields are crying out against you!

Break our hearts of such foolishness and evil, Lord

Draw us by Your Spirit to the waters, we who thirst, to buy wine and milk without money or price

For whoever drinks of the water You give him will never thirst again

It will become a well of water springing up to eternal life

Teach us, Lord, to long for You. Amen

FRIDAY

Hebrews 11:16b *"Therefore God is not ashamed to be called their God, because he has prepared for them a city."*

O Lord, our Lord

How majestic is Your Name in all the earth!

You have set Your glory above the heavens

Out of the mouths of children and infants You have established a stronghold against Your enemies

To still the enemy and the avenger

When I look at Your heavens, the work of Your fingers

The moon and stars, which You have set in place

What is mankind that You are mindful of them?

The Son of Man, that You care for Him?

You have made them a little lower than the angels, and crowned Him with glory and honor

You made Him ruler over the works of Your hands

You put all things under His feet:

All flocks and herds

And also the beasts of the field

The birds of the heavens

And the fish of the sea

Whatever passes along the paths of the seas

Lord, our Lord

How majestic is Your Name in all the earth!

Amen

SATURDAY

Hebrews 11:17 *"By faith Abraham, when he was tested, offered up Isaac, and he who had received the promises was in the act of offering up his only son"*

T his faith You have called us to is heavy, Lord

You gave Abraham Your most solemn promises

You promised him a miracle son

You promised him the land

You promised him he would become a great nation

And You promised him that his offspring would be a blessing to the world

Indeed, You cut a covenant with Abraham

Your Spirit foretold that his children would be sojourners in Egypt for four hundred years, until the iniquity of the Amorites was full

All these things the father of our faith heard, and he believed them

And you counted it to him as righteousness

But righteousness, in this broken and evil world, never comes without a cost

So You said to Abraham, *"Take your son, your only son Isaac, whom you love, and go to the land of Moriah"*

He obeyed You, and when his son was bound on the altar, Abraham's hand reached for the knife to slaughter him

But where was the lamb for the burnt offering?

God Himself would provide the Lamb for the burnt offering

And so You did. You took Your Son, Your only Son, Jesus Christ, whom You loved

He went to Golgotha to fulfill the righteous requirements of the Law

He offered one sacrifice, once for all, when He offered Himself

Behold the Lamb of God, who takes away the sin of the world. Amen

MONDAY

Hebrews 11:18 *"of whom it was said, 'Through Isaac shall your offspring be named.'"*

What can the righteous do, Lord? Your people are turning to lies and false gods for surety

They bow down at foreign temples

They offer up their little ones to the destroyer idol

They do not call on Your Name any longer

They go up on the high places, and under every spreading tree

They prostitute their souls to the gods of the nations around

And if anyone speaks against it, they are pushed out, with words or with silence

And as for those of us who would not betray You, are we really any better?

Our hearts fail us when we would speak truth

Our flesh desires the very same wickedness they do

Our spirit is willing, but we are so weak, Lord

We need You to remind us who we are:

We are the children of promise

Ours are the firstfruits of the covenant bonds, the answer to the faith of Abraham, the first taste of the river whose streams make glad the City of God, the holy habitation of the Most High

And more importantly, we need You to remind us who You are:

You are the Fear of Isaac

The Giver of all good things, the One whose day the fathers rejoiced to see, the One who dwells in unapproachable light, yet has drawn us close to Yourself as part of Your family forever

And we have not received the spirit of slavery to fear, but rather the Spirit of adoption as sons, by whom we cry, *"Abba, Father!"*

Deliver us, Lord, for Your own Name's sake. Amen

TUESDAY

Hebrews 11:19 *"He considered that God was able even to raise him from the dead, from which figuratively speaking, he did receive him back."*

L ord, You said that whoever believes in You would also do the works that You did

They will do even greater things than these, You said

What did that mean, Lord?

Your Spirit has impressed on me, over the years, that You are far more than an example

You are the sinless Lamb of God, slain before the foundation of the world to bring about salvation to all mankind

Therefore I worship You, and lift high Your name

I praise You for Your great and wonderful works

I extol You for Your heart of compassion, that remembers we are but dust

I lift Your praise before all the world that all might know Your saving grace

And in it I confess that I am utterly unworthy

I am sinful and heart-wicked, and were it not for Your work of regeneration in me, I would have destroyed myself by now

Can such a one as I approach You in faith and ask for Your promises to be kept?

Can I truly call You Father, and Brother?

Can these unclean lips proclaim Your truth? Yet You call me to

And this is surely a greater thing, that the righteous requirements of the Law should be fulfilled in me. In me! Because of You

That the Spirit of Him who raised Jesus from the dead should dwell in me

That there is a glory to be revealed in me, one which will never fade or pass away

And in this hope I will ever praise You

My Lord, my Brother, my King. Amen

WEDNESDAY

Hebrews 11:20 *"By faith Isaac invoked future blessings on Jacob and Esau."*

H ow rich Your Word is, Lord; how deeply it delves into the human heart

Exposing sin and foolishness, revealing our inmost thoughts before You

You know how the story of Jacob and Esau unfolded

Why it is that we say "Jacob and Esau," and not "Esau and Jacob"

How they were born with Jacob grasping the heel, deceiving and supplanting from his very birth

How Esau despised his birthright, treating it as a joke or a game before You

How Jacob saw the day of his death approach and called his son before him to bless him

How Rebekah put Jacob forward for the blessing, saying, *"Let any curse be on me"*

How Jacob put on a false identity and took false offerings, and deceived Isaac once again

How Isaac laid his hand on the head of his son – of the heir of the Covenant

And said, *"May God give you of the dew of Heaven*

Let peoples serve you, and nations bow down to you

Be lord over your brothers! Cursed be those who curse you, and blessed be those who bless you"

And through trial and heartbreak Your Spirit would teach Jacob to tell the truth

To point with his life and faith to One who would be the rightful heir of all things

Who would offer His birthright to all men freely as the great gift of grace

Who would say, *"I am the Way, and the Truth, and the Life. No one comes to the Father except through Me"*

As it is written, Jacob have You loved, that God's purpose in election might stand

Who will not fear and wonder? For from You and through You and to You are all things. Amen

THURSDAY

Hebrews 11:21 *"By faith Jacob, when dying, blessed each of the sons of Joseph, bowing in worship over the head of his staff."*

F aith sees, Lord

Faith knows

But most importantly, faith obeys

Long did Jacob walk with You and see Your wonders, until his heart learned Your ways

He saw the ladder that stretched from earth to Heaven, and behold, the angels of God were ascending and descending on it

He was afraid, and said, *"How awesome is this place!"* And he named it Bethel

Laban dealt shrewdly with him, and Jacob learned the value of truth

But he accepted the yoke of servitude, and you made him many through Rachel and Leah

You made him rich and increased his wealth on the earth. Your Spirit kept Laban from doing him harm, and protected him from Esau

You wrestled with him until the breaking of the day, and he prevailed

And You appeared to him again, and said, *"Israel shall be your name; be fruitful and multiply"*

So at the end of Israel's life, they brought his grandsons to him, the older one Manasseh on the right and the younger one Ephraim on his left

But Israel obeyed Your Spirit, and crossed his hands to bless the younger as the greater

In faith he obeyed, because it is God alone who raises up and who sets down

For one day You would reject the tent of Joseph, and not choose the tribe of Ephraim

And You would choose the tribe of Judah, Mount Zion, which You love

You would choose David your servant to shepherd the tribe of Jacob with upright heart

For the salvation of all who would trust in You. Amen

FRIDAY

Hebrews 11:22 *"By faith Joseph, at the end of his life, made mention of the exodus of the Israelites and gave instructions concerning his bones."*

L ord, you are not the God of the dead, but of the living

You sent Your only Son, most beloved of all, to shepherd us

He was sent among His brothers to rescue them

But we hated Him for His innocence and holiness, and we struck Him down

He was stripped of His robes and reviled without cause

He was sold for thirty pieces of silver

He emptied Himself by taking on the form of a servant

He was tempted in all points as we are, yet without sin

He was falsely accused, and led forth as a Lamb to the slaughter

Beside two criminals He was raised up before the scorn and mocking of His people

But after He had laid down His life, He rose again and was highly exalted

And God has bestowed on Him the Name that is above every Name

So that at the Name of Jesus every knee should bow, in Heaven and on earth and under the earth

And every tongue confess that Jesus Christ is Lord, to the glory of God the Father

You did not abandon His soul to Sheol, nor did you let Your Holy One see decay

For all the promises of God in Him are Yes, and in Him Amen, to the glory of God

Jesus knew that the people of God had been promised a Land which would be their inheritance

He said, *"I go to prepare a place for you. You know the Way to where I am going"*

And left His Holy Spirit to guide and empower and illumine us

Lord Jesus, help me to follow You today. Amen

SATURDAY

Hebrews 11:23 *"By faith Moses, when he was born, was hidden for three months by his parents, because they saw that the child was beautiful, and they were not afraid of the king's edict"*

We are strangers and aliens in this world, Lord

You call us for the Lord's sake to be subject to every human institution

To obey the one You have allowed to bear the sword

To make it our ambition to live a quiet life

To work with our hands and mind our own affairs

To walk properly before outsiders and to be dependent on no one

To keep our conduct before the Gentiles honorable

So that when they speak against us as evildoers, they may see our good deeds and glorify God on the day of visitation

Not to join with them in the same flood of debauchery, though they are surprised and malign us

Not to call conspiracy all that this people calls conspiracy, nor to fear what they fear, nor to be in dread

But the Lord of Hosts, Him we shall fear

Bind up the testimony; seal the teaching among the disciples

We will wait for the Lord, who is hiding His face from the house of Jacob, and we will hope in Him

We will render to Caesar the things that are Caesar's, and to God the things that are God's

In faith we will look for His coming, and do all He has commanded us to till then

We will honor everyone, love the brotherhood, fear God, honor the emperor

Having mercy on those who doubt, saving others by snatching them out of the fire

Show us Your great salvation, Lord, and give us faith to follow You out of exile. Amen

MONDAY

Hebrews 11:24 *"By faith Moses, when he was grown up, refused to be called the son of Pharaoh's daughter"*

F aith is a searching spotlight, Lord

It illumines the dark recesses of this shifting world

It reveals what is

It makes known what has been

It proves what shall be

Nothing is hidden that will not be made manifest

Nor is anything secret that will not be known and come to light

To the one who has, more will be given

And from the one who has not, even what he thinks he has will be taken away

What do we have, Lord?

Not the things of this world, which pass away

Not what the Gentiles seek after

Not riches

Not fame

Not people's regard

Not fleeting pleasure

We are Your children, sons of the Most High

Give us faith to confess Your Name, and bear whatever loss should come as joy

Give us the light of Your face, which shall never fade

And remember us in the Day of Your coming

Amen

TUESDAY

Hebrews 11:25 *"choosing rather to be mistreated with the people of God than to enjoy the fleeting pleasures of sin."*

Y ou are sovereign, Lord

You are high and lifted up

The train of Your robe fills the temple

The earth is the Lord's and the fullness thereof, the world and those who dwell therein

Ascribe to the Lord, O heavenly beings, ascribe to the Lord glory and strength

Worship the Lord in the splendor of holiness

The voice of the Lord is over the waters

The God of glory thunders

The Lord, over many waters

The voice of the Lord shakes the wilderness

Yet we still must choose

For You have placed Your Spirit in us

And faithfully every day, as long as it is called Today, He reveals and instructs

Revealing the terrible emptiness of all that is arrayed about us

The destitution of a life lived without God

And revealing the glory of the certainty of the finished work of Jesus Christ

The depth of purpose of a cruciform discipleship patterned after His

As many days as You give me to live, Lord

I will turn aside from evil things, and lay in Your hands all that is dear to me

And seek first Your Kingdom and righteousness

And one day see Your face. Amen

WEDNESDAY

Hebrews 11:26 *"He considered the reproach of Christ greater wealth than the treasures of Egypt, for he was looking forward to the reward."*

L ord, it is hard to see. There is confusion behind and before

Battle rages all around us

The enemy walks about like a roaring lion, seeking whom he may devour

And there are voices from within the very Church:

> *Fear this person or that evil; do not fear God*

> *Believe in this political party or that movement*

> *Do and say what we tell you to, and we will give you what you want*

> *The Gospel cannot save you. Come and get some therapy so you can stay sick like us*

> *The Bible does not really mean what it says. We know what the real truth is*

> *You can love the world and God too*

How long did I walk in these foolish ways, Lord? Yet Your Spirit snatched me out, woke me up

You taught me with revelation to fear You only

You taught me with heartbreak to look for Your coming only

You showed me that You are my shield and very great reward, and to obey You with joy

You showed me the Son of Man lifted up on a cross, and eternal life for all who trust in Him

You taught me that God is true, and every man a liar

You put me to hard service to know that this world is passing away along with its desires, but whoever does the will of God will live forever

And I bless Your holy Name, for the reproach of following You is worth all it costs and more

You, Lord Jesus, are my very great reward. Amen

THURSDAY

Hebrews 11:27 *"By faith he left Egypt, not being afraid of the anger of the king, for he endured as seeing him who is invisible."*

Out of Egypt You have called Your Son, Lord

Out from among the powerful in the world

The wise

The influential

Those who control nations with their words

The reputable

The rich

The intelligent

The unscrupulous

The proud

All those who make their own life, who need no God

But we are not of those who shrink back and are destroyed, but of those who have faith and preserve their souls

We are the poor in spirit

We are the sick, who desperately need a Healer

We are the guilty who need forgiveness

We who cannot keep ourselves alive, who kneel before You in worship

The hungry and thirsty for righteousness

In rags, brutally treated, homeless, the scum of the earth, the refuse of the world

For we are not greater than our Master

And when all the world fades away, we will still see Your face. Amen

FRIDAY

Hebrews 11:28 *"By faith he kept the Passover and sprinkled the blood, so that the Destroyer of the firstborn might not touch them."*

D eath comes with sin, Lord

We know it from the first time we hear Your holy Law

For You are righteousness, and there is no wrong in You

You speak, and the earth trembles

You arise, and the wicked flee

Your voice proclaims truth

Your Word leaves all things bare and exposed before You

You declare to Your people our transgression

To the house of Jacob our sins:

Is such the fast that I choose, a day for a person to humble himself?

Is it to bow down his head like a reed, and to spread sackcloth and ashes under him?

Is not this the fast that I choose:

To loose the bonds of wickedness

To undo the straps of the yoke

And to let the oppressed go free, and break their yoke?

Then we shall call, and the Lord will answer; we shall cry, and He will say, "Here I am"

The destroying angel will pass over us, because of the blood above the doorway

And we will taste and see that the Lord is good

Who has caused us to born again to a living hope through the resurrection of Jesus Christ from the dead

Amen

SATURDAY

Hebrews 11:29 *"By faith the people crossed the Red Sea as on dry land, but the Egyptians, when they attempted to do the same, were drowned."*

You have set life and death before us today, Lord

Life and prosperity, death and destruction

You have called Heaven and Earth to witness

For it is not too hard for us, neither is it far off

It is not in heaven, that we should say, *"Who will ascend to heaven for us and bring it to us, that we may hear it and do it?"*

Neither is it beyond the sea, that we should say, *"Who will go over the sea for us and bring it to us, that we may hear it and do it?"*

But the Word is very near to us

In the beginning was the Word, and the Word was with God, and the Word was God

All things were made through Him

In Him was life, and the life was the light of men

He has ascended to Heaven and sits at the right hand of God

He shall have dominion from sea to sea, and from the river to the ends of the earth

For He delivers the needy when he calls

The poor, and him who has no helper

Lord Jesus, You have given us faith to hear Your Word as it speaks

You have given us boldness to follow wherever Your Spirit leads

And You have given us lips to praise You, and hearts that joy in Your coming

Blessed be the Lord, the God of Israel, who alone does wondrous things

Blessed be His glorious name forever; may the whole earth be filled with His glory! Amen and Amen

MONDAY

Hebrews 11:30 *"By faith the walls of Jericho fell down after they had been encircled for seven days."*

L ord, who is it that builds up and tears down

Who raises nations until they rule over the whole world

Who gives authority to kings

Who waited until the iniquity of the Amorites had reached its full measure, to mete out judgment against them

Who led His people through the desert

Who threw Og king of Bashan on an iron bed of suffering, until he let the children of Israel pass through

When they were few in number, of little account, and sojourners in the land

He allowed no one to oppress them

He rebuked kings on their account

Saying, *"Touch not Mine anointed ones! Do my prophets no harm"*

He is the Lord our God; His judgments are in all the earth

He remembers His covenant forever

The word that He commanded, for a thousand generations

And the Lord said to Joshua, *"See, I have given Jericho into your hand, with its king and mighty men of valor"*

But Rahab the prostitute with all her family He saved alive

Who is king but the Lord? Or who shall stay His hand

He has brought His people out with joy

His chosen ones with singing

Praise the Lord. Amen

TUESDAY

Hebrews 11:31 *"By faith Rahab the prostitute did not perish with those who were disobedient, because she had given a friendly welcome to the spies."*

Not many wise, Lord

Not many powerful

Not many of noble birth

But You chose what is foolish in the world to shame the wise

You chose what is weak in the world to shame the strong

You chose what is low and despised in the world

Even the things that are not

To bring to nothing the things that are

So that no human being might boast in the presence of God

Even someone like Rahab

What do people suppose when they hear the words "friendly welcome" used of a prostitute?

Yet for her faith and works she has been robed with dignity forever

Jeremiah and Ezekiel, some of the greatest of the prophets, were of her lineage

And Jesus Christ Himself was descended from her

He who became to us wisdom from God

Righteousness and sanctification and redemption

So that as it is written:

"Let him who boasts, boast in the Lord"

Give us eyes of faith to understand the times spiritually, to see what is happening

Boldly to act without regard to ourselves or our reputations, when Your Spirit prompts us

And remember us when You come into Your Kingdom, Lord. Amen

WEDNESDAY

Hebrews 11:32 *"And what more shall I say? For time would fail me to tell of Gideon, Barak, Samson, Jephthah, of David and Samuel and the prophets—"*

It seems the world is all about us, Lord

And so it is

It creeps into our minds

It affects our thoughts

It colors our prayers

Fleshly and self-pleasing ways come to us by nature

And many around us assume that we will follow in the same foolishness they do

They are surprised that we do not

But there are many throughout the ages who have been heroes of faith and examples for us

They have heard Your Word

They have feared You

They have turned from evil to do good

They have placed their belief in Your eternal Gospel

They have laid hold of the horns of the altar of grace

They have rejected the world in its many forms

They have claimed Your promises by faith in Christ Jesus

They have conquered by the blood of the Lamb and by His testimony

For they loved not their lives even unto death

Therefore since we are surrounded by such a great cloud of witnesses, let us lay aside our sin

And look to Jesus, who is the great Hope of all who have trusted in Him for their salvation. Amen

THURSDAY

Hebrews 11:33 *"who through faith conquered kingdoms, enforced justice, obtained promises, stopped the mouths of lions..."*

T o do great things, Lord

To aspire to achieve

To conquer in Your name

To make wrong things right

To claim Your promises

To defeat evil

To bring Your Kingdom

All these I have sought after

And found that I was not enough

That my strength could not deliver; my heart could not rise that high

But in the sorrow of that realization, I also found You

And in my joy went and sold all that I had

That You might be my great and only treasure

O Lord, my heart is not lifted up; my eyes are not raised too high

I do not occupy myself with things too great and too marvelous for me

But I have calmed and quieted my soul

Like a weaned child with its mother

Like a weaned child is my soul within me

O Israel, hope in the Lord

From this time forth and forevermore

Amen

FRIDAY

Hebrews 11:34 *"quenched the power of fire, escaped the edge of the sword, were made strong out of weakness, became mighty in war, put foreign armies to flight."*

W ho is the god who will deliver you out of my hands?" the angry king shouted

"We have no need to answer you. Our God is able to deliver us. But even if not, we will not worship your idol," the three Hebrews answered him

And when they were cast into the flames, there was another, one like a Son of the gods, who walked there with them

"I have a message from God for you," the left-handed man said quietly

"Silence!" the king said, and all his servants left him

And when the left-handed man had plunged the double-edged sword he had made into the fat belly of the oppressor, he escaped beyond the idols. He sounded the trumpet in the hill country of Ephraim, and God delivered His people

The blind man said to his attendant, *"Let me lean against the pillars of the house"*

He paused for a moment as he remembered the days of his strength, and how grievous his downfall had been, for the Spirit of the Lord had left him for his sin and his pride

He raised his sightless eyes to Heaven and prayed one last time, *"Let me die with the Philistines."* And he bowed with all his strength, and God honored him, and the house came down; and more were those he killed at his death than those he had killed in his life

The women came out of all the cities of Israel, singing and dancing, with tambourines, with songs of joy, and with musical instruments

"Saul has killed his thousands, and David his tens of thousands," they sang

And the king was wroth; but God would have a man after His own heart to lead His people

They have conquered by the blood of the Lamb and the word of their testimony, for they loved not their lives unto death. Amen, Lord Jesus. Come quickly

SATURDAY

Hebrews 11:35 *"Women received back their dead by resurrection. Some were tortured, refusing to accept release, so that they might rise again to a better life."*

D eath is all around us, Lord. It entered the Garden in the dawn of being

When the quiet suggestion was made that maybe, possibly, You did not mean what You said

And that maybe, possibly, You did not have Eve's best interests at heart

She lingered over the forbidden fruit, to think on what could have been

And in sudden resolve she went up to sit in false tribunal upon the Word of God

To decide for herself what was right and wrong

What was lawful and forbidden

What was life and death

And with her Adam entered into sin for all humanity

For because of that one man's trespass, death reigned through that one man

And all stood condemned by the holy wrath of God

But while we were still weak, at the right time Christ died for the ungodly

The just for the unjust

That He might bring us to God, being put to death in the flesh but made alive in the Spirit

And through the furling shadows of the Death around

We saw the brilliance of the Life to be

For I am sure that neither death nor life, nor angels nor rulers, nor things present nor things to come, nor powers, nor height nor depth, nor anything else in all creation, will be able to separate us from the love of God in Christ Jesus

Then shall come to pass the saying that is written: *"Death is swallowed up in Victory"*

Thanks be to God, through Jesus Christ our Lord. Amen

MONDAY

Hebrews 11:36 *"Others suffered mocking or flogging, and even chains and imprisonment."*

T here is no love lost between this world and grace, Lord, between light and dark

Between love and hatred

Between truth and a lie

Between Christ and Belial

Between good and evil

Between abundant life and death

Between Your blessed holiness and ignorant rebellion

But in following You, I have not yet resisted to the point of shedding my blood

Some have suffered much for Your Name

They have endured the loss of houses, brothers, sisters, father, mother, wife, children, lands

In the new world, when the Son of Man shall sit on His glorious throne

We who have followed Him will also sit on twelve thrones, judging the twelve tribes of Israel

And all who have suffered loss for Your Name's sake will receive a hundredfold

And inherit eternal life

Many who are first will be last, and the last first

But we will fall down before You who lives forever and ever, and cast our crowns before the Throne, saying:

"Worthy are You, our Lord and God, to receive glory and honor and power

For You created all things, and by Your will they existed and were created"

In light of this glory, then, give us steadfastness in these our light and momentary trials. Amen

TUESDAY

Hebrews 11:37a *"They were stoned, they were sawed in two, they were killed with the sword."*

L ord, we are not enough

The forces of evil are too great

There is no fear of God before their eyes

They do not care about men

They do not obey Your Word

If it had not been the Lord who was on our side

–Let Israel say–

If it had not been the Lord who was on our side, when people rose up against us

Then they would have swallowed us up alive, when their anger was kindled against us

The flood would have swept us away

The torrent would have gone over us

Then over us would have gone the raging waters.

Blessed be the Lord, who has not given us as prey to their teeth!

We have escaped like a bird from the snare of the fowlers

The snare is broken and we have escaped!

Our help is in the Name of the Lord, who made heaven and earth

You have all power and wisdom and glory

You have ordained all of our days

Though You slay us, we will serve You

Though all the world be arrayed against us

And when we rise in the morning, we will see Your face. Amen

WEDNESDAY

Hebrews 11:37b *"They went about in skins of sheep and goats,
destitute, afflicted, mistreated"*

L ord, have mercy

For every Christ-follower who has endured shame for being faithful to You

Every person who has lost a friend over Your truth

Every worker who has been fired from a job for their Christian integrity

Every child who has been estranged from a parent for loving Your Gospel

Every husband whose wife has turned away from him because he loved God most

Every wife whose husband has left her because she followed Christ first

Every businessman who has lost a deal for honoring You with his truth-telling

Every counselor who has been attacked by her clients for pointing them to Jesus

Every street preacher who has been shamed for proclaiming Your salvation

Every politician who has been punished for acting with integrity for fear of You

Every actor who has lost opportunities for not dishonoring Your Name

Every singer whose career has suffered because they sang Your praises first

Every elderly person who has finished their race alone for their faith

Every teacher who has been let go for not affirming a student in their sin

Every pastor who has been savagely slandered for trying to shepherd well

Every church member who has been cruelly shunned for pointing out what the
Bible said

Though the fig tree should not blossom, nor fruit be on the vines

The fields yield no food, the flock be cut off from the fold, and there be no herd in
the stalls

Yet I will rejoice in the Lord; I will take joy in the God of my salvation

God, the Lord, is my strength, and He will make me to walk in high places. Amen

THURSDAY

Hebrews 11:38a *"of whom the world was not worthy"*

N ow is the judgment of this world, Lord

Now will the ruler of this world be cast out

Now is My soul troubled

And what shall I say?

"Father, save Me from this hour?"

But for this purpose I have come to this hour

"Father, glorify Your Name"

Then a voice came from Heaven:

"I have glorified it, and will glorify it again"

Surely this is our great hope

That in all of our darkness

We have believed in the Light, and become sons of light

That in all of our defeat

We have seen the King coming, who is our Victory

That in all of our despair

We have set our Hope in the Lamb who was slain, and who rose again

Though now for a little while, if necessary, we have been grieved by various trials

So that the tested genuineness of our faith, more precious than gold that perishes, though it is tested by fire

May be found to result in praise and glory and honor at the Revelation of Jesus Christ

For when Your hour had come to depart, having loved Your own who were in the world –

You loved us to the end. Amen, Lord Jesus

FRIDAY

Hebrews 11:38b *"wandering about in deserts and mountains, and in dens and caves of the earth."*

I am blessed far beyond what I deserve, Lord

Foxes have holes, and birds of the air have nests

But the Son of Man has not a place to lay His head

You said, *"Follow Me, and let the dead bury their own dead"*

You showed me a glimpse of eternal life

You taught me Your holy Law

You showed me how in Your flesh You had kept it fully, satisfying its righteous demands

You gave me Your Spirit to indwell and to illuminate

You set my feet on a rock and gave me a firm place to stand

You put a new song in my mouth, a song of praise to our God

Many will see and fear, and put their trust in God

Is there any good thing You have withheld from me?

Yet all these things: marriage, family, friends, home, career, possessions

All these things will fade away in that great Day

Only what is built on the foundation of Christ will remain

For each one's work will become manifest

Because it will be revealed by fire

Search me, O God, and know my heart; try me and know my thoughts

See if there be any grievous way in me

And lead me in the Way everlasting

Amen

SATURDAY

Hebrews 11:39 *"And all these, though commended through their faith, did not receive what was promised"*

I n this life, Lord

We see Your glory, but must wait behind the veil

We hear Your promises, but must take them on faith

We are fools for Christ's sake, but others are wise

We are weak, but they are strong

They are held in honor, but we in disrepute

When reviled, we bless; when persecuted, we endure; when slandered, we entreat

We have become the scum of the world, the refuse of all things

We have renounced disgraceful, underhanded ways

We refuse to practice cunning or to tamper with God's Word, but by the open statement of the truth we would commend ourselves to everyone in the sight of God

This treasure is ours in jars of clay, to show that the surpassing power belongs to God and not to us

We are afflicted in every way, but not crushed; perplexed, but not driven to despair; persecuted, but not forsaken; struck down, but not destroyed

Always carrying in the body the death of Jesus, so that the life of Jesus may also be manifested in our bodies

Exhibited as last of all, like men sentenced to death, because we have become a spectacle to the world, to angels, and to men

For what we proclaim is not ourselves, but Jesus Christ as Lord

God, who said, *"Let light shine out of darkness,"* has shone in our hearts to give the light of the knowledge of the glory of God in the face of Jesus Christ

And this light momentary affliction is preparing for us an eternal weight of glory beyond all comparison, as we look not to the things that are seen but to the things that are unseen

Amen

MONDAY

Hebrews 11:40 *"since God had provided something better for us, that apart from us they should not be made perfect."*

F or God alone my soul waits in silence; from Him comes my salvation

I have come into the world as light, so that whoever believes in Me may not remain in darkness

He alone is my rock and my salvation, my fortress; I shall not be greatly shaken

I have said these things to you, that in Me you may have peace. In the world you will have tribulation. But take heart! I have overcome the world

How long will all of you attack a man to batter him, like a leaning wall, a tottering fence

Blessed are you when others revile you and persecute you and utter all kinds of evil against you falsely on My account

They thrust him down from his high position, and take pleasure in falsehood

I am the Way, and the Truth, and the Life. No one comes to the Father except through Me

For God alone, O my soul, wait in silence, for my hope is from Him

I am the Resurrection and the Life. Whoever believes in Me, though he die, yet shall he live

On God rests my salvation and my glory; my mighty rock, my refuge is God

How can you believe, when you receive glory from one another and do not seek the glory that comes from the only God?

Trust in him at all times, O people; pour out your heart before him; God is a refuge for us. Selah

But seek first the kingdom of God and His righteousness, and all these things will be added to you

Once God has spoken; twice have I heard this: that power belongs to God, and that to You, O Lord, belongs steadfast love

For God so loved the world, that he gave his only Son, that whoever believes in him should not perish but have eternal life

Render to us, Lord, according to the finished work of Jesus today. Amen

TUESDAY

Hebrews 12:1a *"Therefore, since we are surrounded by so great a cloud of witnesses, let us also lay aside every weight, and sin which clings so closely"*

We need Your vision, Lord

Your people have forgotten what they were saved from, as they dally with sin

They have forgotten what they were saved for, as they scoff at Heaven

And they have forgotten Who they were saved by, as they do not revere You

If we only knew how important Your Word is

How much hangs on the truth

What it matters whether we pursue holiness

The importance of one single soul for eternity

What it means for You to be glorified in our lives

Those who have gone on to glory know that, now

Their souls cry out from under the altar, *"How long, O Lord?"*

Those slain for the Word of God, and for their faithful witness

And their cry goes up:

"O Sovereign Lord, holy and true, how long before you will judge and avenge our blood on those who dwell on the earth?"

They have conquered by the blood of the Lamb and the word of their testimony

For they loved not their lives unto death

Now the salvation and the power and the Kingdom of our God and the authority of His Christ have come

One true God, Creator of Heaven and Earth, righteous and holy

Of Your great mercy, give me eyes of faith to see this truth today, which shall never fade away

And a heart to follow hard after Jesus Christ in it. Amen

WEDNESDAY

Hebrews 12:1b *"and let us run with endurance the race that is set before us"*

T o keep going, Lord

    To tell truth

To repent of sin

To sincerely apologize to those we have wronged

To look also to the interests of others

To crucify the flesh

To resist the devil

To draw near to God, and submit ourselves to You

To cleanse our sinful hands, and purify our double-minded hearts

To be wretched and mourn and weep

To turn our laughter to mourning and our joy to gloom

To humble ourselves before the Lord, that You may exalt us

When You restored the fortunes of Zion, we were like those who dream

Then our mouth was filled with laughter, and our tongue with shouts of joy

Then they said among the nations, *"The Lord has done great things for them"*

The Lord has done great things for us, and we are glad

Those who sow in tears shall reap with shouts of joy

He who goes out weeping, bearing the seed for sowing

Shall come home with shouts of joy, bearing his sheaves with him

To fight the good fight, to finish the race, to keep the faith

Henceforth there is laid up for us the crown of righteousness, and not only for us

But for all who have loved Your appearing, Jesus. Amen

THURSDAY

Hebrews 12:2 *"looking to Jesus, the founder and perfecter of our faith, who for the joy that was set before him endured the cross, despising its shame, and is seated at the right hand of the throne of God."*

O ur gaze has been long on this shattered world, Lord

We have seen friends come and go

We have seen love rise up and then fall down, never to rise again

We have seen faithfulness honored among Your people

And we have seen foolishness take its place, and Your people know not the difference

Your Word has been revered and listened to, as what the Spirit says to the churches

And the subtle voice of the enemy has questioned it, and many have turned away

We have seen spiritual attack come against Your leaders

They falter for the merest instant, and lower their shield of faith

And they are overwhelmed by the fiery darts of the wicked one

The simple do not give heed to their ways, and they walk into destruction

The unscrupulous care nothing for truth, and are richly rewarded for their betrayals

And You, Lord Jesus, when You came to this earth, knew all this. You looked and You saw all Israel scattered on the hills like sheep without a shepherd

You set Your face like a flint to Jerusalem

To the place where, to fulfill all righteousness, You must lay down Your life for all of us

And in the power of the Spirit who had descended on You as a dove

You were led as a Lamb to the slaughter

And when You rose again, all things were made in subjection to You, that God may be all in all

In this faith, Lord Jesus, we will look on You for our salvation. Amen

FRIDAY

Hebrews 12:3 *"Consider him who endured from sinners such hostility against himself, so that you may not grow weary or fainthearted."*

N o one is so hated as he who speaks the truth

This was said by a pagan, yet it is true, and all truth is Your truth

We have known the hostility that hotly opposes truth. It has arisen in the words of ones we were once close to

It has been flung in our faces for speaking Your Name in reverence

For daring to insist that You do love truth

That You keep Your promises

That You bear with our failings patiently

That You are true, and every man a liar

That there is indeed such a thing as right and wrong in Your sight

That bearing false witness is a grievous sin against Your glory

That hiding sin is the error of Achan and will draw Your wrath

That to build a ministry that presumes on grace is to move to crucify Christ again

That we should tremble in Your presence

That holy fear is the beginning of wisdom

That we should buy from You gold refined by fire, so we may be rich

That we should seek from You white garments that we may clothe ourselves and the shame of our nakedness may not be seen

That we should plead with You for salve to anoint our eyes, that we may see

That those whom You love, You reprove and discipline

And that in the end, all hostility toward Your Gospel is against You, not against us

May we not grow weary or fainthearted; and may You find us faithful, Lord. Amen

SATURDAY

Hebrews 12:4 *"In your struggle against sin you have not yet resisted to the point of shedding your blood."*

L ong have I struggled, Lord

From the time when I first saw Your glory

When Your Law first shone a light on the darkness of my heart

When Your Spirit first quickened me to feel conviction of sin

When I first knew that there was a better way

Knew that I was ransomed from the futile ways inherited from my forefathers

From the time when I first truly saw You

And knew that You were holy

Holy, holy, holy is the Lord Almighty; the whole earth is full of Your glory

And I heard the voice of the Lord saying, *"Whom shall I send, and who will go for us?"*

And I said, *"Here am I! Send me"*

And You said, *"Go, and say to this people:*

Keep on hearing, but do not understand;

keep on seeing, but do not perceive.

Until cities lie waste, without an inhabitant

and houses without people

and the land is a desolate waste."

But You have placed Your Name upon me. And I will say in that day:

Behold, God is my salvation; I will trust, and will not be afraid

For the Lord God is my strength and my song, and He has become my salvation

Amen

MONDAY

Hebrews 12:5 *"And have you forgotten the exhortation that addresses you as sons? 'My son, do not regard lightly the discipline of the Lord, nor be weary when reproved by him.'"*

There are several kinds of pain You have allowed us to live with, Lord

There is the pain that comes from wrong decisions we make

From simple sin and rebellion against Your Word

From our foolish rebellion against Your Spirit

From our deliberate disobedience that ends in loss and grief

Then there is the pain that comes from living in a cursed world

The tower of Siloam that falls, and eighteen souls are drawn into eternity

Were they worse sinners than others?

No, but unless we repent, we shall likewise perish

Storms that come up on the sea, wild animals that attack, thorns and thistles that grow in the fields we tend

A world that is broken, a creation that has been groaning in the pains of childbirth until now

But there is yet a different pain that arises, the pain of discipline

And we know in our heart that as a man disciplines his son, so the Lord our God disciplines us

We are to keep Your commandments, by walking in Your ways and fearing You

And even in our affliction and discomfort

We know the reproof is as a Father the son in whom He delights

And we hear the voice of Jesus: *"Can you drink the cup I am going to drink?"*

Jesus Christ who tasted of the wrath of God for us, and drained it to its dregs

We rejoice in such a great salvation, and we call you *Abba, Father.* Amen

TUESDAY

Hebrews 12:6 *"For the Lord disciplines the ones he loves, and chastises every son whom he receives."*

I

t hurts to be corrected, Lord

Something in me rankles at it

I want to be right

To be affirmed

To have others agree with me

To be proved out

To prevail when others falter

To be the one who knows, when all is revealed

To be the one who stands, when all is fallen

Such small and selfish desires that drive me

Teach me the heart of Jesus, Lord

To plow, to sow seed, to water, to harvest, to win souls

To spend and be spent

To be poured out as a drink offering, and to be glad and rejoice with those who are saved

To do nothing from selfish ambition or conceit, but in humility to count others more significant than myself

To gladly accept all of Your Spirit's discipline, for it makes me more like You

So that at the Name of Jesus every knee should bow, in Heaven and on earth and under the earth

And every tongue confess that Jesus Christ is Lord, to the glory of God the Father

Surely this is a life worth living, and a hope worth dying for

Thank You, Lord. Amen

WEDNESDAY

Hebrews 12:7 *"It is for discipline that you have to endure. God is treating you as sons. For what son is there whom his father does not discipline?"*

W e have felt Your hand, Lord

It has been heavy on us

Your Word has called us to lift up our eyes

For You had food to eat that we knew nothing of

Your food was to do the will of Him who sent You, and to accomplish His work

And now we have seen that the fields are white for harvest

Already the one who reaps is receiving wages and gathering fruit for eternal life

So that sower and reaper may rejoice together

You sent us to reap for that for which we did not labor

Others have labored, and we have entered into their labor

It is no longer because of what someone has said that people believe

But they have heard for themselves, and know that this is the Savior of the world

And when the Lord restored the fortunes of Zion

We were like those who dream

Then our mouth was filled with laughter

And our tongue with shouts of joy

Then they said among the nations, "The Lord has done great things for them"

The Lord has done great things for us, and we are glad

It was good for me that I was afflicted, that I might learn Your statutes

That I might be made more like Christ, through whom You have brought many sons to glory

Amen

THURSDAY

Hebrews 12:8 *"If you are left without discipline, in which all have participated, then you are illegitimate children and not sons."*

L ord, when You walked this earth, people brought even their infants to You, that You might touch them

And when Your disciples saw it, they tried to rebuke them

But You called them to Yourself

And You said:

"Let the little children come to Me, and do not hinder them

For to such belongs the Kingdom of God

Truly, I say to you:

Whoever does not receive the Kingdom of God like a little child shall not enter it"

And a great hope rose up within us

We ceased our worldly play

We followed You where You led us

We imitated You in Your humility, Your love, Your compassion, Your obedience

We did not flinch when the world hated us, for it had hated You first

We did not try to serve both God and Money, but freely gave away what You had blessed us with

We broke off our friendship with the world, knowing it was enmity with God

We held up Your glory for the world to see, in all its mesmerizing beauty

And as we walked in Your steps we began to see an amazing thing:

In the mirror of the perfect Law, our reflections began to take on Your resemblance

And in joy we spread out all our treasures at Your feet, longing for Your return

For truly we belong to You. Amen

FRIDAY

Hebrews 12:9 *"Besides this, we have had earthly fathers who disciplined us and we respected them. Shall we not much more be subject to the Father of spirits and live?"*

Y ou work through families, Lord. From the earliest stories in the Bible there have been fathers and mothers and children

You saved Noah from the floodwaters, him and his wife and children

You called Abram out from the pagan temples, with his wife and children

You brought a wife for Isaac from his own people to further his line

You took Joseph from the house of Jacob and set him over the whole land of Egypt, so that he might save his people when the famine came

You called David from tending the sheep and promised to make his house great

You gave his son Solomon wisdom like no other, and promised to hear him when he called, and when You heard, to save

You promised Malachi the prophet that You would send Elijah the prophet before the great and awesome day of the Lord

And he would turn the hearts of the fathers to the children, and the hearts of the children to the fathers, so that You would not strike the land with a curse

When John had baptized You, a bright cloud overshadowed You, and a voice from Heaven said:

"This is My beloved Son, with whom I am well pleased"

But when Your own family sought to draw You away from ministry, You said:

"Whoever does the will of my Father in Heaven is my mother and father and brothers"

Lord Jesus, in You we have found a new family: Adoption as sons through Jesus Christ, according to the purpose of Your Will

In You we have obtained an inheritance, having been predestined according to Your purpose

So that we who were the first to hope in Christ might be to the praise of Your glory

You are our great Father and Brother, Lord. Lead us in Your ways today. Amen

SATURDAY

Hebrews 12:10 *"For they disciplined us for a short time as it seemed best to them, but he disciplines us for our good, that we may share his holiness."*

D avid called You Lord, so how were You his son?

He was a man after God's own heart

From the sheepfolds he came to lead them

Israel's sweet psalmist he became

He defeated his tens of thousands

The giant fell before his hand

The enemies of God he drove from the holy city

But when he would have built You a house, You stopped him

And You said, *"I will build you a house"*

And when he sinned against You, taking away an innocent lamb, You disciplined him

Your sword never departed from David's house

Even his own son, his beloved Absalom, You struck down before You

But You showed him something that was worth all the sorrow and grief:

That You Yourself would become the Son

The innocent Lamb, led to the slaughter for the sins of all men

That the blind might see, the lame walk, the guilty pardoned, the dead rise

That the One who knew no sin might become sin, for our sake

That we might become the righteousness of God

Behold, now is the favorable time; now is the day of salvation!

Hosanna to the Son of David! Blessed is He who comes in the Name of the Lord!

Amen

MONDAY

Hebrews 12:11 *"For the moment all discipline seems painful rather than pleasant, but later it yields the peaceful fruit of righteousness to those who have been trained by it."*

I t seemed that nothing good would ever come from it, Lord

It was all darkness

All loss

All pain

A deep, aching pain that would not go away

Friends glanced and then turned away

Some who had once been friends were friends no longer

Enemies laughed and continued on their way

Nothing left of dreams, love, friendship, calling, community

Nothing left but sadness

But Your Spirit raised my head

And said, *"Behold, the eye of the Lord is on those who fear Him, on those who hope in His steadfast love, that He may deliver their soul from death"*

I believed You

Through the long night I went on, hoping only in the dawn of Your salvation

And years later, when the wounds had healed into scars, someone said to me, "Nothing good will ever come from this"

I smiled at them, through my own tears

And I said, "No. God has a purpose in this. Seek Him in it"

And in their eyes I saw the peaceful fruit of righteousness begin to grow

Let Your steadfast love, O Lord, be upon us, even as we hope in You

Amen

TUESDAY

Hebrews 12:12 *"Therefore lift your drooping hands and strengthen your weak knees"*

Y ou know my drooping hands, Lord

My knees have been weak

My heart has faltered; my steps had nearly slipped

For I was envious of the arrogant when I saw the prosperity of the wicked

For they have no pangs until death; their bodies are fat and sleek. They are not in trouble as others are; they are not stricken like the rest of mankind

Pride is their necklace, and violence covers them as a garment

Therefore Your people turn back to them and find no fault in them

And they say, *"How can God know? Is there knowledge in the Most High?"*

All in vain have I kept my heart clean and washed my hands in innocence

But when I thought how to understand this, it seemed to me a wearisome task

Until I went into the sanctuary of God, and then I discerned their end

Truly You set them in slippery places; You make them fall to ruin

How they are destroyed in a moment, swept away utterly by terrors!

Like a dream when one awakes, O Lord, when You rouse Yourself, You despise them as phantoms

When my soul was embittered, when I was pricked in heart, I was brutish and ignorant; I was like a beast toward You

Nevertheless, I am continually with You; You hold my right hand

You guide me with Your counsel, and afterward You will receive me to glory

Whom have I in heaven but You? And there is nothing on earth that I desire besides You

My flesh and my heart may fail, but God is the strength of my heart and my portion forever. Amen

WEDNESDAY

Hebrews 12:13 *"and make straight paths for your feet, so that what is lame may not be put out of joint but rather be healed."*

L ong have I walked in crooked paths, Lord

My heart has gone after the way of the world:

To gather to myself all that my heart desires, without thought of Your Kingdom that is to come

To receive the glory that comes from others, and not the glory that comes from God alone

To seek to be first, rather than to be a servant

My heart has gone after the way of the flesh:

To gratify the desires of the body, rather than to walk by the Spirit

To satisfy the lust of the flesh, the lust of the eyes, and the pride of life

To meet the passions of the flesh that war against the soul

My heart has gone after the way of the devil:

To speak evil of my brothers, and so to speak evil of the Law, and to judge it

To hide, to conceal, to deceive, to manipulate, to thwart, to misdirect, to curse

To call into question the Word of God and set it at naught

Jesus, Son of David, have mercy on me. Trouble the waters of my helpless soul

Pour Your Spirit out upon me, to give me a new heart and mind

A heart that looks on Your suffering and resurrection anew, and breaks for the sins of the world

A mind that is stayed on the holiness and power of God Almighty, and moves out in faith

Heal me that I may be healed; save me that I may be saved

For You are all my praise. Amen

THURSDAY

Hebrews 12:14 *"Strive for peace with everyone, and for the holiness without which no one will see the Lord."*

L ord, You said, *Blessed are the peacemakers*

I have striven for peace

I have tried to see both sides

I have stood in the gap between warring factions

I have brought brothers and sisters together for reconciliation

I have laid down my own preferences to see differences resolved

I have reasoned and pleaded and pursued

But there comes a point when reason and beseeching can go no further

There comes a point when Truth may not be denied

A point where I can bend no further, or I will break

At that point, You stepped into Creation, You who Yourself are Truth

When we were still the uncircumcision

Separated from Christ, alienated from the commonwealth of Israel, strangers to the covenants of promise

Having no hope and without God in the world

But now in Christ Jesus we who were once far off have now been brought near by the blood of Christ

For You Yourself are our peace, who have made us both one and broken down in Your flesh the dividing wall of hostility

Abolishing the Law of commandments, creating in Yourself one new man in place of the two

To reconcile us both to God in one body through the Cross

And in the holiness of Your perfect sacrifice may we all together see the Lord. Amen

FRIDAY

Hebrews 12:15a *"See to it that no one fails to obtain the grace of God"*

Remember me, Jesus, when you enter into Your Kingdom

I have suffered for my sins; You suffered for me

I have fallen many times; You were steadfast

I have not always been faithful; You were faithful until the end

I have doubted God's Word; You never did

I have not always remembered His mighty works, His miracles of long ago; You called them to mind again and again

I have not kept God's holy Law, to walk in all the way that the Lord God commanded; You delighted in all of His statutes

I have not always resisted the devil so that he flees from me; You rebuked him with the Word

I have not taken every opportunity to encourage my brothers and sisters; You always spoke the truth in love

I have not always spoken Your glories to all around me; You gloried the Father at every step

I have not meditated enough on the holiness of God; You took time to commune alone with Him

I have not wept enough over the brokenness of the world; You longed to gather Your own to You

I am not the Christ –

You are.

I worship, and give You all thanks and praise that Your salvation is all of grace

And that all Your righteous works are imputed to me

You alone, Jesus, are the hope of the world

Give me strength and humility to walk in Your ways today

Amen

SATURDAY

Hebrews 12:15b *"that no 'root of bitterness' springs up and causes trouble, and by it many become defiled"*

F orgiveness is very hard, Lord

Someone sins against us

Their words are sharp and cutting

They take something that we had shared

They ruin something that was beautiful to us

They destroy something we labored long to build

They turn their backs on a friendship that had endured long

And when they see our sorrow over it, they only laugh

And turn away

How can we forgive someone who has taken away that which was dearest of all? When it was their very self that we loved, and not anything peripheral?

And we still love them, even after all is loss and darkness and betrayal

So, bitterness begins to grow up within us

And we find ourselves unable to forgive. Not just that we will not, but that we cannot

But the unflinching command of Jesus sounds in our memory: *"You must forgive"*

And the Spirit faithfully guides us to the only place we can ever do that:

To the Cross.

There we lay them down, let them go, hoping only in this one truth, this promise that You made:

That You will one day make all things new

And in this mighty hope You call us out into a world defiled by its savagery

To hold out in our hands the burning light of Your unending grace. Amen

MONDAY

Hebrews 12:16 *"that no one is sexually immoral or unholy like Esau, who sold his birthright for a single meal."*

W e have been given a great gift, Lord

Indeed, what do we have that we did not receive?

What advantage has the Jew? Or what is the value of circumcision? Much in every way

Theirs were the Law, the Prophets, the Writings

And the Word of the Lord came to them, saying, *"Thus says the Lord of hosts, Render true judgments, show kindness and mercy to one another, do not oppress the widow, the fatherless, the sojourner, or the poor, and let none of you devise evil against another in your heart"*

But they made their hearts diamond-hard, lest they should hear the Spirit speaking to them

We, then, are the true circumcision

Who worship by the Spirit of God and glory in Christ Jesus, and put no confidence in the flesh

Though we have not already obtained this, nor are we already perfect

But we press on to make it our own, since Christ Jesus has made us His own

Shall we then take the members of Christ and join them with a prostitute? Never!

We will flee from sexual immorality, for our bodies are temples of the Holy Spirit

We are not our own, for we were bought with a price

Empower us to walk in the footsteps of Jesus

To speak Your Name with reverence

To obey You only

To place our faith in Your Gospel of Grace

And to long for Your coming

Amen. Come, Lord Jesus

TUESDAY

Hebrews 12:17 *"For you know that afterward, when he desired to inherit the blessing, he was rejected, for he found no chance to repent, though he sought it with tears."*

Men say foolish things in Your Name, Lord

They say:

"God never turned anyone away"

"You can repent whenever you want"

"God will always be merciful"

"Even after you die, there may be a chance of salvation"

"Even if you kill yourself, God will forgive you"

But these are just the words of men

Your Word says something different:

"Behold, now is the accepted time; now is the day of salvation"

"Choose you this day whom you will serve"

"Keep on hearing, but do not understand; keep on seeing, but do not perceive"

"If they do not hear Moses and the Prophets, neither will they be convinced if someone rises from the dead"

"I never knew you. Depart from me, you who practice lawlessness"

Worship is not a game; church is not a game; life is not a game

Eternity is near at hand for all of us

Where are their gods, the rock in which they took refuge, who ate the fat of their sacrifices and drank the wine of their drink offering?

See now that I, even I, am He; and there is no god beside Me

I kill and I make alive, and there is none that deliver out of My hand

Blessed are all who take refuge in You, Lord. Amen

WEDNESDAY

Hebrews 12:18 *"For you have not come to what may be touched, a blazing fire and darkness and gloom and a tempest"*

L ord, You reign

Let the earth rejoice; let the many coastlands be glad

Clouds and thick darkness were all around You

Righteousness and justice were the foundation of Your throne

Fire went before You and burned up Your adversaries all around

Your lightnings lit up the world; the earth saw and trembled

The mountains melted like wax before the Lord

Before the Lord of all the earth

Zion heard and was glad

The daughters of Judah rejoice because of Your judgments, O Lord

Sacrifice and offering You did not desire, but a body was prepared for You

Rejoice greatly, O daughter of Zion!

Shout aloud, O daughter of Jerusalem! Behold, your King is coming to you

Righteous and having salvation is He

Humble and mounted on a donkey, on a colt, the foal of a donkey

O you who love the Lord, hate evil!

He preserves the lives of His saints; He delivers them from the hand of the wicked

Light is sown for the righteous

And joy for the upright in heart

Lord Jesus, we worship before You in Spirit and in truth, and we bring You all we are

Thanks be to Your holy Name. Amen

THURSDAY

Hebrews 12:19 *"and the sound of a trumpet and a voice whose words made the hearers beg that no further messages be spoken to them."*

L ord, You are holy. You were before all things, and in You all things hold together

High and lifted up is Your throne

You spoke, and light and darkness came into existence

Through You all things were made; without You nothing was made that has been made

You formed the earth; You sank its bases and laid its cornerstone

When the morning stars sang together, and all the sons of God shouted for joy

You shut in the sea with doors, and made clouds its garment

And said, *"Thus far shall you come, and no farther; here is where your proud waves halt"*

You commanded the morning since days began, and caused the dawn to know its place

A wandering Aramean You called to be the father of many

He went down into Egypt and sojourned there, few in number

And there he became a nation great, mighty, and populous

But the Egyptians treated us harshly and humiliated us, and laid on us hard labor

Then we cried to the Lord, the God of our fathers

And the Lord heard our voice and saw our affliction, our toil, and our oppression

You brought us out of Egypt with a mighty hand and an outstretched arm, with great deeds of terror, with signs and wonders

And You have promised us this land, a land flowing with milk and honey

For surely all Your promises are Yea and Amen in Christ Jesus

Lord Jesus, You have satisfied the righteous Law on our behalf, and our eyes are on You. Amen

FRIDAY

Hebrews 12:20 *"For they could not endure the order that was given, 'If even a beast touches the mountain, it shall be stoned.'"*

T he letter kills, but the Spirit gives life

We have need of the Law, Lord

Sin is crouching at our door

It has been since the days of our fathers

When Cain brought an offering of the fruit of the ground, You did not have regard for it

For You had shown them that blood must be shed to atone for sin

That their sin had come between them and the delights of Eden

That corruption had entered into Your good and beautiful Creation

That their nakedness must be covered

That they must rule over sin

And when Cain rose up to slay his brother, and You pronounced judgment on him for it

He cried out to You and said, *"My punishment is more than I can bear"*

And truer words were never spoken

For none of us can bear the weight of sin

Much less the eternal consequences for it

We needed someone to go up on the Mountain for us

Someone faithful as a Son over Your house

Someone to be led out as a Lamb to the slaughter, to take our punishment

And to be raised again to newness of life

We have need of a Savior, Lord, who kept Your Law perfectly

And we bless Your holy Name, Jesus. Amen

SATURDAY

Hebrews 12:21 *"Indeed, so terrifying was the sight that Moses said, 'I tremble with fear.'"*

L ord, You called Moses from the wilderness. He had left all to follow You

He refused to be called the son of Pharaoh's daughter

He acknowledged his sin and looked to You for forgiveness

He chose rather to be mistreated with the people of God than to enjoy the fleeting pleasures of sin

He considered the reproach of Christ greater wealth than the treasures of Egypt, for he was looking to the reward

He was not afraid of the anger of the king, for he endured as seeing Him who is invisible

And by faith he kept the Passover and sprinkled the blood, so that the Destroyer of the firstborn might not touch them

You called him Friend, and walked and talked with him, and his face shone from Your presence

When Aaron and Miriam spoke against him, You vindicated him

When Korah rose up with all his people, You threw them down

Moses asked to see Your glory, and You hid him in the cleft of the rock as You passed by, proclaiming Your Name:

The Lord, the Lord, a God merciful and gracious, slow to anger, and abounding in steadfast love and faithfulness, keeping steadfast love for thousands, forgiving iniquity and transgression and sin, but who will by no means clear the guilty, visiting the iniquity of the fathers on the children and the children's children, to the third and the fourth generation

Yet for all this, when he saw Your holy Law revealed on Sinai, he trembled with fear

Who will not fear, O Lord, and glorify Your Name? For You alone are holy

All nations will come and worship You, for Your righteous acts have been revealed

Yes, Lord God the Almighty, true and just are Your judgments. Amen

MONDAY

Hebrews 12:22 *"But you have come to Mount Zion and to the city of the living God, the heavenly Jerusalem, and to innumerable angels in festal gathering"*

O Lord, our Lord, how majestic is Your Name in all the earth

You have set Your glory above the heavens

From the lips of children and of infants You have ordained praise

Because of your enemies, to silence the foe and the avenger

How is it that I am able to be in Your presence? For I was once an enemy of grace

I was once darkness

I was lost in my foolishness and pride

My hand was against everyone

I did not know over what I stumbled

By nature a child of wrath, carrying out the desires of the body and the mind

Yet You left the ninety and nine, and You pursued me

Far beyond what any other would have done

For when I was yet a sinner, Christ died for me

Set my feet on a firm place, gave me a new heart, spoke His Gospel of grace to me

And brought me out into the light of life

It is by faith that I see Mount Zion; blessed are we who have not seen and have believed

But O, what is before me now!

The great cloud of witnesses, the adoration of the heavenly beings, the very Throne of God

The mercy-seat, where my heart was set free to worship You forever

Surely eternity will not be long enough to declare Your praises

O Lord, our Lord, how majestic is Your Name in all the earth! Amen

TUESDAY

Hebrews 12:23 *"and to the assembly of the firstborn who are enrolled in heaven, and to God, the judge of all, and to the spirits of the righteous made perfect"*

T hings get so messed up, Lord

Our sin is ever before us

We have wronged each other deeply

We have spoken what is not true

We have done what Your holy Law forbids

We have not sought Your glory in all things

We have missed opportunities to speak Your Name

We have harbored bitterness and resentment against each other in our hearts

We have not always kept our eyes on You

And now, Lord, for what do we wait? Our hope is in You

For Your soul was troubled. And what would You say? *"Father, save Me from this hour"?*

But for that purpose You came to that hour. So You said: *"Father, glorify Your Name"*

Then a voice came from Heaven: *"I have glorified it, and will glorify it again"*

Now is the judgment of this world; now will the ruler of this world be cast out

And You, when You were lifted up, drew all men unto Yourself

We believe in You, Lord Jesus, and in the One who sent You

The light is among us for a little longer; let us walk in it, lest darkness overtake us

And as grains of wheat we offer up our lives, even as You did, that we might bear much fruit

For we know that Your commandment is eternal life

And in this blessed hope we wait for the dawning of Your Kingdom. Amen

WEDNESDAY

Hebrews 12:24 *"and to Jesus, the mediator of a new covenant, and to the sprinkled blood that speaks a better word than the blood of Abel."*

L ong have we wandered, Lord

We have gone far from what You made us to be

We have been unfaithful to the good covenant You made with us

We have dishonored the good land You placed us in, with houses we did not build, and vineyards we did not plant

We did what was evil in Your sight

We abandoned the Lord, the God of our fathers, who had brought us out of the land of Egypt

We went after other gods, from among the gods of the peoples who were around us, and bowed down to them

We provoked You to anger

For in our hearts we abandoned You and served the Baals and the Ashtaroth

We did not listen to our judges, and we whored after other gods and bowed down to them

The gods of the nations around us whom You gave into the hand of Joshua

And Your anger was kindled, and You left those nations around us, to test us

In order that the generations of Israel might know war, to teach war to those who had not known it before

Our sons and daughters fell by the hand of the Amorite; our brothers and sisters were struck down by Canaan; the blood of our people flowed dark in the Jordan

And in our sorrow and loss we turned back to You, and repented of our sin

And You met us there, and Your Spirit grieved with us

A mighty vision You gave of a new Judge, to mediate an eternal Covenant

With upright heart He would shepherd us and guide us with His skillful hand

And bring us home to glory. Amen, Lord Jesus

THURSDAY

Hebrews 12:25 *"See that you do not refuse him who is speaking. For if they did not escape when they refused him who warned them from earth, much less will we escape if we reject him who warns from heaven."*

 ll my life You have called me, Lord

Early Your Spirit spoke to my heart

Convicting of sin and revealing Your holiness in Your perfect Law

Out of Egypt You called Your son, from the land of slavery into the land of promise

And from the burning bush to the terrible dark slopes of Sinai, You taught me holy fear

In faithfulness You established my steps before You, to teach Your people from Your holy Word

To exalt Your glories, and describe Your ways

To shepherd the flocks of Israel that were scattered on the hills

But one day You sent a man to say, *"There were two men, one rich and the other poor – Thou art the man!"*

And the foolishness of my heart rose up before me, and I bowed down in humility before You

To turn from sinful longing, and in grief accept the sting of Your chastening rod

To look on the One who knew no sin, yet became sin for me

Behold, and see if there is any sorrow like His sorrow!

He was oppressed, and He was afflicted, like a lamb that is led to the slaughter; yet He opened not His mouth

Out of the anguish of His soul He would see and be satisfied; by His knowledge did the Righteous One make many to be accounted righteous, and He bore their iniquities

And having loved His own who were in the world, He loved them to the end

Behold the Lamb of God! Lord Jesus, I surrender to Your perfect will today. Amen

FRIDAY

Hebrews 12:26 *"At that time his voice shook the earth, but now he has promised, 'Yet once more I will shake not only the earth but also the heavens.'"*

ll Creation must go through a resurrection, Lord

There are many who say that it will not happen

They say: *Where is the promise of His coming*

For ever since the fathers fell asleep, all things are continuing as they were from the beginning of Creation

For they deliberately overlook this fact:

That the heavens existed long ago

And the earth was formed out of water and through water by the Word of God

And by means of these the world that then existed was deluged with water and perished

But by this same Word the heavens and earth that now exist are stored up for fire

Being kept until the Day of Judgment and the destruction of the ungodly

But the Day of the Lord will come like a thief, and the heavens will pass away with a roar

And the heavenly bodies will be burned up and exposed

And the earth and the works that are done on it will be exposed

How are we to stand in such a Day, Lord? Yet even in the asking, we Your own know the answer

To grow in the grace and knowledge of our Lord and Savior Jesus Christ

To be diligent to be found by You without spot or blemish, and at peace

And to count the patience of our Lord as salvation

When You shake the heavens, Lord, remember us

To You be the glory, both now and to the Day of eternity

Amen

SATURDAY

Hebrews 12:27 *"This phrase, 'Yet once more,' indicates the removal of things that were shaken—that is, things that have been made—in order that the things that cannot be shaken may remain."*

I think all of the Christian life is a shaking, Lord

First You show us who we are in the mirror of Your perfect Law

We are convicted and undone

We humble ourselves and ask for Your mercy

Your Spirit meets us there, and we are born again

In joy we go out to serve You

But the world we encounter is no longer a friend to us

It tempts us, seduces us, uses us, beats us down. Our hearts are crushed by our loss

Your Spirit meets us again, and shows us treasures in Heaven

In hope we enter into the community of Your people, the Church

But there we find that everyone is a sinner, just like we are

We sin against them, and they retaliate against us

We repent to each other, but things get complicated

The Spirit shows us that the passions of our flesh war against Him

Broken-hearted, we go on walking in Your way, missing the faces of those we loved

Like a roaring lion the devil assails us to take us down

We resist him, firm in our faith, and he flees from us

And we begin to know that there is only one thing sure in all this world:

That all authority in Heaven and on earth has been given to Jesus Christ

And we are Your witnesses in Jerusalem and Judea and Samaria, and to the ends of the earth. Let Your Kingdom come, Lord. Amen

MONDAY

Hebrews 12:28 *"Therefore let us be grateful for receiving a kingdom that cannot be shaken, and let us offer to God acceptable worship, with reverence and awe"*

L ord, You are holy

There is none holy like You

There is none besides You

There is no rock like our God

You will judge the righteous and the wicked

Your Word forever comes to pass

Your Spirit moves in Your people to accomplish Your will, and we offer ourselves freely on the day of Your power

Who can ever stay Your hand? Who can ever thwart Your designs

The evil one himself acts only at Your command; he presents himself after going to and fro in the earth, and walking up and down in it

When disaster comes and the righteous cry out to You, it comes about for their good

When the wicked are suffered to rise, they will one day be cast down

When the righteous fall, You Yourself restore them again

Your Kingdom is forever, and Your dominion endures through all generations

You are righteous in all Your ways, and kind in all Your works

You are near to all who call on You, to all who call on You in truth

In the face of such glory, how can our worship be acceptable? Yet You have called for Yourself a people

You have set on us the Name of Your Son Jesus, in whom You are well pleased

And in full confidence we draw near to Your throne of grace, to worship You in Spirit and in truth forever

Amen. May it be, Lord

TUESDAY

Hebrews 12:29 *"for our God is a consuming fire."*

The voice of the Lord flashes forth flames of fire

As fire consumes the forest and flame sets the mountains ablaze, so is the Holy One of Israel

A flaming sword You set between us and the Garden

A smoking firepot and a flaming torch went before Abram as the seal of Your Covenant

In a burning bush that was not consumed You revealed Yourself to Moses; with a pillar of fire and smoke You brought Your people out of bondage

You descended on Sinai in fire, and smoke billowed up from it like a furnace. Out of the midst of the fire the Lord spoke, but there was no form, only a voice

The people cried out at Your holiness, and the radiance shone from Your servant's face when he came down from the mountain, until he put on a veil

Fire broke out in the company of the wicked, and those who spoke against You were destroyed

The prophets spoke of Your coming, that before You went a devouring fire

The Light of Israel would become a fire and His Holy One a flame

Who can endure the day of Your coming, and who can stand when You appear? But You would purify the sons of Levi and refine them like gold and silver

Is not My Word like fire, declares the Lord, *and like a hammer that breaks the rock in pieces?*

He is like a brand plucked from the burning, Joshua the high priest standing to intercede for us

Every branch that does not bear fruit He will cut down and throw into the fire

But in that fiery wilderness we drink from the spiritual Rock that follows us, and that Rock is Christ

For everyone will be salted with fire

And when the great Day of the Lord comes like a thief, and the heavens pass away with a roar, we will stand before You in the holiness of Him whose eyes are like a flame of fire. Amen

WEDNESDAY

Hebrews 13:1 *"Let brotherly love continue."*

The day grows long, Lord

We have labored into the night for Your Name

But the opposition has been fierce

The enemy has subtly worked against us

The wheat in the fields are choked with tares

It is white for the harvest, but the workers are few

Those we thought were on our side have forgotten Your Name

They have not feared Your Word

They have not walked with Your Spirit

They have not longed for Your coming

Because they loved this present world, they have turned aside into the way of Demas

They have been handed over to Satan to be taught not to blaspheme

Are we then all that remains? Is our faithfulness all the Church has to depend on

No

For there is a Remnant

There has always been a Remnant

And together we confess: *I am not the Christ*

Help us to love one another and pray for those who have stumbled, Lord

To forgive, when seventy times seven has long passed

To imitate the One who sticks closer than a brother

To eat Your flesh, drink Your blood, confess Your Name before a watching world

As Your little children, let us not love in word or talk but in deed and truth. Amen

THURSDAY

Hebrews 13:2 *"Do not neglect to show hospitality to strangers, for thereby some have entertained angels unawares."*

We have never known a mere mortal, Lord

You have called us to two great commands:

Love the Lord with all your heart and with all your soul and with all your mind

Love your neighbor as yourself

All the Law and the Prophets hang on these

But we forget

Desires come up within us for what others have

Anger flares up when we are hurt by each other

Revenge lurks in our hearts to get even

Scorn arises and we throw people away after we have used them

And our witness before the world is tainted, and sin and destruction creeps in

Teach us to excel in the grace of giving

To feed the hungry

To give the thirsty something to drink

To invite the stranger in

To clothe the naked

To look after the sick

To visit those in prison

And to do all this not out of guilt, or fear of law

But knowing that whatever we do for the least of these, we have done for You

And be poured out in our lives as a drink offering, for love of You, Christ Jesus. Amen

FRIDAY

Hebrews 13:3 *"Remember those who are in prison, as though in prison with them, and those who are mistreated, since you also are in the body."*

Our hearts tell us to move on, Lord

To avoid their gaze

To avoid asking the Question

To not listen, when they answer

To prefer not to think about their pain

To tell ourselves: *"They deserve it"*

To secretly hope that their mistreatment will stay contained; that none of it will get on us

And we can continue on our easy way

But Lord, we have forgotten

When all avoided our gaze, yet You did not

When Your holy Law asked us the Question, and we had no answer

When none would listen to our cry, yet Your Spirit was there

When none would enter into our pain, except the holy sinless Lamb of God

When the echo of our just sentence for sin was all we could hear for the world

Yet Your Word spoke into that prison, and You came to that desolate place in our hearts

You knew we deserved it; if anyone ever knew, You did

But You took all of our judgment onto Yourself at the Cross

And when You rose again in glory and power, You brought us with You out into everlasting life

Show us that we must not – ever – move on, until we have declared Your praises to the dying

And by the Gospel of Jesus Christ You have brought many sons to glory. Amen

SATURDAY

Hebrews 13:4 *"Let marriage be held in honor among all, and let the marriage bed be undefiled, for God will judge the sexually immoral and adulterous."*

L ord, You judged it good to create

You made man in Your image; male and female You created us

And You blessed us. You said: *Be fruitful and multiply, and fill the earth and subdue it*

For this reason a man shall leave his father and mother and cleave to his wife, and they shall be one flesh

What therefore God has joined together, let man not separate

Yet we have gone astray, and have turned every one to his own way

We cover the Lord's altar with tears, weeping and groaning because He no longer regards the offering or accepts it with favor from our hand

Why does He not?

Because the Lord was witness between us and the wife of our youth

To whom we have been faithless, though she was our companion and our wife by covenant

Did He not make us one, with a portion of the Spirit in our union?

And what was the One God seeking? Godly offspring

So Christ loved the Church, and gave Himself up for her

That He might sanctify her, having cleansed her by the washing of water with the Word

And present her to Himself in splendor, holy and without blemish

This mystery is profound; but in our redeemed flesh we are the Temple of the living God

May we be found among those considered worthy of that age

Sons of the resurrection, holy children of the God of Abraham and Isaac and Jacob

Amen

MONDAY

Hebrews 13:5 *"Keep your life free from love of money, and be content with what you have, for he has said, 'I will never leave you or forsake you.'"*

T he Lord is my Keeper

The Lord is the Shade at my right hand

The Lord is my Light and my Salvation

The Lord is my Rock

The Lord is my Banner

The Lord is my Hiding Place

The Lord is a Shield about me

My Glory, and the Lifter of my head

The Lord is my Strength and my Song

He has become my Salvation

The Lord is my Refuge

The Lord is my Portion; be gracious to me according to Your promise

The Lord is the Righteous One

The Lord is my King, who ordains salvation for Jacob

The Lord is my Stronghold, a shelter to the poor

The Lord is my Strong Tower, to whom I run and am safe

The Lord is the Everlasting God, the Creator of the ends of the earth

The Lord is the Mighty One who speaks and summons the earth

The Lord is my Bridegroom rejoicing over me

The Lord will keep my going out and my coming in, from this time forth and forevermore

Amen

TUESDAY

Hebrews 13:6 *"So we can confidently say, 'The Lord is my helper; I will not fear; what can man do to me?'"*

There is a place of safety, Lord

It is not in the highest tower

It is not in the midst of the greatest army

It is not in the strategy of the wisest counselors

It is not in the company of the cleverest men

It is not surrounded by many friends

It is not found in beauty

Nor in confidence

Or in money

Or in power

O men, how long will my honor be turned into shame? *Selah*

How long will you love vain words and seek after lies?

But know that the Lord has set apart the godly for Himself

The Lord hears when I call to Him

Be angry, and do not sin; ponder in your own hearts on your beds, and be silent. *Selah*

Offer right sacrifices, and put your trust in the Lord

There are many who say, *"Who will show us some good? Lift up the light of Your face upon us, O Lord"*

You have put more joy in my heart than they have when their grain and wine abound

There is only One who has made a right sacrifice; and His name is Jesus

In peace I will both lie down and sleep, for You alone, O Lord, make me dwell in safety. Amen

WEDNESDAY

W e have countless guides in Christ, Lord

But not many fathers

Many have been the voices that professed to speak for You

Who led us down various ways

To have all we want

To become rich

To reign as kings

To look on those condemned to death

As spectacles to the world, to angels, and to men

Those who are fools for Christ, while we are wise for Christ

Who are weak, but we are strong

Who are held in disrepute, but we in honor

Who to the present hour hunger and thirst

Who are poorly dressed and buffeted and homeless

Who labor, working with their own hands

Who bless when reviled, endure when persecuted, entreat when slandered

Who have become like the scum of the world, the refuse of all things

For God has exhibited them last of all

But the Kingdom does not consist in talk but in power

God grant us eyes of faith to see that this world is passing away

And to set our eyes on Christ alone. Amen

THURSDAY

Hebrews 13:7b *"Consider the outcome of their way of life,
and imitate their faith."*

L ord, You know how jaded my heart is

How many times I have seen in others (or in my self) what I thought was
faithfulness

What I thought was truth

What I thought was pleasing to You

What I thought would bring salvation

What I hoped would endure, though the mountains fell into the heart of the sea

And I was wrong

It was lies, it was sin, it was damnation, it did not endure

Yet You still have some who have not bowed the knee to Baal

Who have not sought to conflate Christ and Belial

Who have not worshiped in the temple of Molech

Who tremble in Your presence

Who speak Your Word with longing for Your coming

Who ask boldly for Your Spirit to work, and step into obedience

Who humble themselves before You, and gladly make the good confession:

"I am not the Christ."

These I will follow, as they follow Jesus Christ

As in the innocence of their spiritual childhood they take You at Your Word

That You are a consuming fire

And that You will surely one day make all things new

Little children, let us keep ourselves from idols. Amen

FRIDAY

Hebrews 13:8 *"Jesus Christ is the same yesterday and today and forever."*

L ord, who is like You?

For we know the grace of our Lord Jesus Christ, that though You were rich, yet for our sake You became poor

That we by Your poverty might become rich

You entered into the evil of our world and our hearts

You spoke truth, for surely You are truth

You obeyed the Law, for You were faithful as a Son in God's house

You listened to the Spirit, who descended on You as a dove

You sought the Father's will and set it above Your own

You caught the shrewd in their wisdom, turning their questions back on them

You turned away from the desires and ways of this world

You resisted the devil and spoke the Word, and he fled from You in the desert

You set Your face like a flint to Jerusalem

You accepted the Hosannas of the people, yet You knew that death awaited You

You wept over Your beloved people, in returning and rest to be saved, yet we would not

From the very cross You forgave Your enemies, Your brothers; You forgave us

And in the final hour You gave up Your spirit to God, and went under, with none to save

But in the power of an indestructible life You crushed Death itself, and rose again

Worthy is the Lamb who was slain, to receive power and wealth and wisdom and might and honor and glory and blessing!

From of old You are glorious, You are good, You are holy, You are my great and only hope

Teach me today to fix my eyes on You, and to look for Your coming. Amen

SATURDAY

Hebrews 13:9 *"Do not be led away by diverse and strange teachings, for it is good for the heart to be strengthened by grace, not by foods, which have not benefited those devoted to them."*

Y ou spoke to us in the days of Your flesh, Lord:

"It is not what goes into a person that defiles a person, but what comes out"

And You said it with authority, for it was You who created us

Not for foods, that we should be devoted to them

Not for festivals or days, that we should find salvation in observing them

Not for traditions, that we should be in bondage to them

Not for sayings of man, that we should found our lives on them

Not for visions, or the worship of angels, puffing us up in our sensuous minds

For these are a shadow of the things to come; but the substance belongs to Christ

"Do not handle; do not taste; do not touch!"

In Christ we died to these elemental spirits of the world, which are destined to perish with use

Though they have an appearance of wisdom, they have no power to save

They are like children sitting in the marketplace, calling out, *"We played the flute for you, and you did not dance; we sang a dirge, and you did not weep"*

John the Baptist came eating no bread and drinking no wine, and they said he had a demon

The Son of Man came eating and drinking, and they said You were a glutton and a drunkard, the Friend of tax collectors and sinners

Yet wisdom is justified by her children

And when You came preaching Your Gospel for all men to repent and believe, for the Kingdom of God was coming

We left everything and followed You. And for what – to receive a hundredfold? Surely, but that is not what our hearts long for

It was to receive You, Lord, by the grace in which we now stand. May it be. Amen

MONDAY

Hebrews 13:10 *"We have an altar from which those who serve the tent have no right to eat."*

I was glad when they said to me, *"Let us go to the house of the Lord"*

Too long have I had my dwelling among those who hate peace

Woe to me, that I sojourn in Meshech

That I dwell among the tents of Kedar

I am for peace; but when I speak, they are for war

O Jerusalem, Jerusalem

The city that kills the prophets and stones those who are sent to it!

Behold, your house is forsaken

You will not see Him until you say, *"Blessed is he who comes in the name of the Lord"*

Blessed is the poor in spirit

Blessed are those who mourn

Blessed are the meek

Blessed are those who hunger and thirst for righteousness

Blessed are the merciful

Blessed are the pure in heart

Blessed are the peacemakers

Blessed are those who are persecuted for righteousness' sake

Blessed are all who are spoken evil of for Christ's sake

For all these things we have received at the altar;

We have received from Him who has broken down in His flesh the dividing wall of hostility

We worship You, Lord. Amen

TUESDAY

Hebrews 13:11 *"For the bodies of those animals whose blood is brought into the holy places by the high priest as a sacrifice for sin are burned outside the camp."*

Y ou appeared in the cloud, Lord Jesus, over the mercy-seat

In fear the high priest came into the Holy Place, with a bull from the herd for a sin offering and a ram for a burnt offering

He put on the holy linen coat and had the linen undergarment on his body

He offered the bull as a sin offering to make atonement for himself and his house

He took a censer full of coals of fire from the altar before the Lord, and two handfuls of sweet incense beaten small

And he brought it inside the veil and put the incense on the fire before the Lord

That the cloud of the incense might cover the mercy-seat over the testimony, so he did not die

Two male goats he took from the congregation of the people of Israel, one for a sin offering and one for a burnt offering, one for the Lord and the other for Azazel

He took the goats and set them before the Lord at the entrance to the Tent of Meeting

He killed the goat of the sin offering that was for the people and brought its blood inside the veil to do with it as he had done with the blood of the bull

Sprinkling it over the mercy-seat and in front of the mercy-seat, to make atonement for the Holy Place

Because of the uncleannesses of the people of Israel and because of their transgressions, all their sins

No one could be in the tent of meeting from the time he entered to make atonement in the Holy Place until he came out and had made atonement for his house and the assembly of Israel

And Aaron laid both his hands on the head of the live goat, and confessed over it all the iniquities of the people of Israel, and all their transgressions, all their sins

He put them on the head of the goat and sent it away into the wilderness

And in all this we have seen a great vision, Lord: A vision of Your finished work

For by Your perfect sacrifice, the just shall live by faith. Amen

WEDNESDAY

Hebrews 13:12 *"So Jesus also suffered outside the gate in order to sanctify the people through his own blood."*

Y ou have been there, Lord

In that moment when we see that evil is beginning to hold sway

When truth is not spoken

When Your Word is not heard

When Your Spirit is not followed

When a lie is quietly protected

When hesitation is punished with distance

When questioning is punished with rebuke

When faithfulness is painted as backwardness

When obedience to You is condemned as fearfulness

When people are lovers of self, lovers of money, proud, arrogant, abusive, disobedient to their parents, ungrateful, unholy, heartless, unappeasable, slanderous, without self-control, brutal, not loving good, treacherous, reckless, swollen with conceit, lovers of pleasure rather than lovers of God

When a community of faith has the appearance of godliness, but denies its power

And faithful obedience means we have to go away

Indeed, the hour is coming when whoever kills us will think he is offering service to God

You were there. You know what it means to be alone, to lose friends for faithfulness

Yet You were not alone, for the Father was with You

You have said these things to us so that we may have peace

For in this world we will have tribulation

But we take heart, Lord Jesus, for You have overcome the world. Amen

THURSDAY

Hebrews 13:13 *"Therefore let us go to him outside the camp and bear the reproach he endured."*

L ord, we confess that it was not because we saw signs that we sought You, but because we ate our fill of the loaves

We have worked for the food that perishes instead of for the food that endures to eternal life, which the Son of Man will give to us, on whom the Father has set His seal

What must we do, then, to be doing the works of God?

This is the work of God, to believe in Him whom He has sent

Then what sign do You do, what works do You perform? For our fathers ate the manna in the wilderness; as it is written, He gave them bread from Heaven to eat

But the bread of God is He who comes down from Heaven and is the life of the world

Sir, give us this bread always

I am the bread of life; whoever comes to Me shall not hunger, and whoever believes in Me shall never thirst. For this is the will of my Father, that everyone who looks on the Son and believes in Him should have eternal life, and I will raise him up on the last day

But how do You now say, *"I have come down from Heaven"*?

It is written in the prophets: "And they will all be taught by God." I am the living Bread. And the bread that I will give for the life of the world is My flesh. Whoever feeds on this bread will live forever

This is a hard saying; who can listen to it?

Do you want to go away as well?

Lord, to whom shall we go? You have the words of eternal life, and we have believed, and have come to know, that You are the Holy One of God

Truly I say to you, in the new world, when the Son of Man will sit on His glorious throne, you who have followed Me will also sit on twelve thrones, judging the twelve tribes of Israel

What then is our reward? Surely it is You, Lord. Amen

FRIDAY

Hebrews 13:14 *"For here we have no lasting city, but we seek the city that is to come."*

U nless the Lord builds the house, those who build it labor in vain

Unless the Lord watches over the city, the watchman stays awake in vain

If it had not been the Lord who was on our side–

Let Israel now say–

If it had not been the Lord who was on our side when people rose up against us

Then they would have swallowed us up alive when their anger was kindled against us

Then the flood would have swept us away, the torrent would have gone over us

Then over us would have gone the raging waters

But our help is in the Name of the Lord, who made Heaven and earth

God is our Refuge and Strength, a very present Help in trouble

Therefore we will not fear though the earth gives way, though the mountains be moved into the heart of the sea

There is a river whose streams make glad the City of God

The holy habitation of the Most High

God is in the midst of her; she shall not be moved

God will help her when morning dawns

Great is the Lord and greatly to be praised, in the City of our God!

Beautiful in elevation, His holy Mountain is the joy of all the earth

Mount Zion, in the far north, the City of the great King

Walk about Zion, go around her, number her towers, consider well her ramparts, go through her citadels

That you may tell the next generation that this is God, our God forever and ever. He will guide us forever. Amen

SATURDAY

Hebrews 13:15 *"Through him then let us continually offer up a sacrifice of praise to God, that is, the fruit of lips that acknowledge his name."*

Y ou are worthy, Lord

From the highest heavens to the lowest depths, all things are under Your hand

You are before all things, and by Your will they come to be

Is anything too hard for the Lord?

Awake, awake, put on strength, O arm of the Lord, as in days of old, in generations of long ago

Was it not You who cut Rahab in pieces, who pierced the dragon?

Was it not You who dried up the sea, the waters of the great deep?

You, You are He who comforts us

Who are we that we are afraid of man who dies, of the son of man who is made like grass

And have forgotten the Lord, our Maker, who stretched out the heavens and laid the foundations of the earth?

And where is the wrath of the oppressor?

He who is bowed down shall speedily be released; he shall not die and go down to the pit

You are the Lord our God, who stirs up the sea so that its waves roar – the Lord of Hosts is Your name

But I will not make a sacrifice to the Lord that costs me nothing

I will confess my iniquity; I am sorry for my sin

Do not forsake me, O Lord! O my God, be not far from me

O Lord, all my longing is before You

Let me hear in the morning of Your steadfast love, for in You I trust

Make me know the way I should go, for to You I lift up my soul. Amen

MONDAY

Hebrews 13:16 *"Do not neglect to do good and to share what you have, for such sacrifices are pleasing to God."*

I t takes me so long to learn, Lord

O foolish, and slow of heart to believe all that the prophets have spoken!

Was it not necessary that the Christ should suffer all these things and enter into His glory?

To stretch out His hand to the leper, and say, *"I will; be clean"*

To say to the centurion, *"Go, let it be done for you as you believed"* and his servant was healed

To rise and rebuke the winds and the sea, saying, *"Peace, be still"* and there was a great calm

To say to the paralytic, *"Take heart, My son, your sins are forgiven."* And under the charge of blasphemy, to show His authority and say, *"Rise and walk"*

To bless the woman who touched His garment and say, *"Take heart, daughter, your faith has made you well"*

To exhort His disciples because of the people, harassed and helpless like sheep without a shepherd, that they should pray to the Lord of the harvest to send out workers

To send His disciples out to the lost sheep of the house of Israel, instructing them, *"You received without paying; give without pay"*

And in His final hour, to offer Himself up a living sacrifice, perfect and spotless, the greatest gift mankind has ever known

Shall I not offer up all that I am and all that I have, to see Your Kingdom come?

Shall I not give generously without thought of return?

Shall I not see in the least of these the face of my Master, and joy to share with them?

And in all this, not for the sake of giving, or of doing; but because Christ is being formed in me, by the power of Your Spirit

I must decrease, Lord, and You must increase

May it be so. Amen

TUESDAY

Hebrews 13:17a *"Obey your leaders and submit to them, for they are keeping watch over your souls, as those who will have to give an account."*

We have gone astray like lost sheep, Lord

Seek Your servants, for we do not forget Your commandments

Who among us has clean hands and a pure heart

Who does not lift up his soul to what is false

Who does not swear deceitfully

Who shall ascend the hill of the Lord?

And who shall stand in His holy place

Who will receive blessing from the Lord

And righteousness from the God of his salvation

Such is the generation of those who seek You

Who seek Your face, O God of Jacob

Selah

But it has pleased the King of glory to set under-shepherds over us

Men set apart for Your service, to lead Your sheep, to feed Your lambs

They are not the Christ

But for Your sake we will obey them and submit to them

For it is You we come to, laboring, heavy laden

We have heard that Your yoke is easy and Your burden is light

To learn of You, Lord, for You are gentle and lowly in heart

And find rest for our souls

Amen

WEDNESDAY

Hebrews 13:17b *"Let them do this with joy and not with groaning, for that would be of no advantage to you."*

T he Gospel is Christ, not me

It is God's salvation of men, not men reaching for God

It is the new birth, not more rules

It is the power of the Cross, not human resolve

It is the Resurrection, not human ideas

It is through the Word of God, which is higher than my thoughts

It is by the Spirit of God, Whose ways are higher than my ways

It is the finished work of Jesus, applied by grace to my account to satisfy the holy Law

It is a righteousness by faith from first to last

Yet if I am truly in Christ, this same Gospel will be worked out in my life

It will work humility in my heart

It will draw me into fellowship with other believers

It will lead me to offer up my body a living sacrifice, pure and pleasing to God

Eager to maintain the unity of the Spirit in the bond of peace

To bear with my brothers and sisters in love

One body, one Spirit

—Just as we were called to the one hope that belongs to our call—

One Lord, one faith, one baptism

One God and Father of all, who is over all and through all and in all

When You ascended on high You led a host of captives, and gave gifts to men

Lead me in Your way everlasting, Lord. Amen

THURSDAY

Hebrews 13:18 *"Pray for us, for we are sure that we have a clear conscience, desiring to act honorably in all things."*

W hat is holiness, Lord?

Ever since You rescued us from the kingdom of darkness and transferred us into the Kingdom of Your beloved Son, we have pursued it

Ever since we realized the price that was paid for our souls, we have treasured it

Ever since we began to turn away from the vanity of this world, we have given all we have for it:

> To be separated from all things earthly for Your sake

> To feel the weight of glory in Your presence

> To be set apart, vessels for honorable use; Your use

> To come out from among them and be separate

> To touch no unclean thing, that You may receive us

> To worship the Lord in the splendor of holiness

> To walk on the Way of Holiness, the highway in the desert

> To cleanse ourselves from every defilement of body and spirit

> To lay hold of the forgiveness we have in Jesus Christ, resting in Your finished work

Is there any among us who has done this perfectly? No, but we may fix our gaze on the perfect Lamb of God every day, through the Word, in the Spirit, by faith

For the Law is holy, and the commandment is holy and righteous and good

Which Law You came not to abolish, but to fulfill

You alone are holy, Lord Jesus; yet You call us to follow in Your steps

Your divine power has granted to us all things that pertain to life and godliness

And in our hearts we honor You as holy

Amen

FRIDAY

Hebrews 13:19 *"I urge you the more earnestly to do this in order that I may be restored to you sooner."*

We pray, Lord

We lift before You our humble petitions

We open our hearts to You as our Creator

But much more importantly as our Father

We have deadly enemies

The world, the flesh, and the devil

Evil without and within

Is there anything that defines us more truly than our need? Yet Your Spirit reminds us that it is our very sickness that qualifies us for Your care

Friends betray us, leaders betray us, followers betray us, even our own hearts betray us

So we do not come proclaiming the testimony of God with lofty speech or wisdom

And we decide to know nothing except Jesus Christ and Him crucified

And our ministry is in weakness and fear and much trembling

Our speech and message not in plausible words of wisdom, but in demonstration of the Spirit and of power

So that our faith might not rest in the wisdom of men but in the power of God

And in the midst of all this, we finally see that there is a greater truth than our need, not taught by human wisdom but by the Spirit

It is the truth of what You have done for us through the Cross

What no eye has seen, nor ear heard, nor the heart of man imagined: What God has prepared for those who love Him

In this vision we will follow you, witness for You, suffer for You, pass into glory with You

For by Your mercy we have the mind of Christ. Amen

SATURDAY

Hebrews 13:20 *"Now may the God of peace who brought again from the dead our Lord Jesus, the great shepherd of the sheep, by the blood of the eternal covenant"*

F rom the cosmic war that awoke between You and sin with the mighty pronouncement of the proto-evangelium: *"I will put enmity between you and the woman"*

From the moment when waves lifted the ark high, and the face of the preacher of righteousness was hidden from the earth in the safety of Your Covenant

From out of the fearful shadows of the mud-brick temples of idolatry, when You first said to Your servant, *"Go to a land I will show you"*

From the sacred, flickering light of the torch and the firepot as they passed between the slaughtered bodies of the sacrifices, and Your servant first knew Your Covenant for certain

From the voice of the angel that stopped his knife, hanging over his beloved son, and You provided a lamb for the burnt offering at the cost of Your own Son

From the fiery serpent that was set upon the pole, that whoever saw it should live, and through it the briefest glimpse down through the ages to the Son of Man who would one day be lifted up

From the tablets of stone with Your holiness written upon them, that Your people should walk in Your ways; one day to be kept perfectly by Jesus Christ Himself

From the days when you drew the sweet Psalmist of Israel to be a man after Your own heart, and promised that the Messiah would one day sit on his throne

From the words of the son of man who prophesied to the house of Israel, that the Lord God would remove their hearts of stone, and give them hearts of flesh

From the prophet who blew a trumpet in Zion, and it was spoken that in the great and awesome Day of the Lord His Spirit would be poured out on all flesh

From the voice crying in the wilderness: *"Comfort, comfort ye My people, says your God. Speak tenderly to Jerusalem, that her warfare is ended, and her iniquity is pardoned"*

From the Spirit descending like a dove, and Your voice sounding from Heaven: *"This is My beloved Son, with whom I am well pleased. Listen to Him"*

From the eyes of the Lord Jesus looking up from His agony, blessing the saving faith of the thief on the cross: *"Today you will be with Me in Paradise"*

To You alone be all glory in the Church and in Christ Jesus, forever and ever. Amen

MONDAY

Hebrews 13:21a *"equip you with everything good that you may do his will, working in us that which is pleasing in his sight"*

The fields are white for the harvest, Lord

The end of all things is near

The wrath of God is revealed from heaven against all ungodliness and unrighteousness of men

But to those who by patience in well-doing seek for glory and honor and immortality, You will give eternal life

For the word of the Cross is foolishness to those who are perishing, but to us who are being saved it is the power of God

Where is the one who is wise? Where is the scribe? Where is the debater of this age? Has not God made foolish the wisdom of this world?

You chose the foolish to shame the wise, the weak to shame the strong

You chose what is low and despised in the world, even the things that are not, to bring to nothing things that are

The free gift was not like the trespass, then

For if many died through one man's trespass, the free gift by the one man Jesus Christ abounded for many

We have need of endurance, that when we have done the will of God we may receive what was promised

And what was the one God seeking? Godly offspring

That the fullness of the Gentiles might come in, we need Your Spirit to equip us

Mend our nets, O Lord, and enlarge our hearts, that we may run in the way of Your commandments

Not from fear of Law, but from love of You, in a new heart that has been born of God

To have Christ formed in us, Your beloved Son, with whom You are well pleased

This is our great and only hope, Lord

Amen

TUESDAY

Hebrews 13:21b *"through Jesus Christ, to whom be glory forever and ever. Amen."*

L ord, You were in the beginning with God

All things were made through You, and without You was not anything made that was made

In You was life, and the life was the light of men

You were the true Light, which gives life to everyone, and You came into the world

You came to Your own, and Your people did not receive You

But to all who did receive You, who believed in Your Name, You gave the right to become children of God

Born not of blood or of the will of the flesh or of the will of man, but of God

For though the Lord is high, He regards the lowly, but the haughty He knows from afar

All the kings of the earth shall give You thanks, O Lord, for they have heard the words of Your mouth

They shall sing of the ways of the Lord, for great is the glory of the Lord

May You have dominion from sea to sea, and from the River to the ends of the earth!

May desert tribes bow down before You and Your enemies lick the dust

May all kings fall down before You; all nations serve You

For You deliver the needy when he calls, the poor, and him who has no helper

You have pity on the weak and needy, and save the lives of the needy

May Your people blossom in the cities like the grass of the field!

May people be blessed in You; all call you Blessed

For from You and through You and to You are all things

Amen

WEDNESDAY

Hebrews 13:22 *"I appeal to you, brothers, bear with my word of exhortation, for I have written to you briefly."*

L ord, there is so much

You have delivered us from the domain of darkness and transferred us to the Kingdom of Your beloved Son

The times of ignorance You overlooked, but now You command all people everywhere to repent

Because You have fixed a day on which You will judge the world in righteousness, by a Man whom You have appointed

And of this You have given assurance to all by raising Him from the dead

For You have raised up a Horn for Your people

Praise for all Your saints

For the people of Israel who are near to You

Praise the Lord!

Praise the Lord from the heavens; praise Him in the heights!

Praise Him, all you angels; praise Him, all you hosts

Praise Him, sun and moon! Praise Him, all you shining stars

Let them praise the Name of the Lord! For He commanded and they were created

He established them forever and ever; He gave a decree, and it shall not pass away

Praise the Lord from the earth, you great sea creatures and all deeps

Fire and hail, snow and mist, stormy wind fulfilling His Word

Kings of the earth and all peoples, princes and all rulers of the earth

The Mighty One, God the Lord, speaks and summons the earth from the rising of the sun to its setting

Amen

THURSDAY

Hebrews 13:23 *"You should know that our brother Timothy has been released, with whom I shall see you if he comes soon."*

E very day and what it will bring is known by You, Lord, but not by us

Today or tomorrow we will go into such and such a town

Spend a year there, trade, make a profit

Yet we do not know what tomorrow will bring

What is our life? For we are a mist that appears for a little time and then vanishes

Our days are like grass

We flourish like a flower of the field

The wind passes over it, and it is gone

And its place knows it no more

But the steadfast love of the Lord is from everlasting to everlasting on those who fear Him

And His righteousness to children's children

To those who keep His covenant and remember to do His commandments

Bless the Lord, O you angels, you mighty ones who do His Word

Bless the Lord, all His hosts, His ministers who do His will

Bless the Lord, all His works, in all places of His dominion

Bless the Lord, O my soul

For the Lord is at hand

Let us not be anxious about anything, but in everything by prayer and supplication with thanksgiving let our requests be made to God

And all things will work together for good in Christ Jesus, as we are called according to His purpose

Amen

FRIDAY

Hebrews 13:24 *"Greet all your leaders and all the saints. Those who come from Italy send you greetings."*

W e are Your people, Lord, the sheep of Your pasture

Sometimes we meet another saint, and the distance between us vanishes instantly

The way they say Your Name

The prayer they say over their meal

The way they flinch when someone else misuses Your Name

Their reverence in a place of Your worship

The way they speak the Word

The way they listen to the Spirit

The way they remain silent, when the days are evil

The way they step in boldly, when many would look the other way

The way their hearts open so readily to the hurting, the lost, the despairing, the friendless, the sorrowing, the destitute

Their generosity with earthly goods, as if their treasure actually were in Heaven

An unutterable joy that pervades their every act and word

And at the same time, a deep sadness in their eyes from wounds that will never be healed until You return

There is a kinship we instantly have with each other, that cannot be demonstrated from aspect or lineage or affect or situation

It is not so much something about us, ourselves, as it is something about where we are headed

Our eyes lifted from this ruined world, that is so swiftly passing away around us, and fixed on Jesus Christ and His coming Kingdom

Our hearts set on finding our way home.

Amen

SATURDAY

Hebrews 13:25 *"Grace be with all of you."*

G race begins with Law, Lord

So You taught us from the words of the prophet:

The people who survived the sword found grace in the wilderness

When Israel sought for rest, and the Lord appeared to him from far away

You have loved us with an everlasting love

Therefore You have continued Your faithfulness to us

Faithfulness to make a covenant with us

To lead us with cloud and fire through the wasteland

To feed us with the bread of the angels

To refresh us with water from the rock

To stagger us with the burden, as we cried out under the lash

To test us with fiery serpents, with scorpions and thirsty ground where there was no water

That we might listen to the Word of the Lord, and obey

Raising our eyes to the perfect sinless Sacrifice

To Him who is the end of the Law for all who believe

It is for this we have toiled, longed, striven, hoped, sacrificed, prayed, suffered, endured

But in the end it is all of grace, free grace from first to last; not of works, that anyone should boast

And so we go out into all the world and proclaim this Gospel to all creation: That the dwelling place of God is at last with man.

The Most Holy Place.

May it be, Lord Jesus. The Spirit and the Bride say, "Come." Amen.

LightPath Publishing
100 S. Lynnhaven Drive
Staunton, VA 24401

lightpathpublishing@gmail.com

Psalm 119:105